Ali Ferguson's beautiful textile art takes inspiration from ordinary people and everyday life. In this fascinating book, Ali shares the stories and thinking processes behind pieces of her work, alongside the techniques that she uses, instructions for making projects and a thoughtful curation of related work from other contemporary textile artists working with similar themes.

Part One looks at capturing inspiration, showing the many ways that Ali is continually gathering and storing ideas, including in her 'stitcher's sketchbook'. Part Two shows readers how ordinary things such as old letters and postcards, photographs, vintage magazines and old sewing paraphernalia can provide endless inspiration for creating personal textile art. Part Three explores Ali's love of using words as inspiration. It shows different ways of incorporating writing into stitched textiles; for example, using pencil and stencil, rusting powder, typewriters and inkjet printing, in addition to hand stitching. The final section looks at clothing and accessories, including textile jewellery, pockets and beautifully adorned decorative garments that have the reader's own personal stories firmly at their heart.

This book is an absolute treasure trove of ideas for any artist or embroiderer who wants to explore new sources of inspiration close to home and create personal, meaningful textile art.

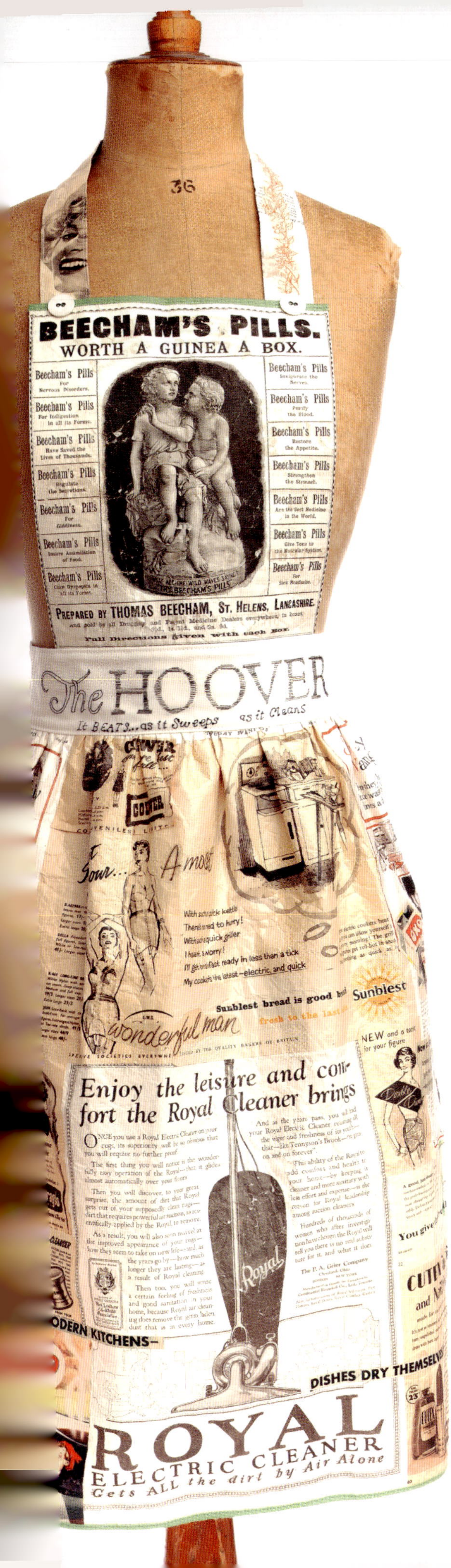

Life Stories

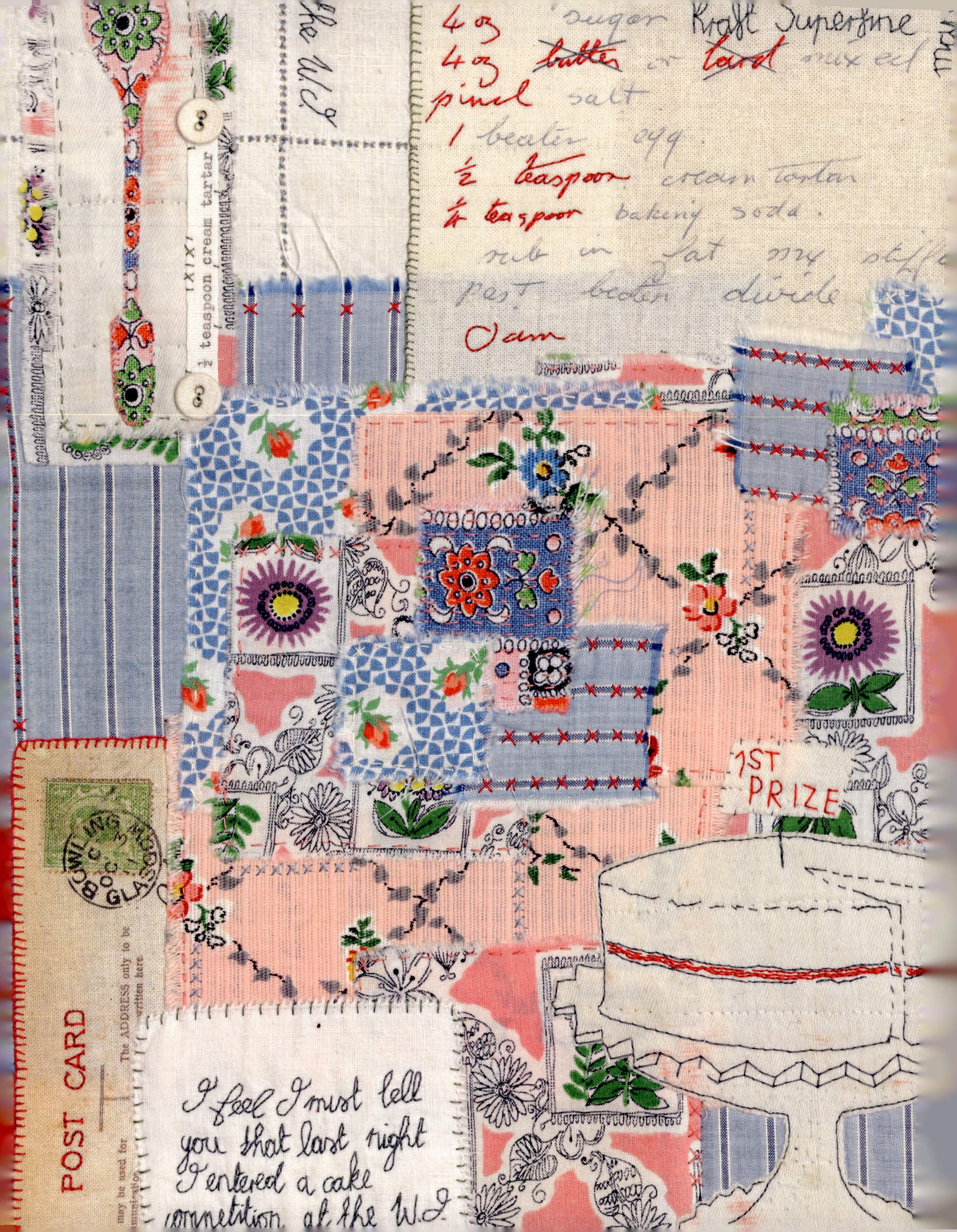

the W.I.
4 oz sugar Kraft Superfine
4 oz butter or lard mixed
pinch salt
1 beaten egg
½ teaspoon cream tartar
¼ teaspoon baking soda
Jam
½ teaspoon cream tartar
1ST PRIZE
POST CARD
I feel I must tell you that last night I entered a cake competition at the W.I.

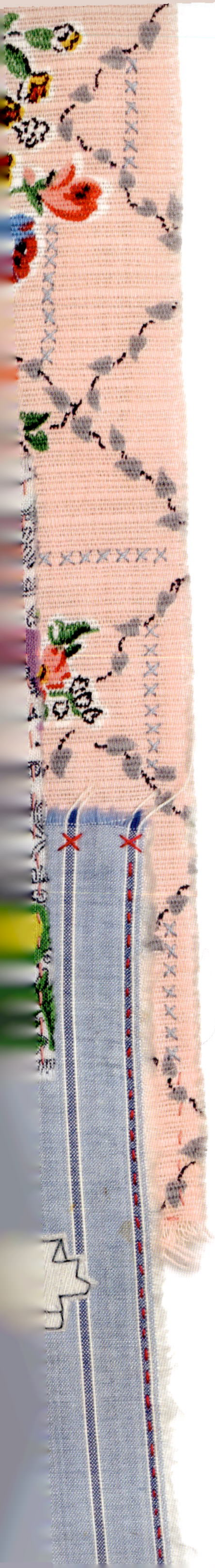

Ali Ferguson

Life Stories

TEXTILE ART INSPIRED
BY PEOPLE AND MEMORIES

BATSFORD

First published in the United Kingdom in 2026 by
Batsford
43 Great Ormond Street
London
WC1N 3HZ

An imprint of B. T. Batsford Holdings Limited

ISBN 978 1 83733 025 6

A CIP catalogue record for this book is available from the British Library.

10 9 8 7 6 5 4 3 2 1

Reproduction by Rival Colour Ltd, UK
Printed by Toppan Leefung Printing International Ltd, China

This book can be ordered direct from the publisher at
www.batsfordbooks.com, or try your local bookshop

Distributed throughout the UK and Europe by Abrams & Chronicle Books, 1st Floor, 22–24 Ely Place, London EC1N 6TE and 57 rue Gaston Tessier, 75166 Paris, France

www.abramsandchronicle.co.uk
info@abramsandchronicle.co.uk

FSC www.fsc.org MIX Paper | Supporting responsible forestry FSC® C104723

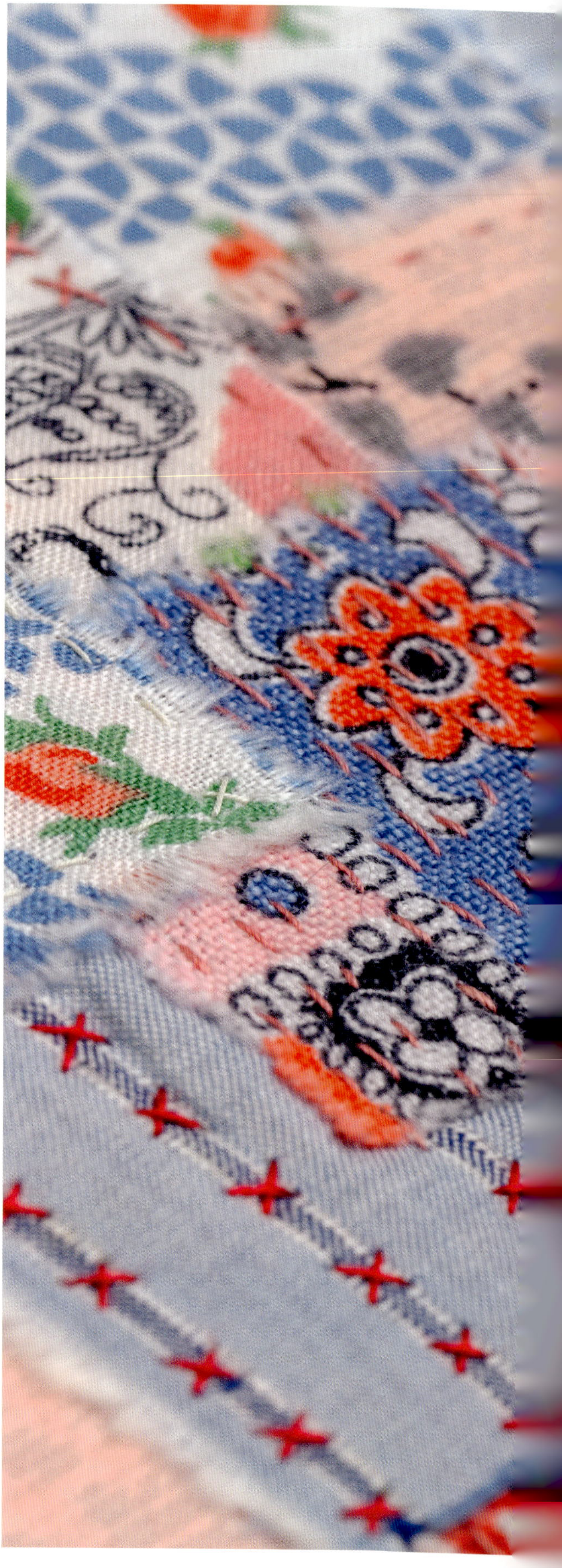

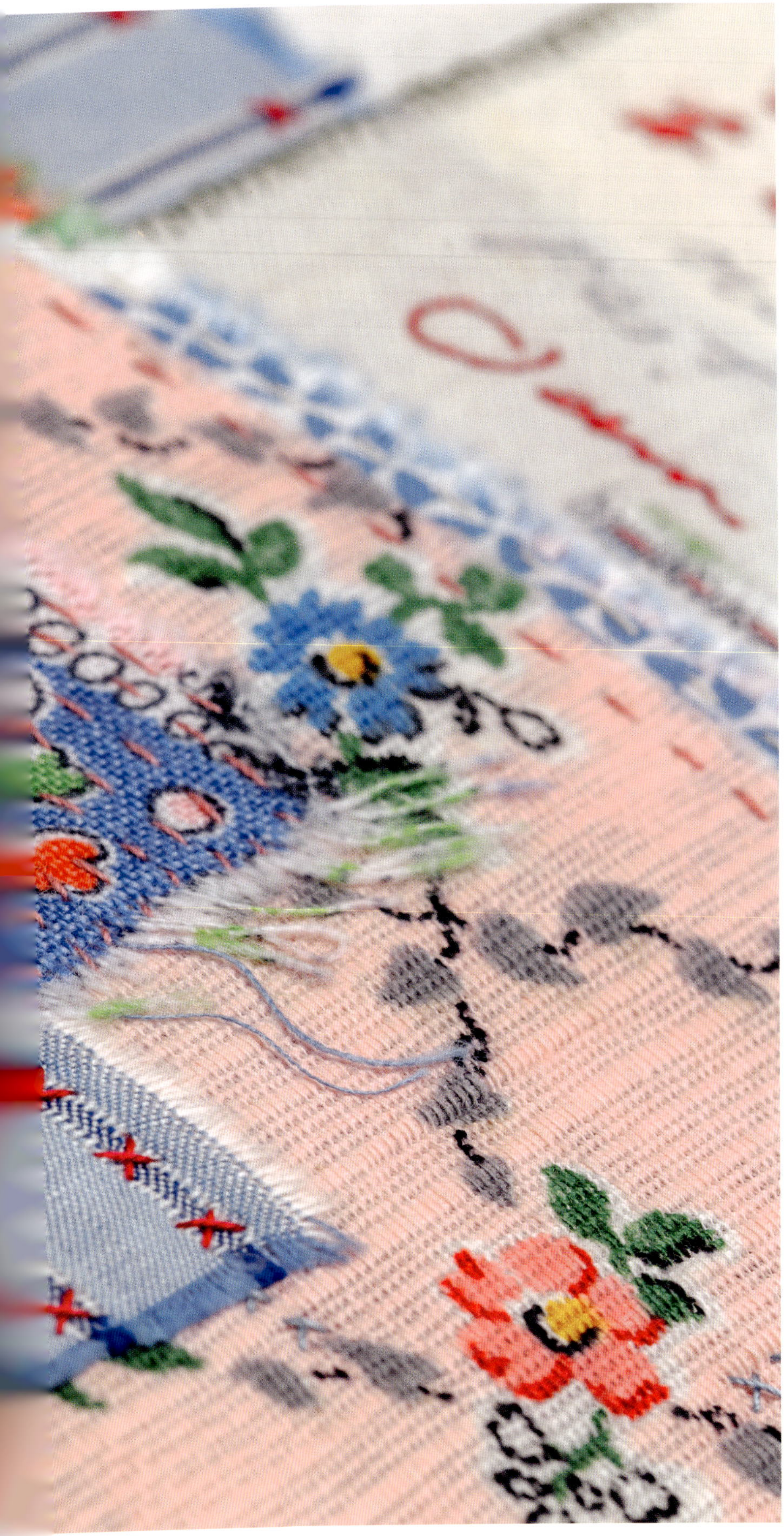

Contents

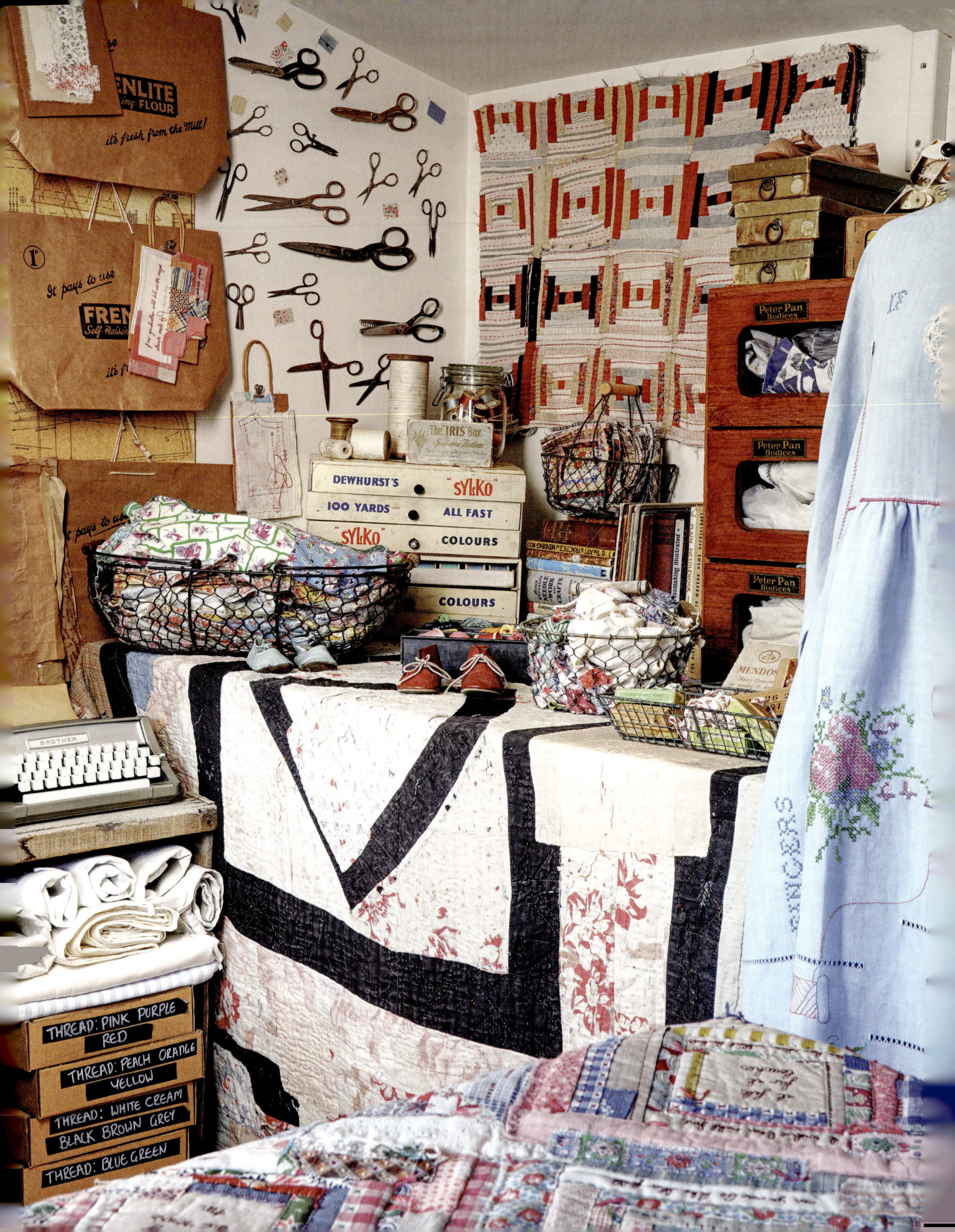
ENLITE
FLOUR
it's fresh from the Mill!
It pays to use
FREN
DEWHURST'S
SYLKO
100 YARDS
ALL FAST
SYLKO
COLOURS
COLOURS
Peter Pan Bodices
Peter Pan Bodices
Peter Pan Bodices
THREAD: PINK PURPLE RED
THREAD: PEACH ORANGE YELLOW
THREAD: WHITE CREAM BLACK BROWN GREY
THREAD: BLUE GREEN

Introduction

Imagine that you're walking through the door of The Purple Thread Shed, my quirky studio which sits at the bottom of my garden in a small village just outside Edinburgh. You'll find yourself immersed in a little world of carefully curated 'stuff'. Old scissors dance up the walls, soft leather baby shoes nestle on shelves, spools of coloured silk thread are heaped in old bread tins and small sets of drawers are home to precious letters, postcards and photographs.

These little snippets of life surround me as I work, and they continually spark ideas that have me delving into my stash of vintage linens and old garments. Before long, a cloth collage will emerge as I rip, layer and patch scraps of fabric together before continuing my storytelling with needle and thread.

Life Stories invites you to join me in this world where we'll explore my three favourite sources of inspiration: collected stuff, words and clothing.

My fascination with each of these leads me in different directions, but they always bring me back to the same place – creating textile art with a palpable sense of story about ordinary people and everyday life. This is the essence of this book.

I've divided it into four chapters, but in truth I can't completely separate them, as one idea frequently leads to another and everything intermingles. I'll apologize in advance; this book may have you lying awake at 3 am with ideas and stories whirring around in your head!

My aim is to inspire you to create using your own collections of stuff, to use some of those family treasures that lie forgotten at the bottom of drawers, and those bits and pieces that you couldn't resist buying but don't quite know what to do with. I'd love it if something I mention in passing sparks a curiosity that sends you off on a delicious hunt for information. I want to show you how, by using meaningful materials, words and motifs, you can turn all of this into personal textile art.

OPPOSITE: A corner of my studio in the garden of my home in Roslin, Scotland.

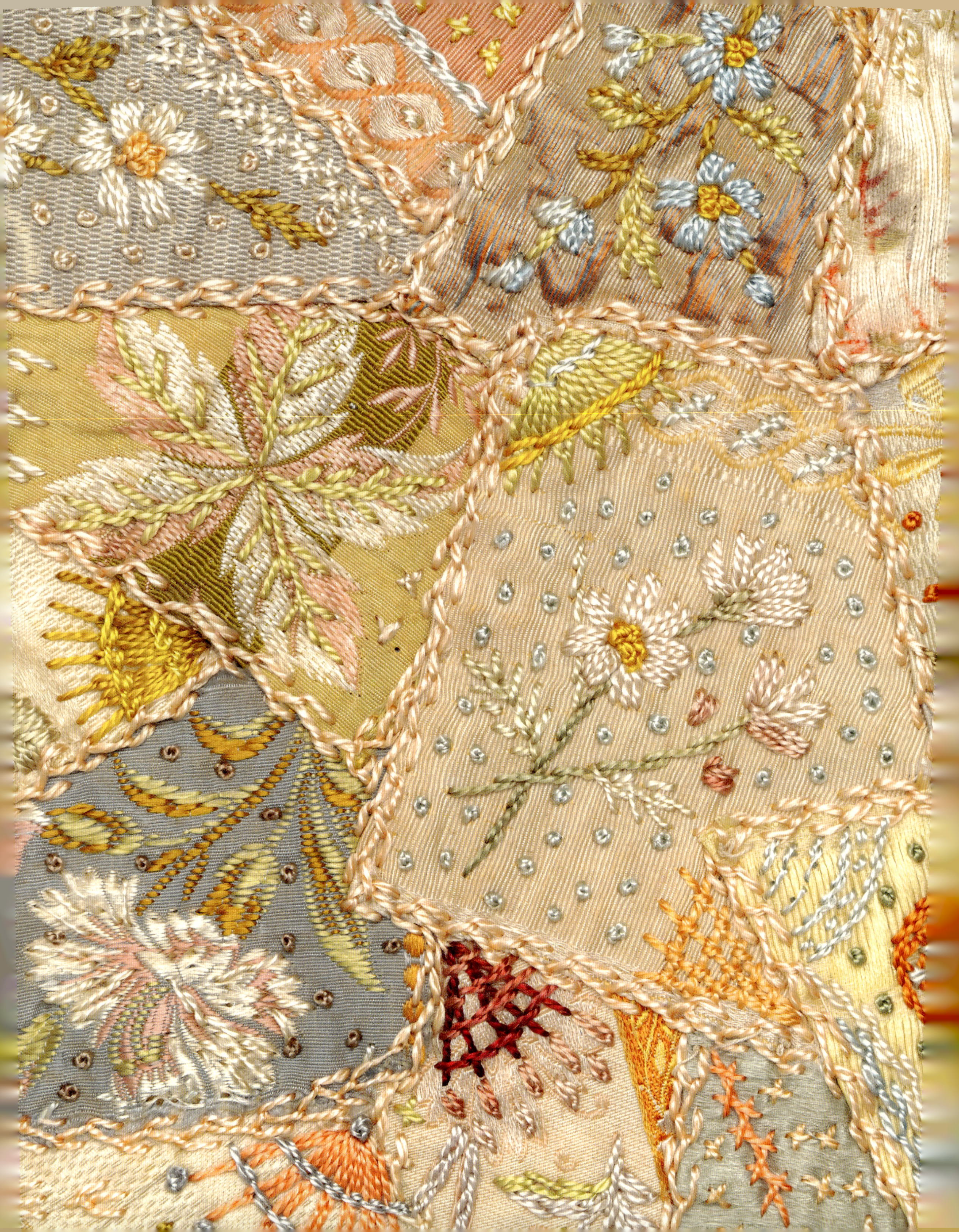

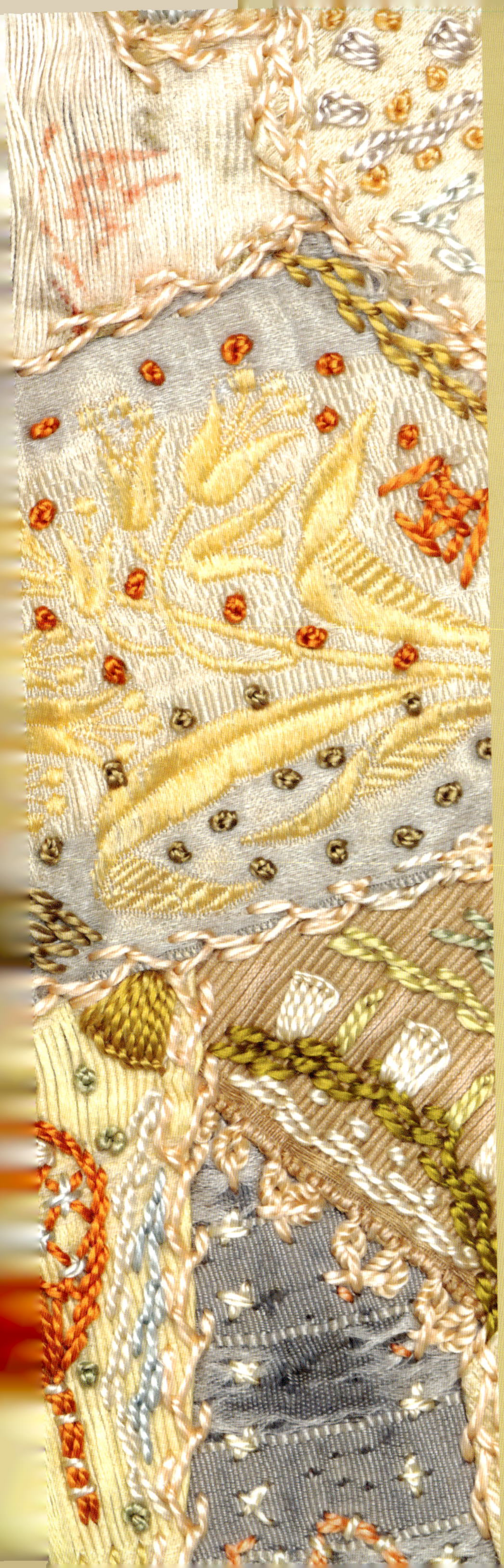

Creating from a 'place of story'

When I'm teaching, I like to start my workshops by gathering everyone around the table. I'll show my workshop samples and share the stories behind each piece.

I'm softly spoken, and I take my time. I'm sure this is annoying for some – after all, when you go to a workshop there is that excited anticipation of starting work and getting stitching!

But it's very deliberate. I've discovered that by starting in this way it allows people to physically settle, it quietens their minds and helps them to leave behind the rush of travel and an early start. There's something relaxing about listening to stories; it's a nighttime ritual for young families across the world for a reason.

As I share the personal stories and emotions behind my work, this awakens people's own stories, memories and thoughts and we find ways of stitching some of these into their pieces.

I call this very natural process finding your 'place of story'.

Capturing inspiration

I invite you to settle down while you read this book, to grab a cuppa and take time over the pages. I'd recommend having a notebook on hand, to jot down thoughts that come to mind or to make notes of things you would like to know more about. I always have a bundle of papers close by, usually torn sheets of brown parcel paper held together by a bulldog clip, ready for whenever inspiration strikes.

CONTINUALLY GATHERING

I talk at length in my book *Cloth Stories* about my use of meaningful materials, words and motifs, but I'll summarize them again here, because they continue to be my three main ingredients for making personal story-based art. While other artists may spend hours sketching or taking photographs as inspiration for their work, I'm continually gathering these three elements.

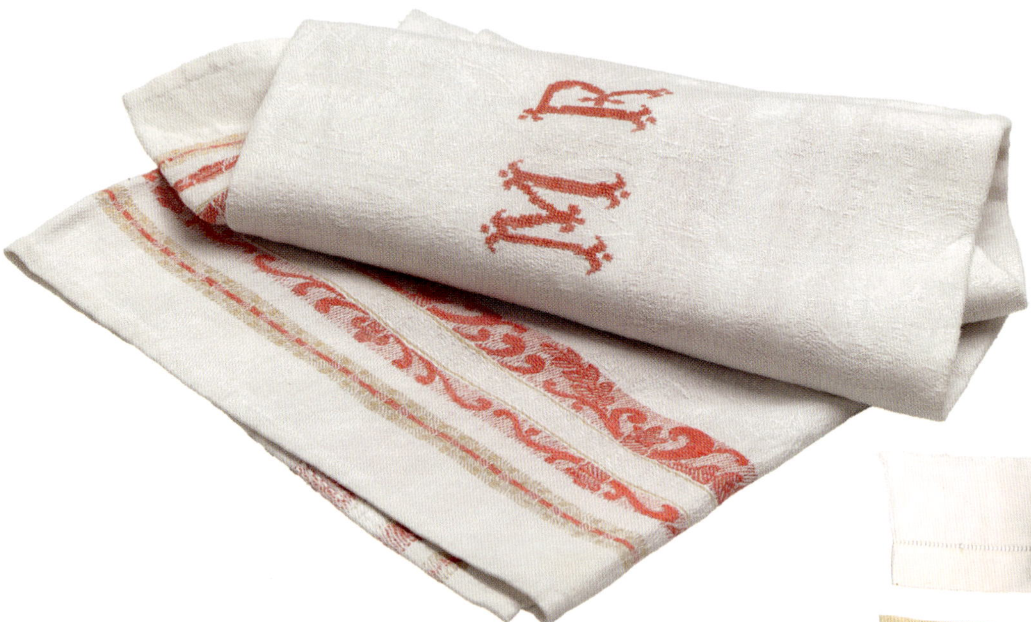

ABOVE: I can't resist antique French linens with beautifully embroidered initials.

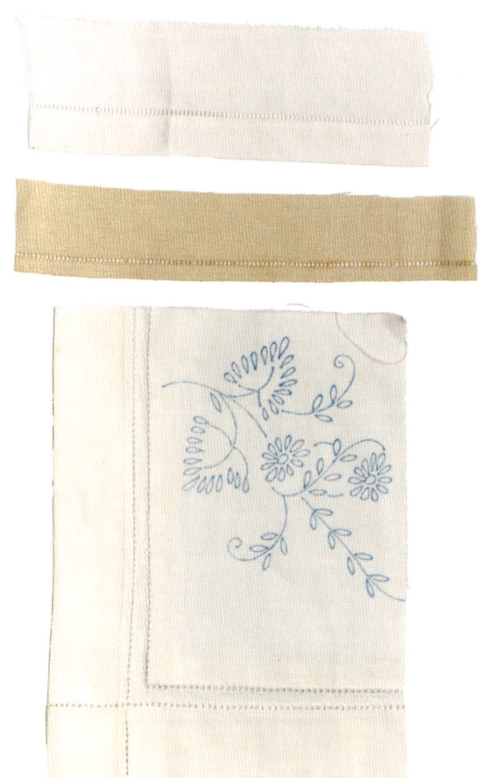

RIGHT: I especially love the corners and edges of vintage linen tablecloths.

GATHERING MEANINGFUL MATERIALS

By meaningful materials I mean materials that will help tell the story of your piece – whatever that happens to be. This often involves a specific search for just the right thing. The question to be foremost in your mind at the start of any project is: 'What materials would help tell my story?'

I work wherever possible with vintage materials. I share a love with so many artists for the old, used, washed and worn, and am always on the lookout for bits and pieces. My favourites are what I would call 'homely' fabrics – cotton prints particularly from the 1930s and 1940s, old French fabrics and torchons, old cotton shirting in stripes and checks and whatever else calls out to me.

I buy mostly small scraps rather than longer lengths of fabric, as they offer me more selection and suit my style of working. Nothing gets wasted. As the scraps get smaller, they go into boxes and baskets to be used as random patches on my cloth collages.

I'm always on the lookout for old quilts and covers made from cotton patches. These were commonly made by reusing fabric scraps, often from items of clothing that had been outgrown or damaged beyond mending. I'll carefully unpick larger patches of fabric (and get very excited when I find a garment shape left intact), but will also rip sections from quilts made from smaller patches, giving combinations of fabric that I would never think of putting together. I look for damaged quilts for cutting.

THIS PAGE: My gatherings of 'meaningful materials' will often include 'homely' fabrics such as these. Used, washed and worn, they bring their own stories to my work.

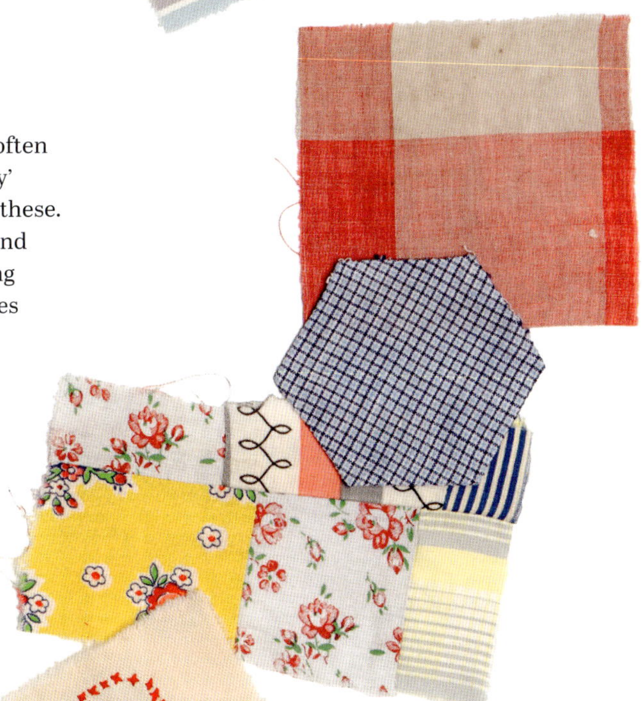

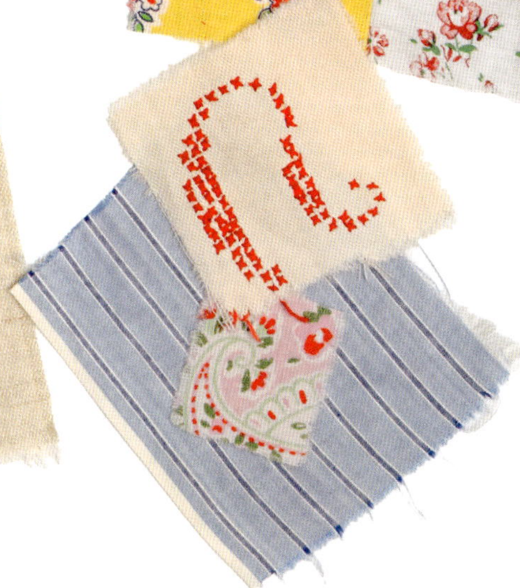

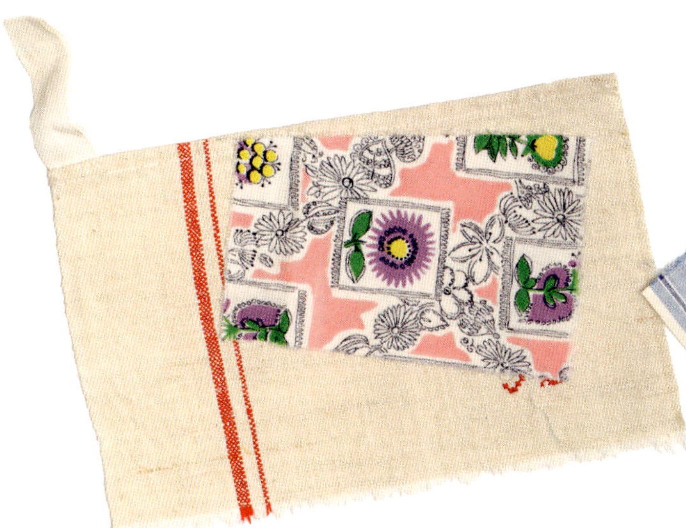

GATHERING WORDS

Words and text feature in most of my artwork. Certain words and phrases literally jump off the page when I am reading them, immediately conjuring up pictures in my mind or sending me off on wild trains of thought.

I'm continually inspired by words from old books, vintage magazines and the personal letters of complete strangers, but I'll also find them closer to home with personal memories, scribbled reminders and shopping lists scripted by my grandchildren, for example.

You'll find references to 'found words' throughout this book – in fact, I've so much to say that I've dedicated the whole of the third chapter to them!

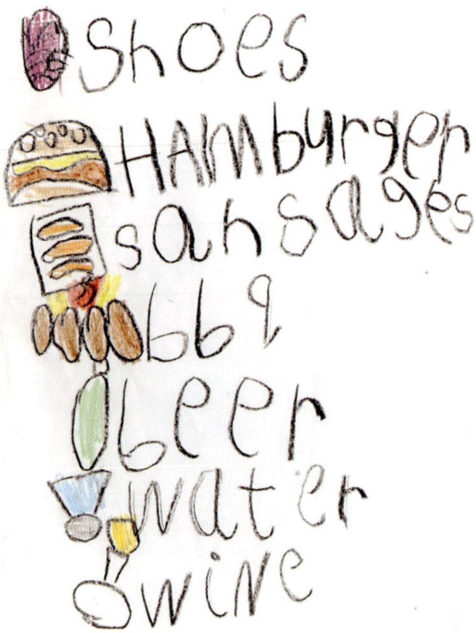

RIGHT: My granddaughter's list for a holiday barbeque became the inspiration for the small cloth collage below.

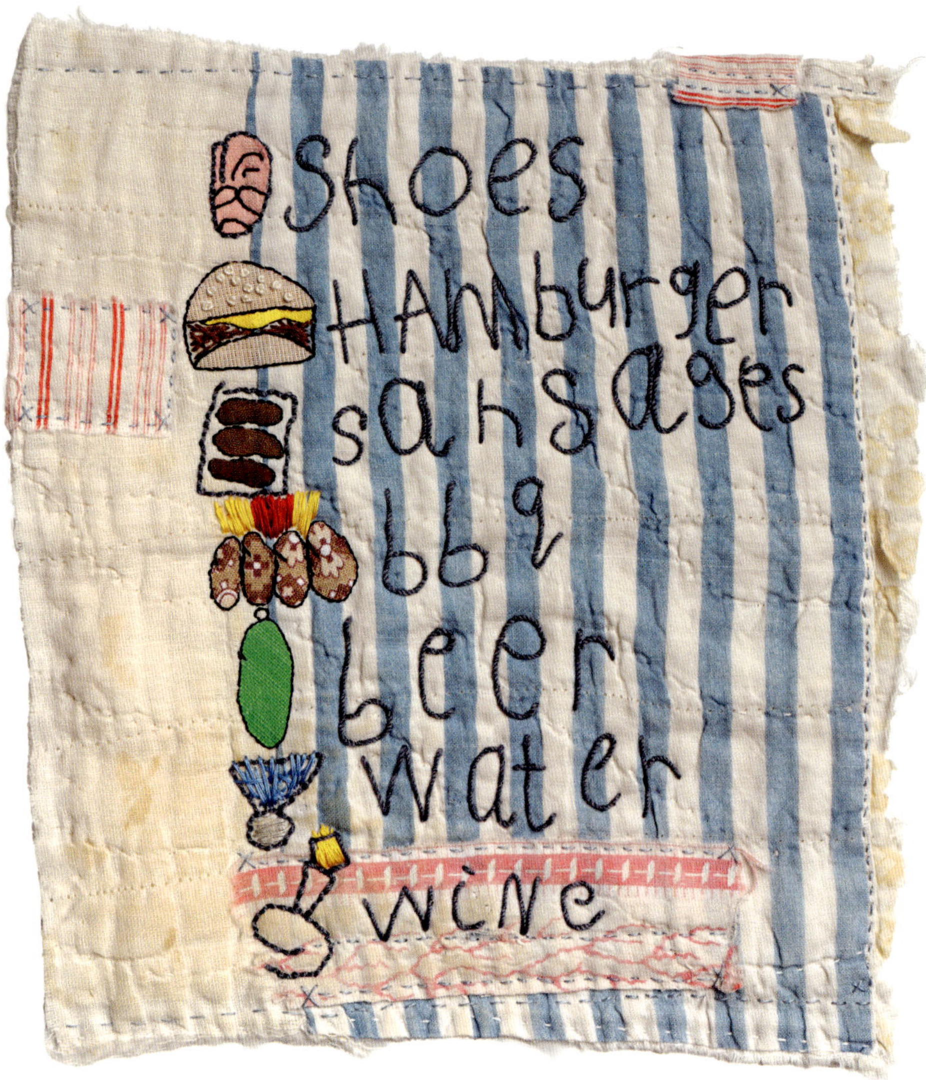

RIGHT: *Beer, Water, Wine*, 18 × 19cm (7 × 7½in). The words are couched onto a scrap of old quilt, with the drawings interpreted in hand stitch and simple appliqué using Bondaweb.

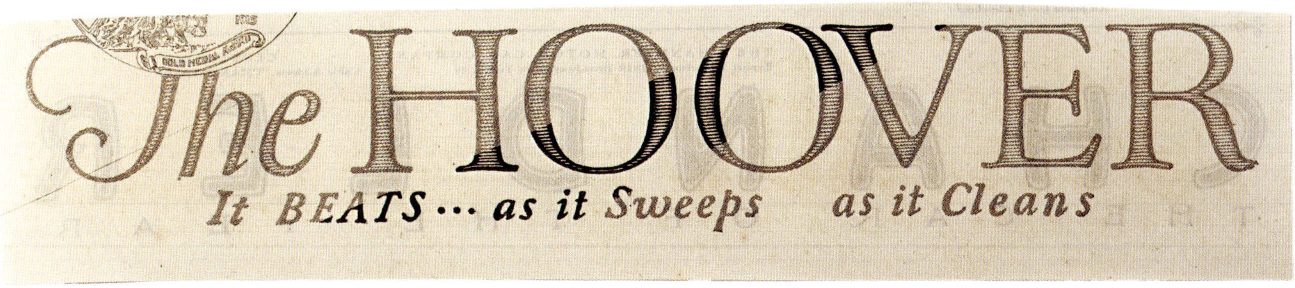

GATHERING MOTIFS

By motifs I mean something that will help illustrate your story. For me, this often takes the form of a simple stitched line drawing, an embroidered illustration or an appliquéd shape. I often refer to vintage haberdashery for motifs to use in my cloth collages and find illustrations in old books and magazines to be great sources of inspiration. For example, the typeface used in an advertisement for Hoover inspired my apron *Beats as it Sweeps as it Cleans* (see page 49).

Motifs don't just have to be illustrations, though; in the following pages you'll see that I use photographs, garments, shoes and other collected items in my stitched pieces, as well as old coat hangers and bobbins as methods of display. If these things are chosen for a reason, rather than being randomly added for their appearance, then they play a part in illustrating the story of the piece.

This process of gathering is ongoing. If I see a sentence or a picture in a magazine that appeals to me, I'll take a copy or cut out the page and save it for future use.

I'm discerning in my gatherings – things must speak to me by awakening a memory, an emotion or a curiosity. My interest lies in the domestic, so my gatherings revolve around the lives of ordinary people and simple everyday things.

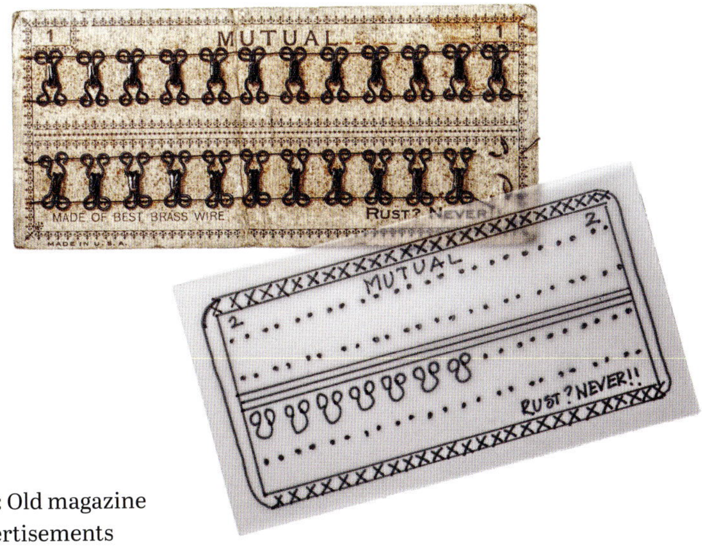

TOP: Old magazine advertisements are a continual source of inspiration, such as this 1920s Hoover advert.

ABOVE AND BELOW: I drew simplified versions of these old haberdashery cards and then traced them onto vellum to use as motifs in my sewing box studies (page 60).

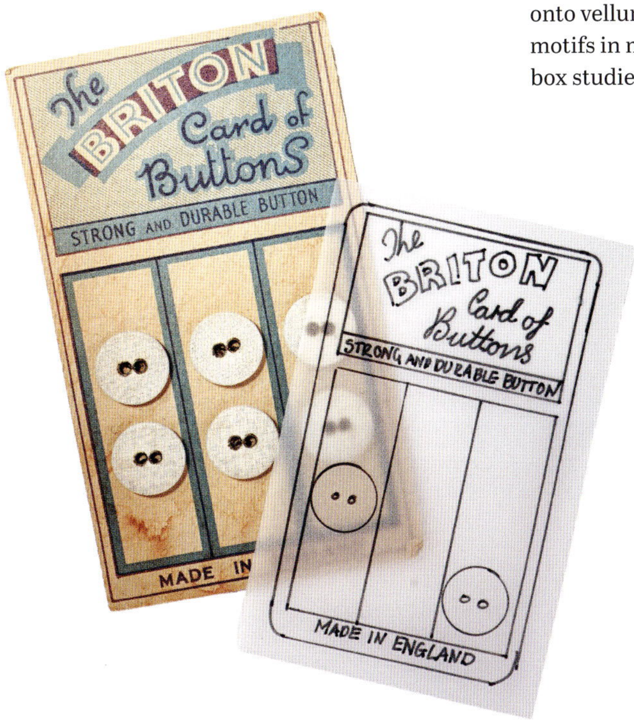

Threads of thought

I find my own 'place of story' by sitting down and capturing my thoughts and ideas onto paper in the form of a mind map. I've developed this over the years into my own way of working, which I call creating *threads of thought*. These were at the heart of my book, *Cloth Stories*, so I won't go into the process here, except to say that it's a great way to get ideas flowing.

I find that creating my *threads of thought* allows one thought to lead to another, taking me in different and sometimes unexpected directions. It leads me beyond my first and most obvious ideas. Each 'thread' causes me to explore several different pathways, unlocking memories and emotions along the way. I include the headings of materials, words and motifs to help me explore different possibilities for these.

There are examples later in this book.

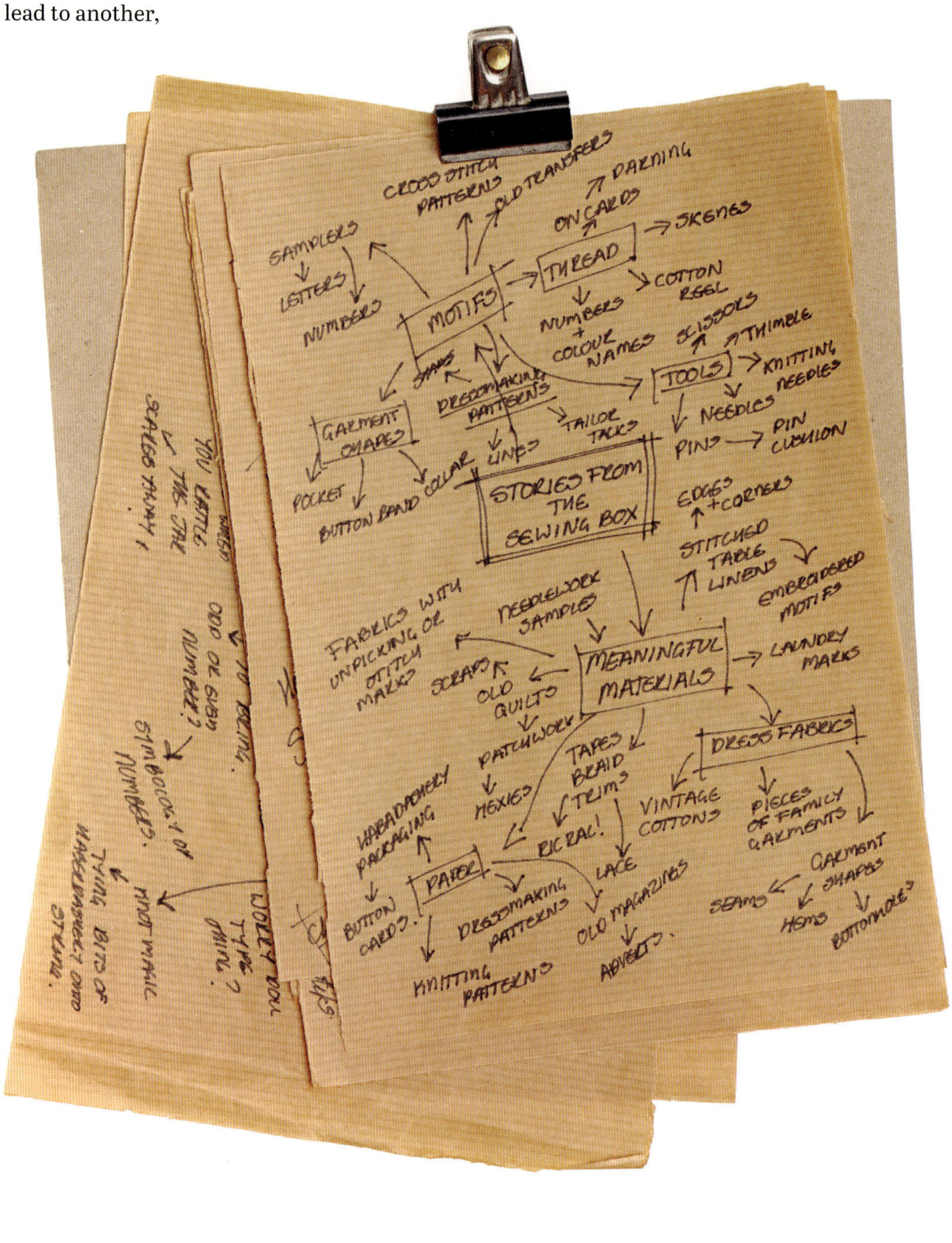

RIGHT: Crisp, white sheets of paper can be daunting, so I draw my *threads of thought* and scribble my notes on scraps of brown parcel paper.

Gathering your thoughts

At the start of any project my table is strewn with paper. As well as my *threads of thought*, there will be ideas for words and motifs, photographs for inspiration, pages of printed research and drawings. As the project progresses, scraps of fabric, threads and small samples may also be added to the pile. All my ideas and workings out are done on scraps of paper.

While I am working, I store all these things in a cardboard box. I find that everything is then easily accessible. I can add to the box as I go along and discard things that are no longer of interest. There comes a point, however, when I like to create order out of the chaos, and this is where a sketchbook comes in. The very process of transferring materials from box to page helps me to collate my thoughts, as well as my notes and resource materials.

My sketchbooks become future reference books, I return to them repeatedly as any one idea and the subsequent *threads of thought* can inspire further bodies of work. Sometimes I will rewrite or redraw things directly into the pages or write things out more neatly, but often the original papers get taped or stitched into the pages.

I do this at the end of a project, which may sound back to front, but it works for me. As a future resource, I want my sketchbook to be visually pleasing and stimulating, so I take time in creating it. This becomes a creative process in itself.

BELOW: My box of source materials, notes and samples for my *Polka Dots and Postcards* project on page 38.

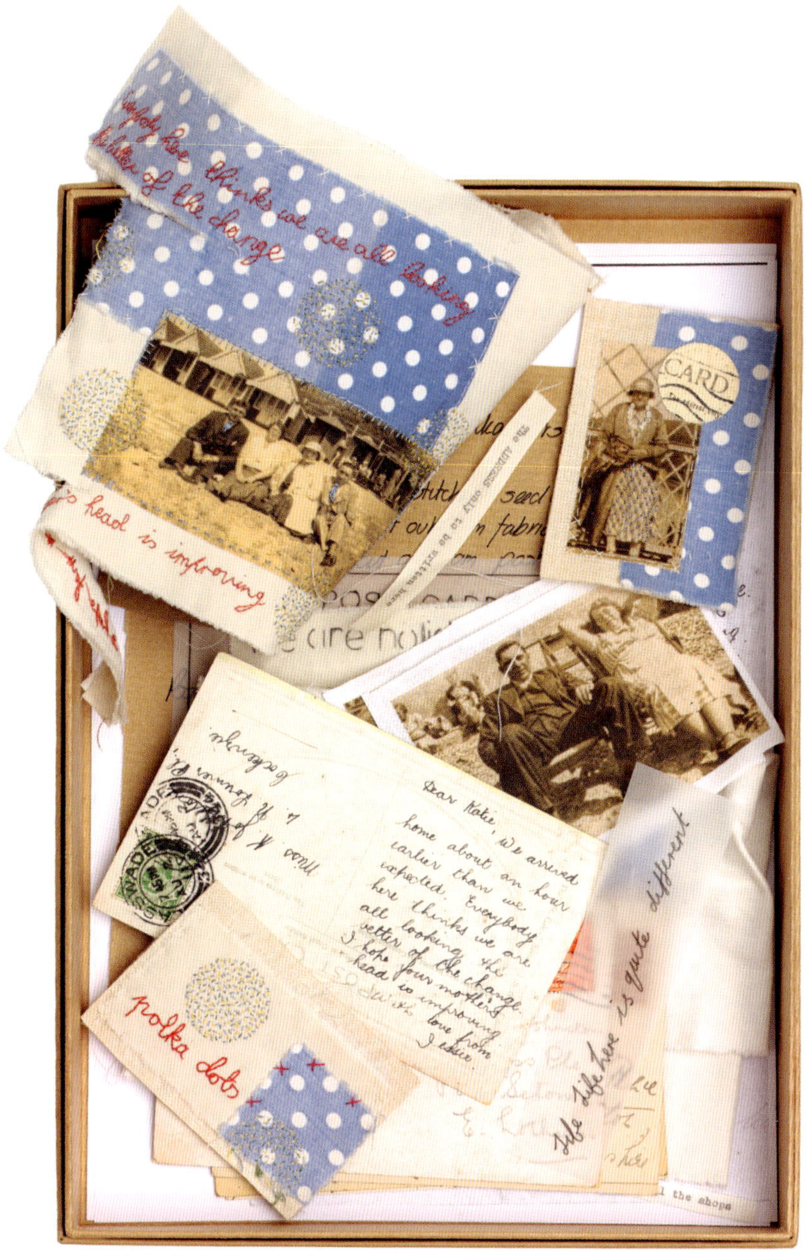

A stitcher's sketchbook

I think a stitcher's sketchbook should appeal to the senses. I love to hear the crinkle of a page as you turn it, to feel fabric scraps and soft old paper and to feast my eyes on pages layered with papers, cloth and stitch. I often make my own sketchbooks out of interesting papers such as brown parcel paper (great for the crinkle), vellum and coloured papers. If pages become torn or loose through use, I simply mend them with patches of cloth glued or stitched over the damage.

Here are some ideas for creating interest:

- Fold or tear some of the pages so that they aren't uniform in size.
- Use tape, paperclips, split pins and bulldog clips as well as stitching to attach things into the pages.
- Insert additional information into the pages using luggage labels, small concertina books or stitched pamphlets.
- Hold or hide things safely in envelopes or bags.
- Pin fabric samples onto the pages with entomology pins, or simply staple or use paper clips.
- Layer materials on your pages and allow them to get messy.

The resulting sketchbook is not only beautifully tactile, but also completely practical. My favourites bulge at the seams with information and inspiration spilling out of the pages.

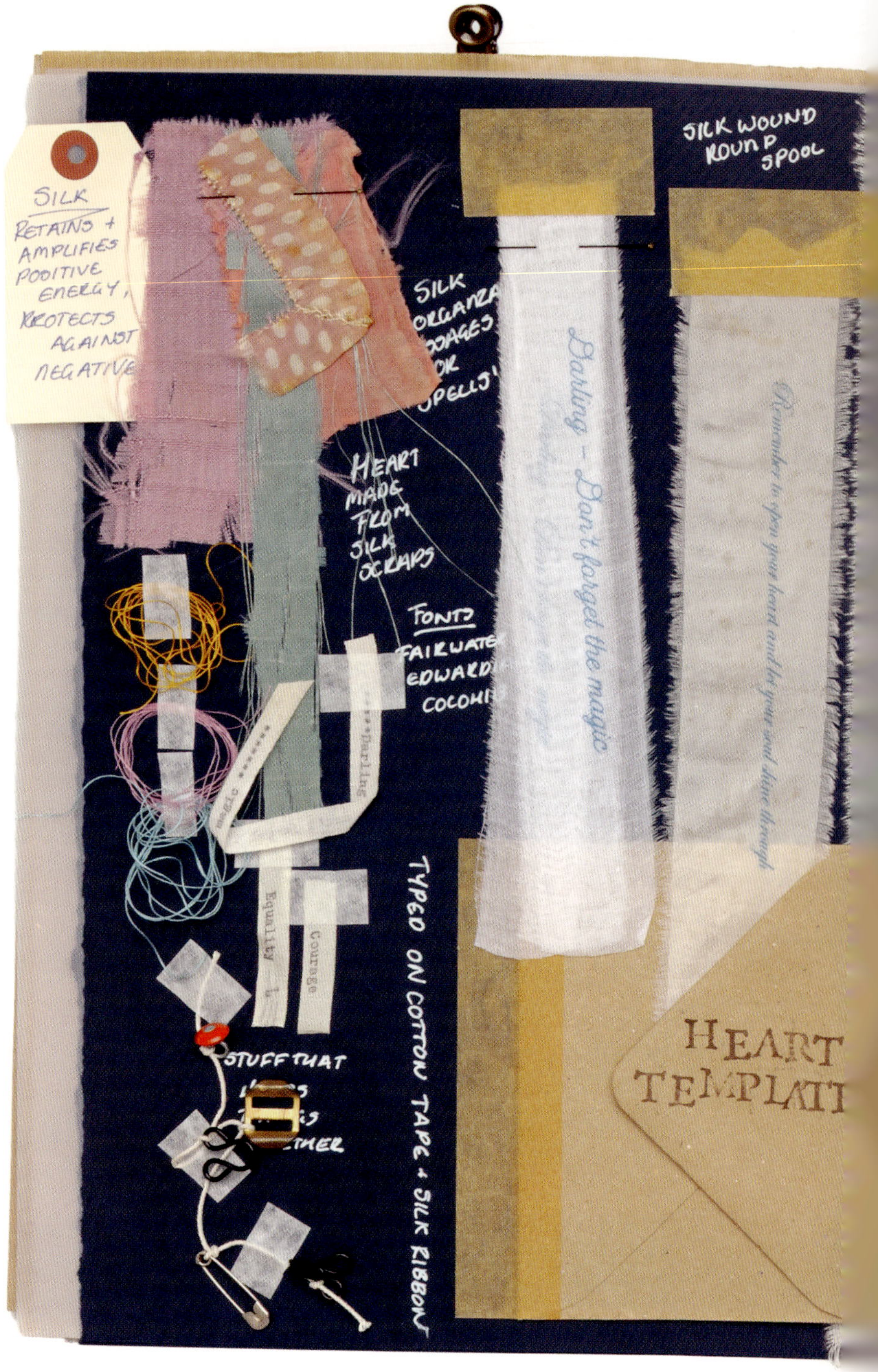

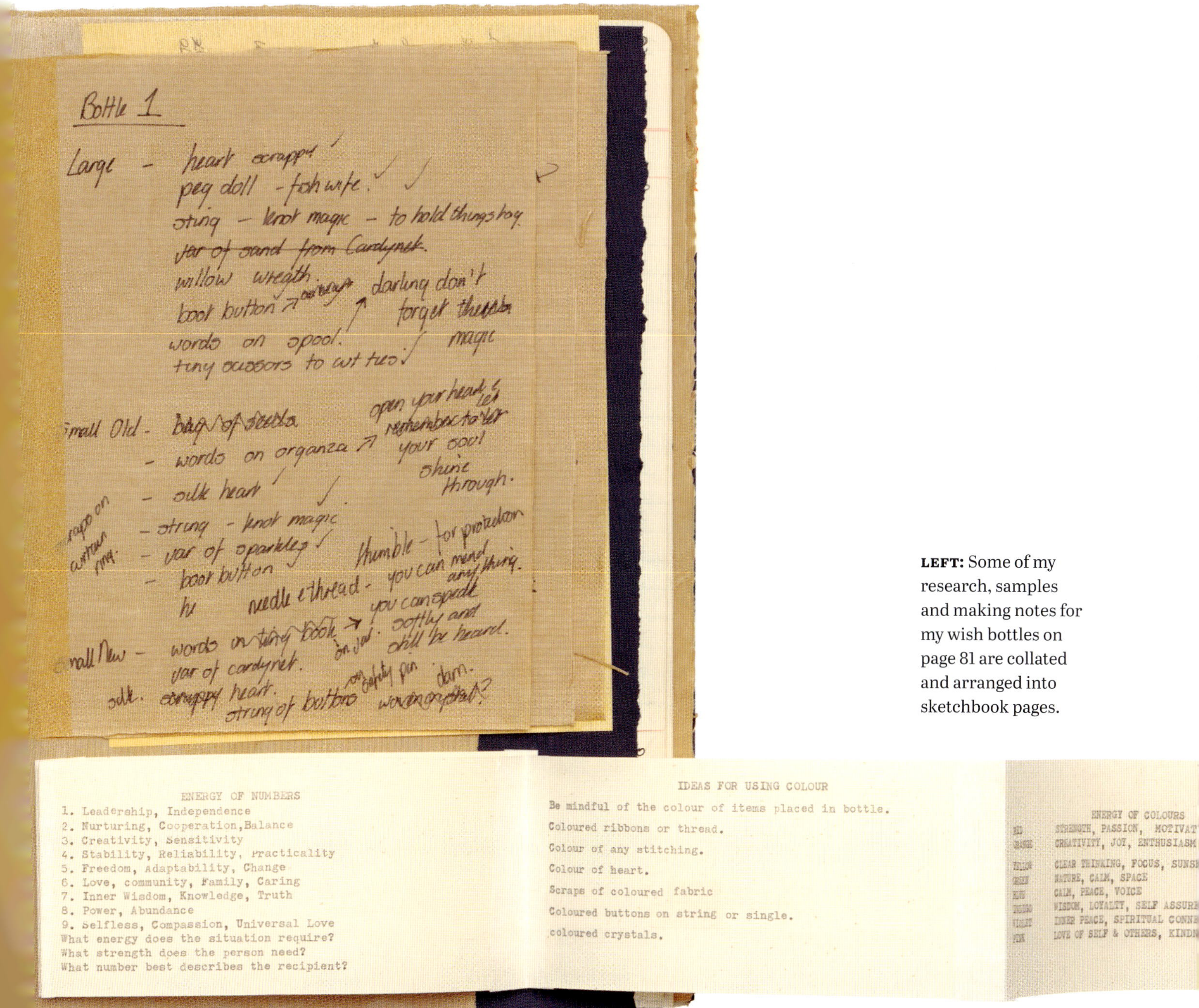

LEFT: Some of my research, samples and making notes for my wish bottles on page 81 are collated and arranged into sketchbook pages.

Hand stitching

I describe myself as being a 'stitcher' rather than an 'embroiderer'. I'm not always neat and I'm certainly not precise. I think that our way of stitching is personal, like our handwriting. I could produce beautifully neat and precise stitches if I put all my energy and attention into the formation of each one, but my personal style is much more fluid – it becomes rhythmic and intuitive, and the result can be slightly (but beautifully) wonky.

I tend to use only a few favourite stitches – running stitch, back stitch, cross stitch and herringbone. I also love seed stitch – I find it soothing and almost meditative forming the repetitive, tiny stitches. I call seed stitch 'worry stitch' after a slight obsession with it during lockdown! Another favourite is blanket stitch, which I often use as an edging.

I use these stitches to create patterns that I repeat across all my work. Again, I'd liken stitching to handwriting, where you gradually develop your personal way of forming marks until they become so familiar that they flow from your needle just like ink from a pen.

As with everything, I turn to the past for inspiration. I was gifted the piece of crazy patchwork shown opposite (dated 1890) many years ago, and I think it played a big part in helping me find my own style of creating cloth collages. It helped me ignore the voice in my head whispering 'less is more' and gave me permission to add lots of detail, which I love.

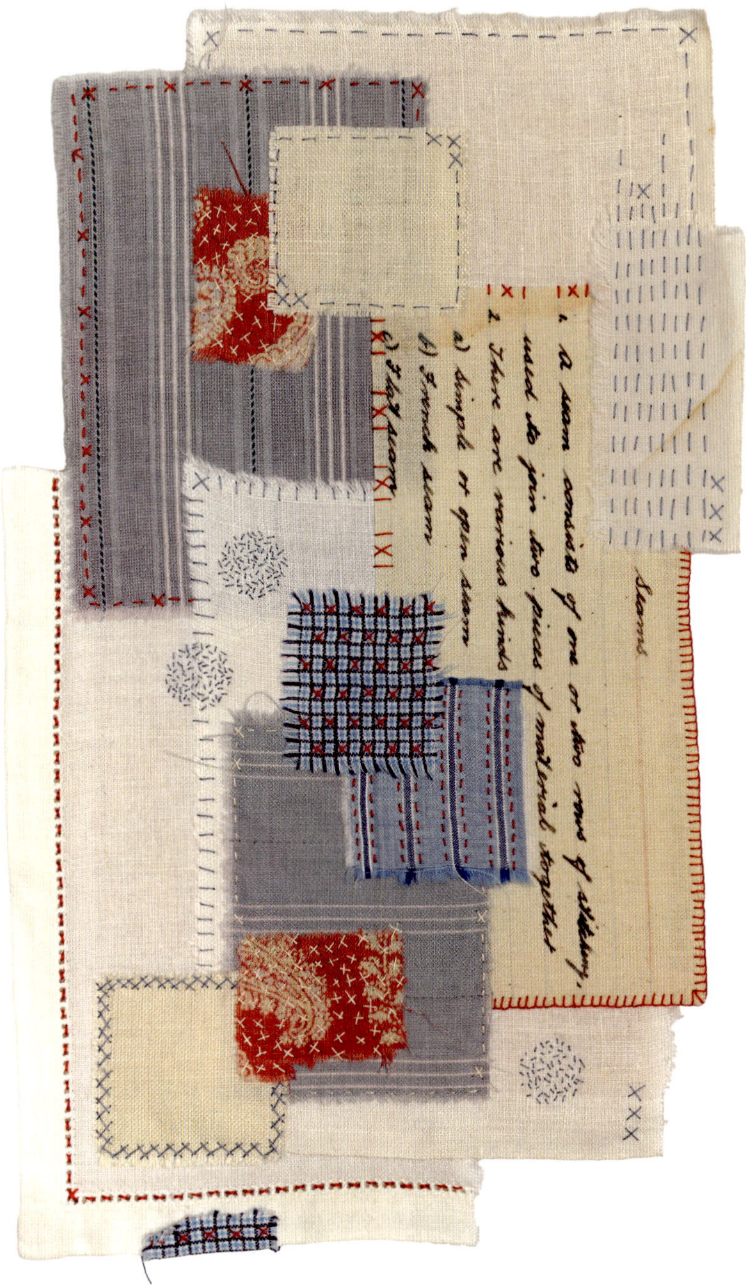

LEFT: *Stitch sample*, 17 × 28cm (6½ × 11in). Small sample showing some of my favourite patterns of stitching using a limited palette of stitches – running stitch, cross stitch, seed stitch, straight stitch, blanket stitch and herringbone.

OPPOSITE: *Antique crazy patchwork*, 22 × 29cm (8½ × 11½in). This crazy patchwork piece made from silk scraps and stitched in 1890 is a wonderful sample showcasing many decorative embroidery stitches.

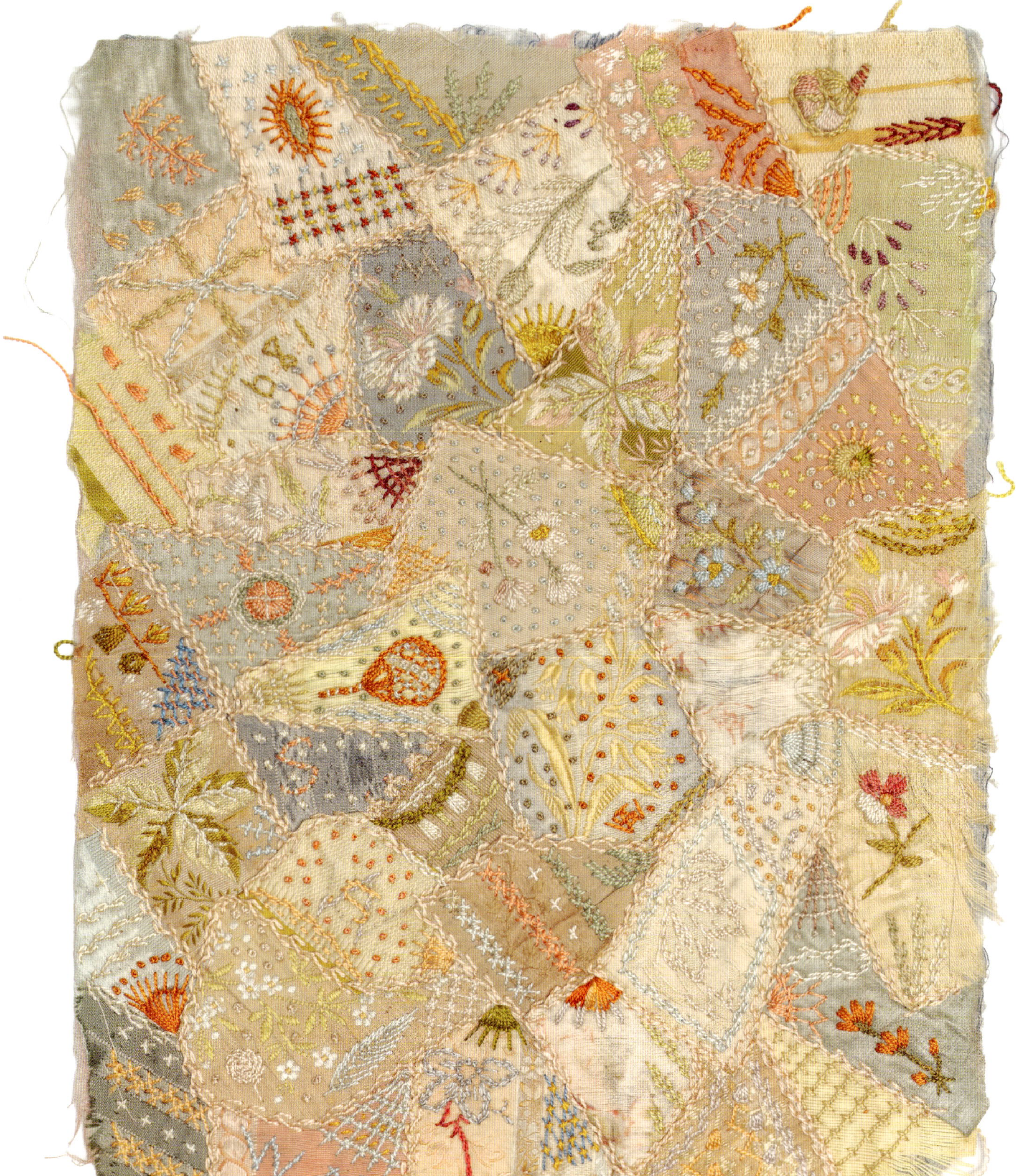

BELOW: Allow your stitching to be intuitive; start with a simple running stitch and then let the fabrics tell you what to do next.

I work with a fine thread – one strand of stranded cotton, vintage silk threads or old sewing threads from reels. I mostly use a no 8 or 9 embroidery (or crewel) needle.

Some fabrics will tell you what they want! For example, I find that gingham squares love to have crosses stitched in them, but of course, they may tell you differently. As work progresses, I sometimes change my mind about a previous decision, and I often unpick areas and redo them.

If you don't know where to start with your own stitching, then I suggest that you choose one patch of cloth and stitch round the edges in a running stitch, perhaps adding a few crosses at the corners. I promise that as you do this, your next idea will come along. Just take it one step at a time, and you'll soon find that you are engrossed in this intuitive way of working – it's rather like doodling with a needle and thread.

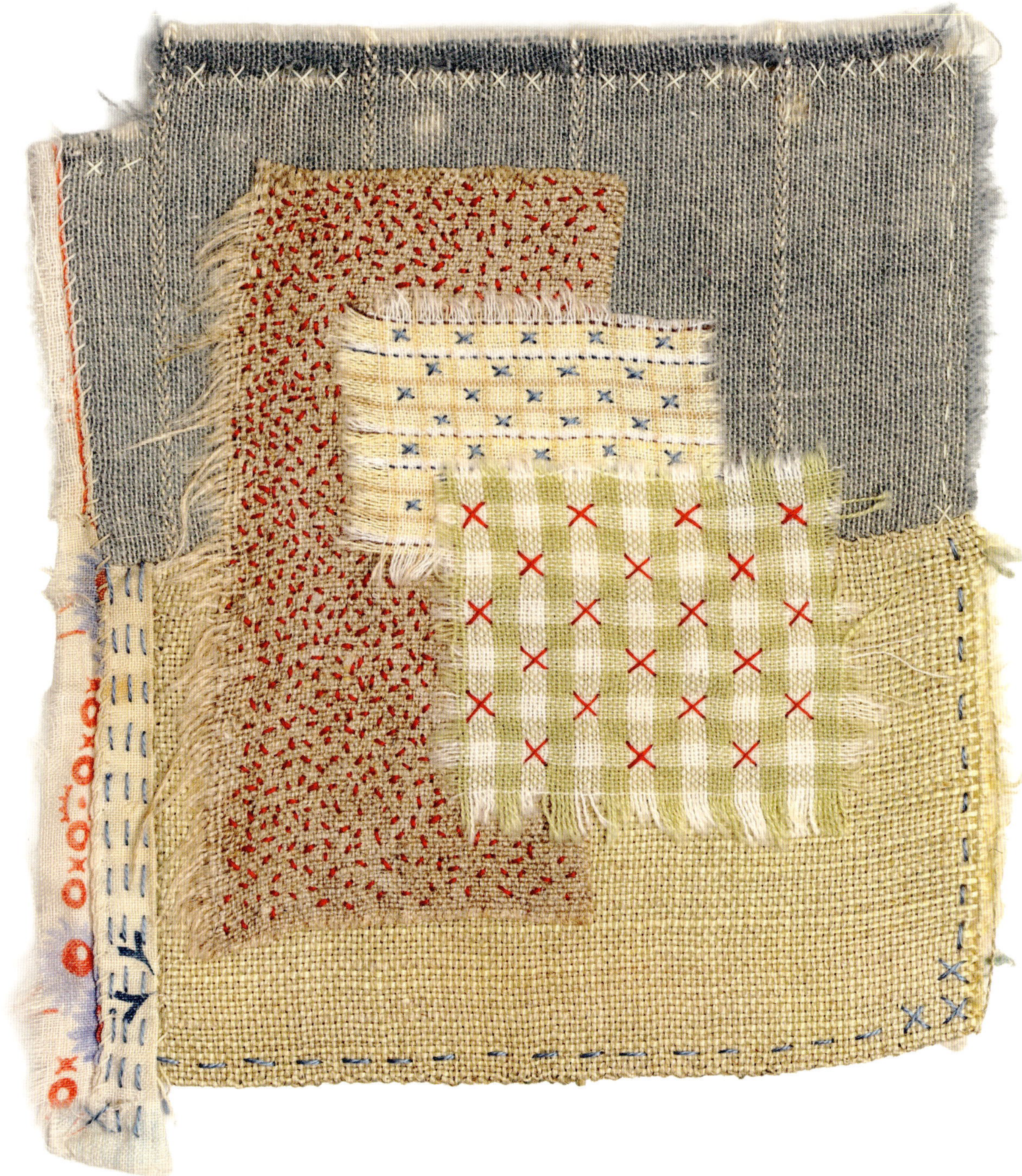

Stitched motifs

To create my stitched motifs, I draw my outline on tissue paper, stick this onto my fabric with small bits of masking tape and then stitch through the tissue with a running stitch. For the best results, keep a good tension when stitching and make evenly sized and spaced stitches. After stitching, carefully tear away the tissue, keeping your thumb over the stitches as you do so to protect them. After the tissue has been removed, you can go back and fill in the spaces (double running stitch) to create a solid line if you wish.

If the project is washable, you can draw or print your motif outline onto sticky water-soluble embroidery stabilizer (more about this on page 74).

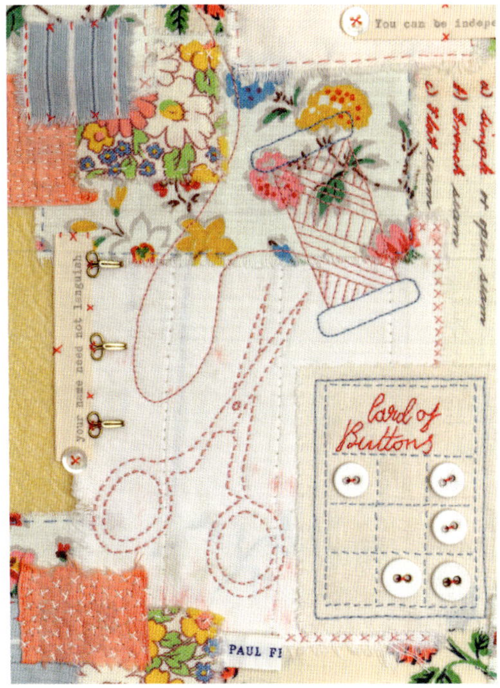

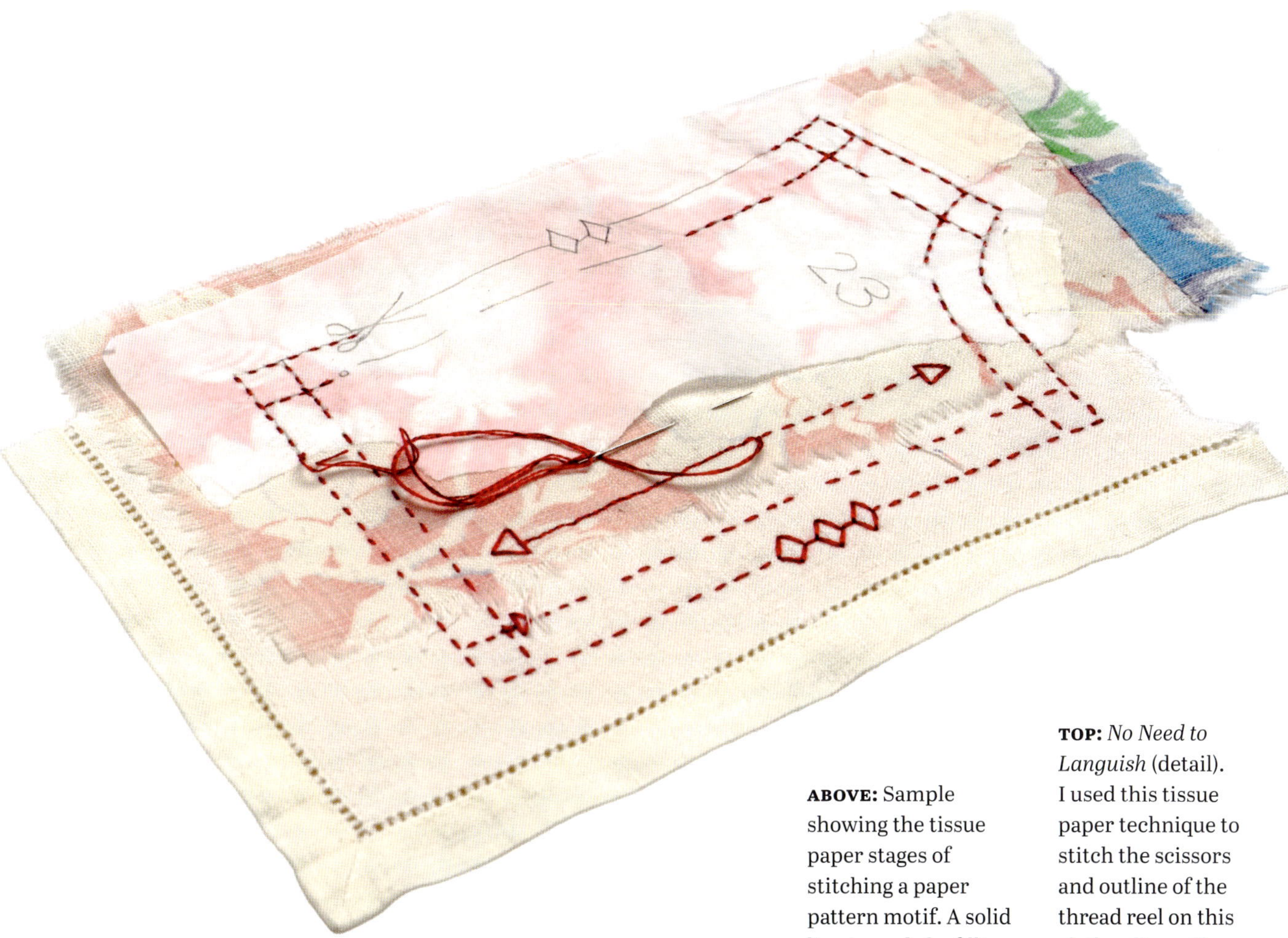

ABOVE: Sample showing the tissue paper stages of stitching a paper pattern motif. A solid line is made by filling in the gaps between stitches once the tissue is torn away.

TOP: *No Need to Languish* (detail). I used this tissue paper technique to stitch the scissors and outline of the thread reel on this cloth collage. The thread detail was added once the tissue had been removed.

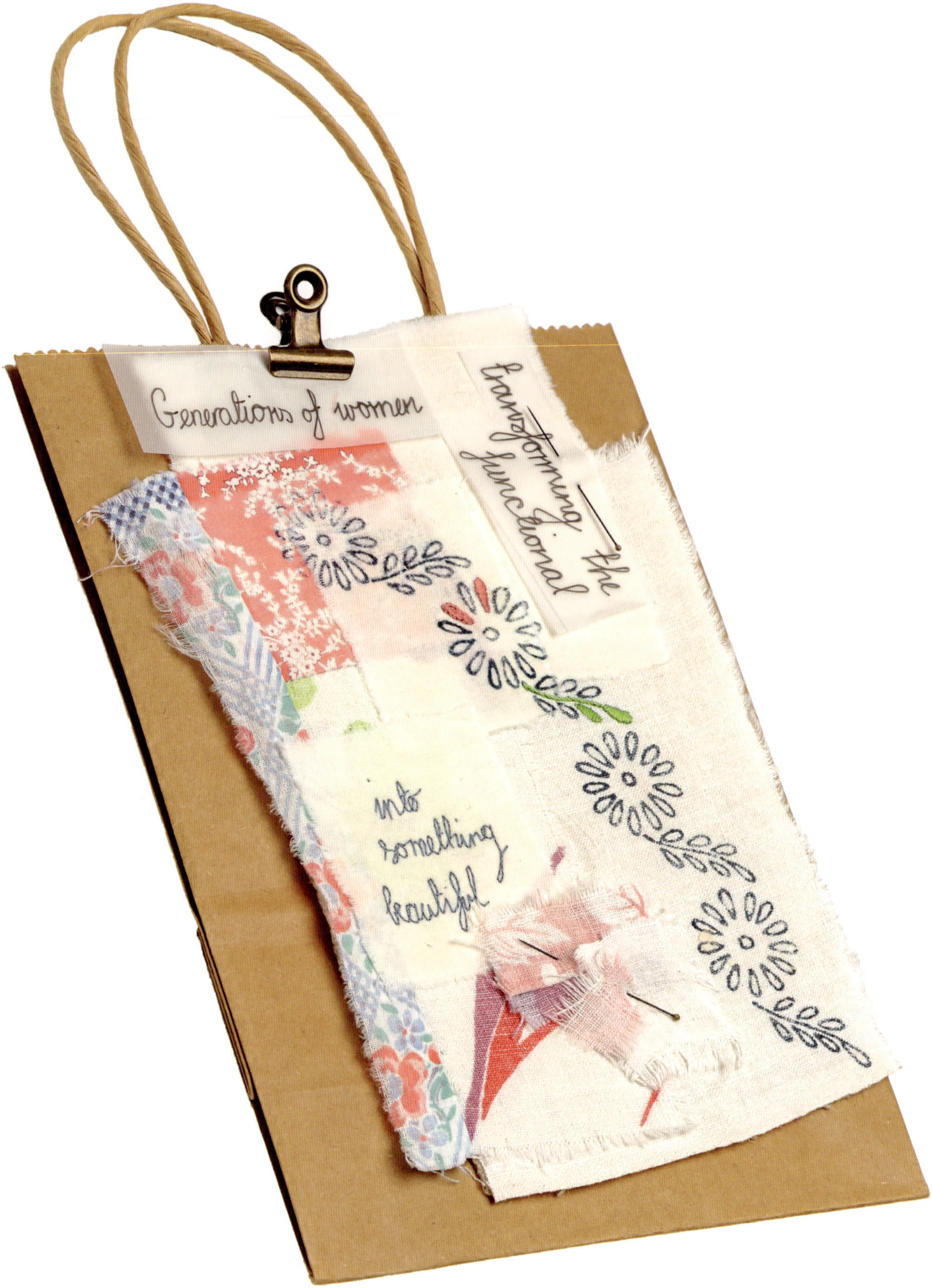
Generations of women
transforming the functional
into something beautiful

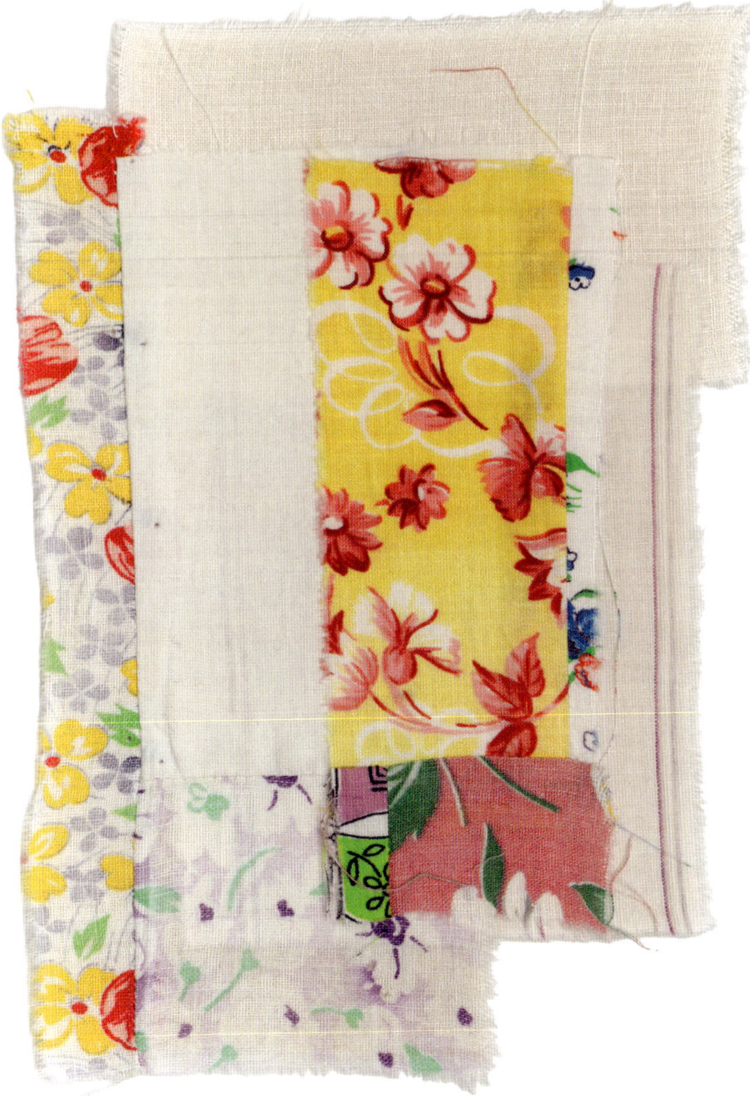

Sampling

There will be times throughout the making when you need to experiment, and it's always worthwhile taking time to create a sample before trying something you are unsure of directly onto your work. Do so, for example, when you're not sure how an idea will look, don't know how a material will react or you just want to practise something that you've never done before. It could be as simple as trying out an unfamiliar stitch.

I often have little sampler backgrounds prepared and ready to stitch. I make them out of scraps of fabric attached to a background with fusible web – I use Bondaweb or Mistyfuse.

Smaller samples are pinned into my sketchbooks, but larger ones pinned to paper bags are hung around my studio.

LEFT: A sampler background prepared and ready to stitch. Scraps of fabric attached onto a foundation of old woollen blanket.

OPPOSITE: I clip my colourful samples onto paper bags and hang them in my studio for inspiration.

RIGHT: Here I played with embroidery stitches and a transfer design on an old linen tablecloth.

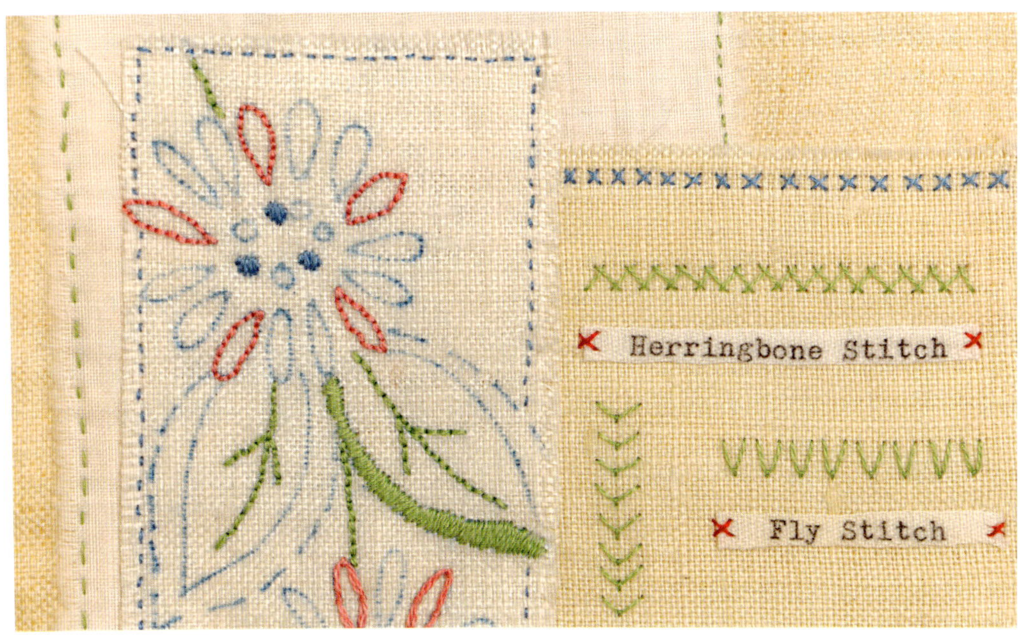

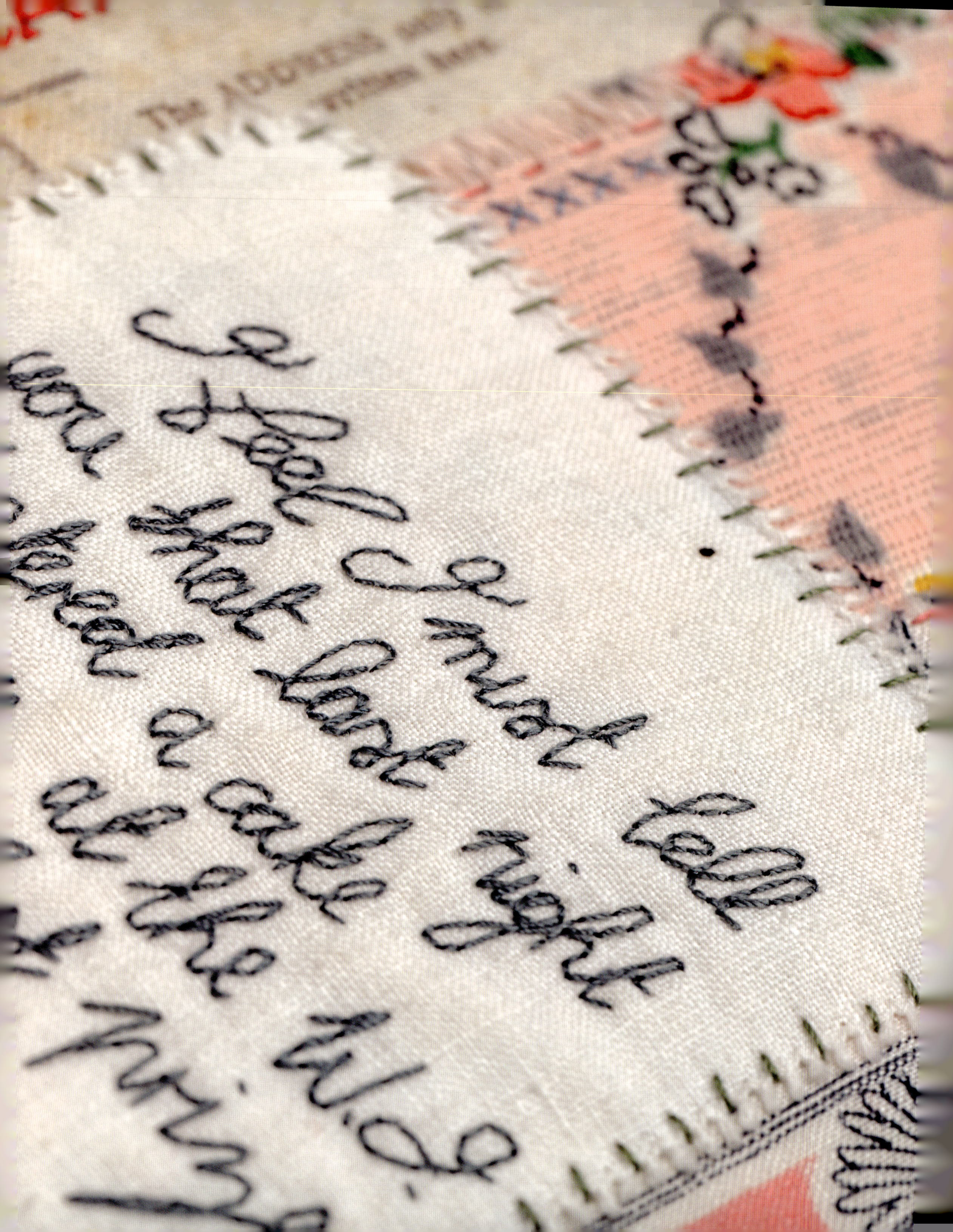

The ADDRESS only
written here
I feel I must tell
you that last night
had a cake
at the W.I.

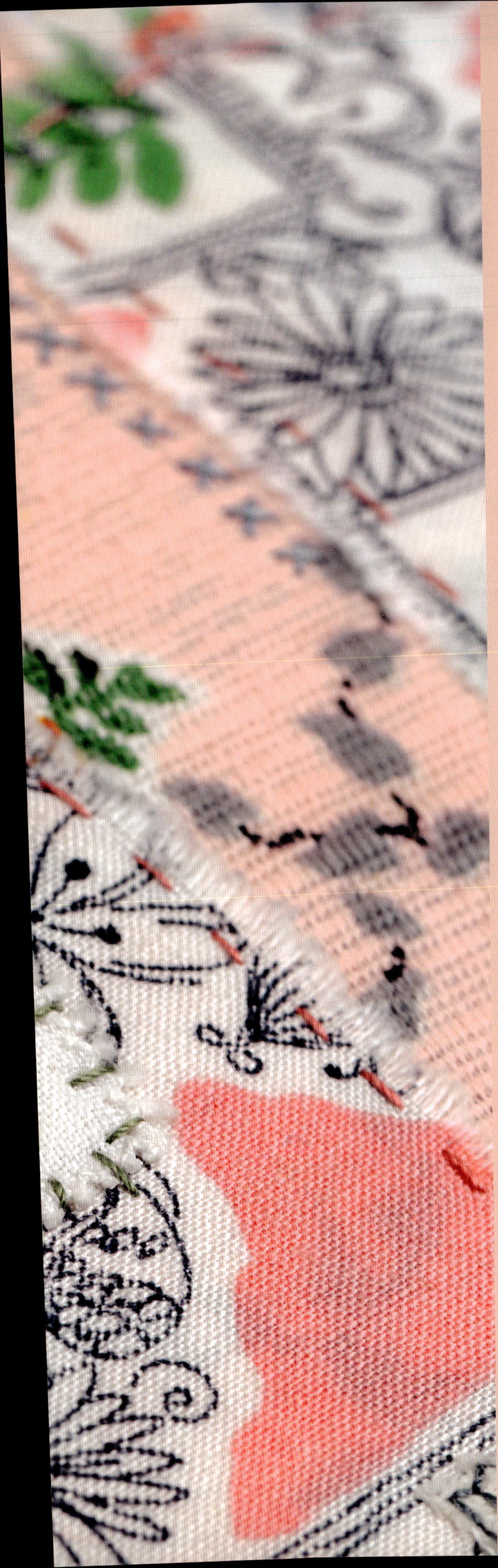

Collected stuff

So many of the textile artists and stitchers that I meet throughout my travels are also by nature collectors of vintage treasures. Some unseen force seems to draw us towards the old and the discarded and we just don't have it in us to leave behind that bundle of letters, envelope of photos, tin of buttons or box of wooden cotton reels.

Perhaps it is the tactile qualities of an old item that attracts us, or the sense of story that we feel as we discover each dent, mark and patina. Perhaps it's the fear that if we don't step in, said item will be condemned to landfill.

But maybe it's just that there is an inherent part of us that has a need to surround ourselves with things that we believe to be beautiful, things that have clearly worked hard for a living and things that we know to be steeped in (hi)story.

A love of collecting

'Someone else's memories and no-one left to care.'
***The Light a Candle Society*, Ruth Hogan**

These words felt particularly poignant when I read them in Ruth Hogan's book, *The Light a Candle Society*. Of course, some of us may be the ones left who do care, fortunate enough to be the guardians of treasured personal items carrying memories and stories of our own families. Sadly, I don't have many personal family items apart from photographs, so I do rely on sourcing things at antique fairs, flea markets and from online traders and auction sites.

Taking inspiration from the past

I collect for different reasons, but mainly the following:

- Because I'll use the item in my work: vintage fabrics, lace, trimmings and garments, of course, but I'm also on the lookout for things to use for display purposes such as old bobbins, tins, old coat hangers and anything else that catches my eye.

- To give me inspiration around a subject: things such as old washing tongs, clothes pegs and kitchen utensils are part of my exploration of domestic lives. Handling these things triggers memories or imaginings. I might sketch them or print with them as inspiration for motifs, but equally, the item itself could become an integral part of the finished work.

- As a resource for learning; for example, vintage books and magazines and my absolute holy grail – old school domestic science jotters and handwritten recipe books.

- Because they fascinate me; there are certain things that I can't walk away from, no matter how hard I try: among them are men's detachable shirt collars, baby shoes in the softest of leather and haberdashery items.

BELOW: I can't resist the sculptural qualities of old detachable collars. They can be strong motifs in telling men's stories.

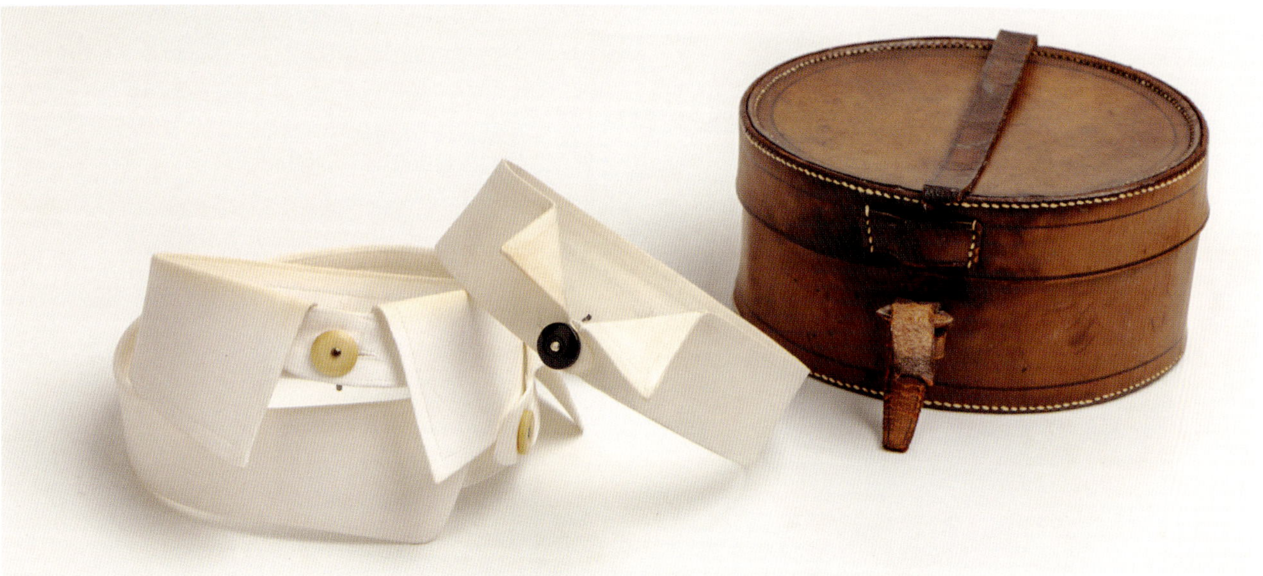

Letters and postcards

These are some of the most valued items in my collections, each one being unique and completely irreplaceable. Sometimes it's the letters themselves that inspire a piece of work, but often all it takes is a sentence or two to set my mind whirring.

I'm often curious as to how these deeply personal letters and other correspondence came to be for sale. I feel a sense of delight when I come across them, guilt as I read them, along with a feeling of sadness that they have been discarded – the thoughts of the author no longer of interest or relevance.

The letters that I love the most tell the most mundane stories, offering glimpses into the everyday lives of the author and the social history of the time they were written. For example:

'Will you have your bath Friday night and so save time over the weekend?'

These words come from a wonderful collection of 60 handwritten letters penned by Ada to her boyfriend, Lackie, during World War II. It's a stark reminder of how time spent together can be a rare and precious commodity, not only back then, but for so many around the world today.

Ada wrote several letters to Lackie each week. Although she frequently had very little news, she could spin it out over several pages, and I suspect that Lackie hung on every inconsequential word. Her writing is frequently interrupted by the sounds of sirens and the subsequent visits to the air raid shelter. I can spend hours reading each one, following the ups and downs of her moods and smiling at her sense of humour.

Ada's letters inspired my 'Story Shirt' featured on pages 96–97.

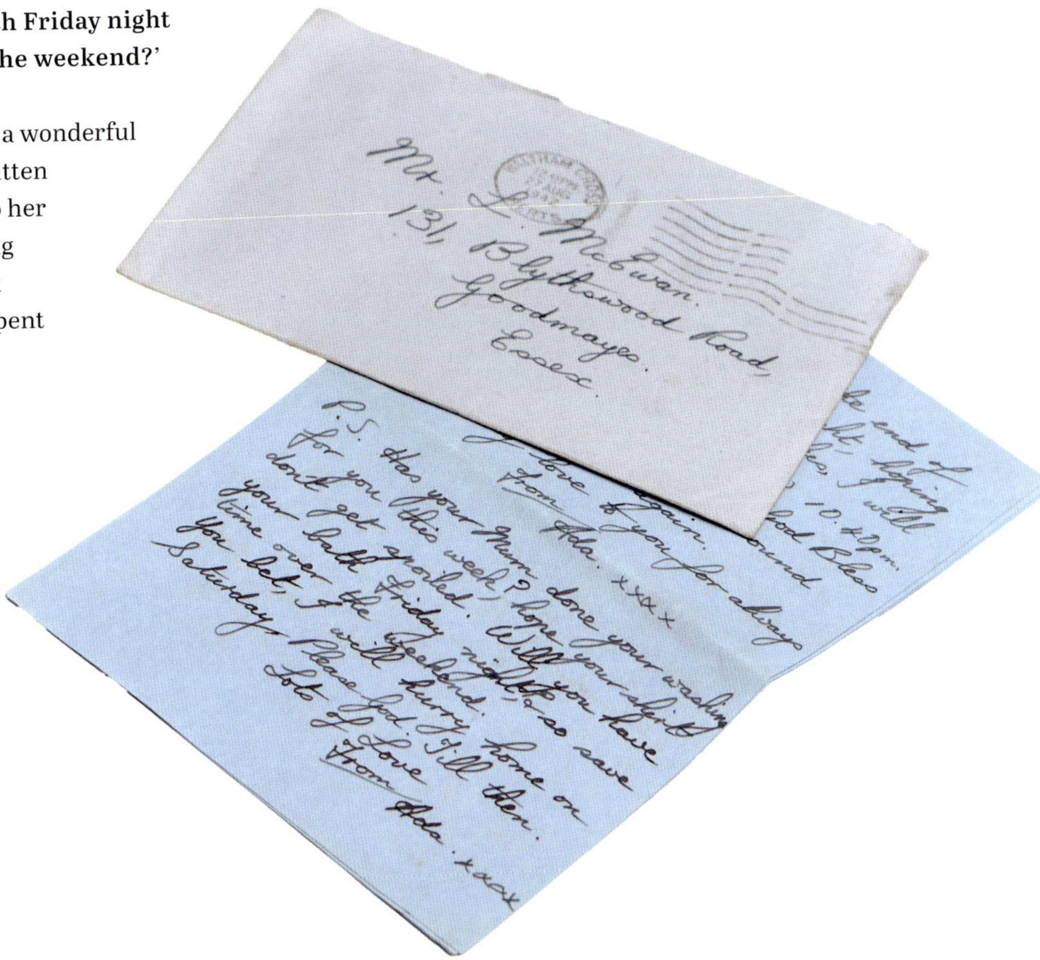

RIGHT: One of Ada's many letters to Lackie during WWII with its poignant PS 'Will you have your bath Friday night...'

A way of life

BELOW: Sketchbook pages showing my *threads of thought* around my research on Scottish fishwives.

OPPOSITE: After my initial explorations take me in many different directions, I start to pin down the ideas that I wish to take forward.

Several years ago I was researching the story of Maggie Dickson, an East Lothian fishwife who was publicly hanged in Edinburgh in 1723 for the crime of concealing a pregnancy. The story goes that as her body was carted home by her friends, she rather miraculously revived, much to the surprise of everyone! She was thereafter known as 'Half-Hung Maggie'.

Although the story of Maggie Dickson was dramatic (please do look it up!) and there are so many different *threads of thought* that you could choose to follow, it was the lives of the fishwives that I uncovered during my reading that captivated me. I spoke at length to a wonderful friend whose family were fisherfolk and she gifted me a collection of family postcards.

In among the postcards were several that had been sent home by the men when they were away at sea. Dated in the early 1900s and starting 'Dear wife', 'Dear mother' and 'Dear sister', they carried news of the important events of the day: the weather, the catch, health and finances. They were the connection between home and the men, who could be at sea for weeks in the most dangerous conditions. It struck me that today's equivalent would be a text message or quick phone call.

The pieces that I originally created were included in Anne Kelly's book *Textile Travels*, but I was recently drawn to revisit my collection of postcards and my original sketchbooks. I did some more research and drew new *threads of thought* before creating these new pieces of work.

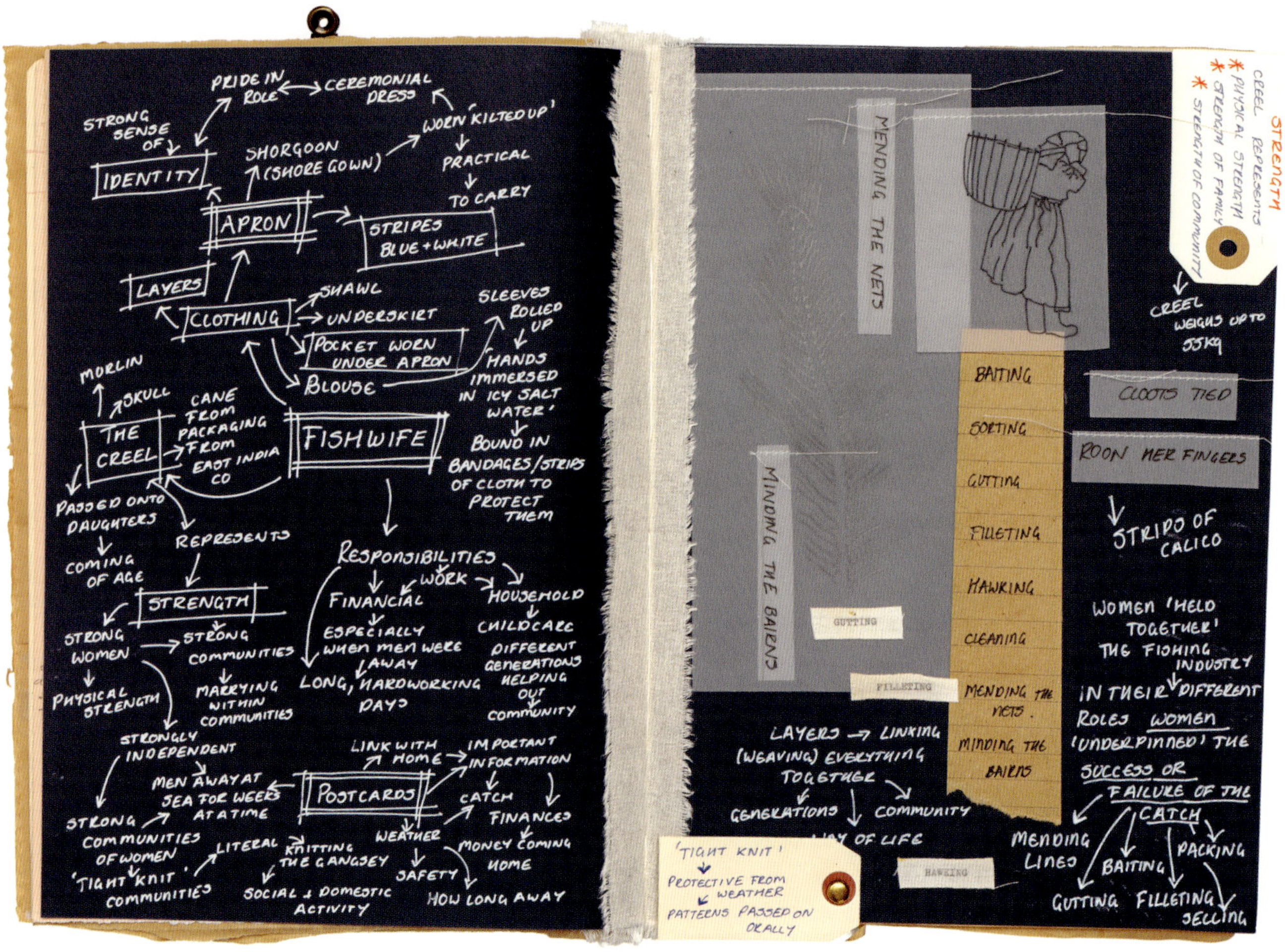

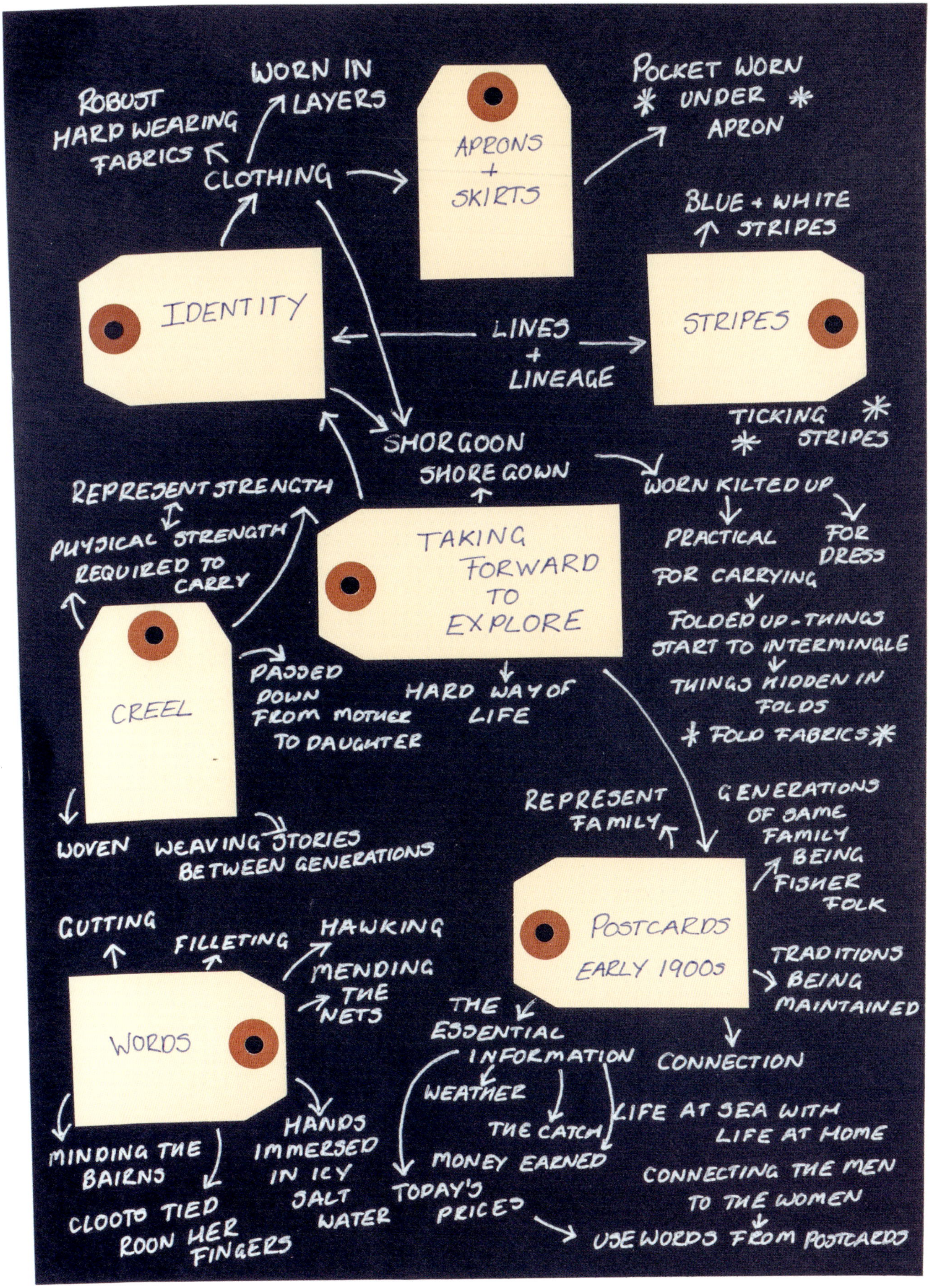
ROBUST HARD WEARING FABRICS
WORN IN LAYERS
CLOTHING
APRONS + SKIRTS
POCKET WORN * UNDER * APRON
BLUE + WHITE STRIPES
IDENTITY
LINES + LINEAGE
STRIPES
TICKING * * STRIPES
SHORGOON
SHORE GOWN
WORN KILTED UP
PRACTICAL FOR CARRYING
FOR DRESS
FOLDED UP - THINGS START TO INTERMINGLE
THINGS HIDDEN IN FOLDS
* FOLD FABRICS *
REPRESENT STRENGTH
PHYSICAL STRENGTH REQUIRED TO CARRY
TAKING FORWARD TO EXPLORE
CREEL
PASSED DOWN FROM MOTHER TO DAUGHTER
HARD WAY OF LIFE
WOVEN
WEAVING STORIES BETWEEN GENERATIONS
REPRESENT FAMILY
GENERATIONS OF SAME FAMILY BEING FISHER FOLK
POSTCARDS EARLY 1900s
TRADITIONS BEING MAINTAINED
CONNECTION
GUTTING
FILLETING
HAWKING
MENDING THE NETS
WORDS
THE ESSENTIAL INFORMATION
WEATHER
THE CATCH
MONEY EARNED
TODAY'S PRICES
LIFE AT SEA WITH LIFE AT HOME
CONNECTING THE MEN TO THE WOMEN
USE WORDS FROM POSTCARDS
MINDING THE BAIRNS
CLOOTS TIED ROON HER FINGERS
HANDS IMMERSED IN ICY SALT WATER

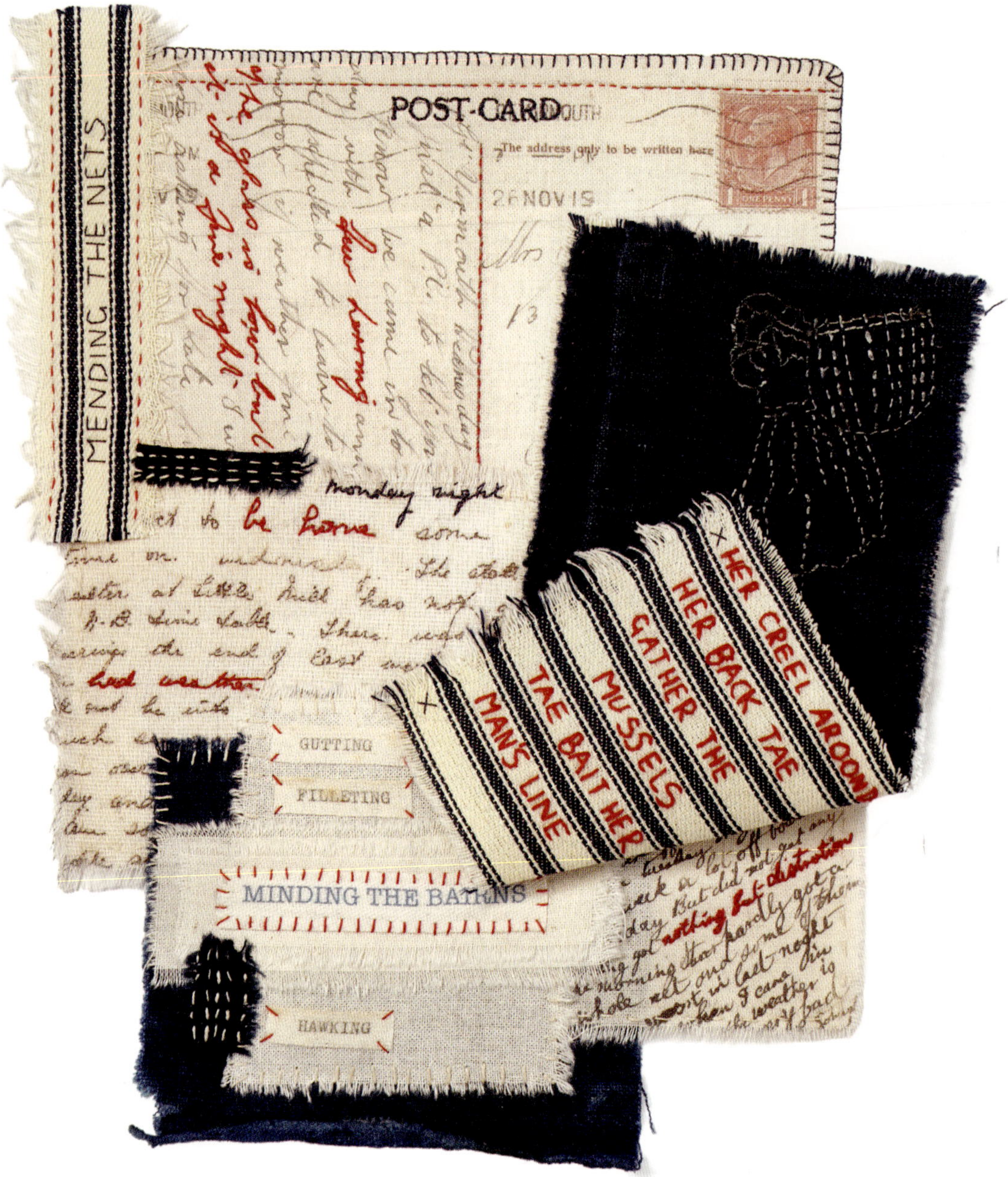

The thinking behind the making

During this process, words and phrases resonated with me such as 'identity', 'strength' and 'community'. The aprons and skirts worn by the Scottish fisherwomen strongly related to their identity and that of the community. They not only gave me my colour palette of navy, white and red, but also the stripes led me to consider 'line' and 'lineage', this being a way of life that passed down through generations.

When I asked myself 'what materials would help tell my story?' my answer was 'poor' fabrics such as vintage ticking, calico and muslin. I tore strips of calico and layered these to represent the bandages that the women wore round their hands to protect them from their razor-sharp knives and the icy salt water as they gutted and filleted the fish.

I included a stitched motif of a woman with her 'creel' (the basket worn on her back) gathering mussels. To me the 'creel' symbolizes strength. These women were physically strong (their baskets could weigh up to 55kg (8st 9lb) when full and they would walk for miles while carrying them), but they also had a strong sense of family and community and were fiercely independent.

ABOVE: *Minding the Bairns*, 18 × 23cm (7 × 9in). Cloth collage with postcards and words inkjet printed onto fabric and cotton tape. Text is hand stitched in back stitch and couched.

The words are the focus of these small pieces. Words from the postcards are printed onto calico and muslin using my inkjet printer with sentences highlighted in tiny back stitches, along with my own words telling snippets of the women's story such as: 'cloots tied roond her fingers tae protect them' (cloths tied round her fingers to protect them), and 'minding the bairns' (looking after the children).

My words are printed onto old cotton tape using my home printer, typed onto tape using an old typewriter as well as handstitched. I'll say more about these processes in the next chapter.

These pieces are small, but I'm already thinking how they could lead to bigger pieces of work and how I could scale everything up in size. I think it's interesting how, when you complete some projects the door in your mind doesn't quite close – it's left slightly ajar so that in future, perhaps as you are flicking through your sketchbook, new ideas start to form, and new *threads of thought* call out to you.

BELOW: *Cloots Tied*, 17 × 27cm (6½ × 10in). It can be really effective to highlight carefully selected words and phrases from printed text with hand stitching.

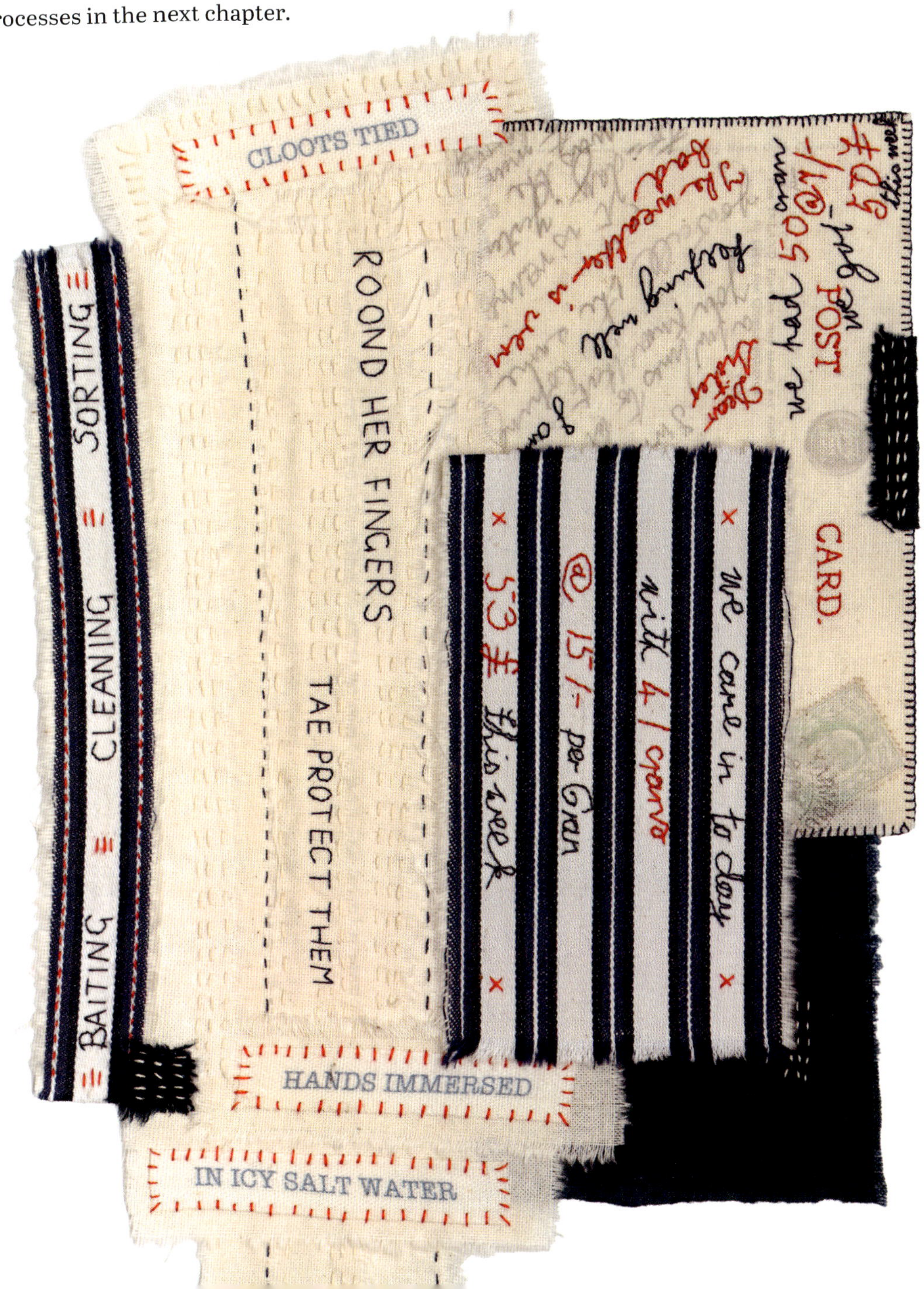

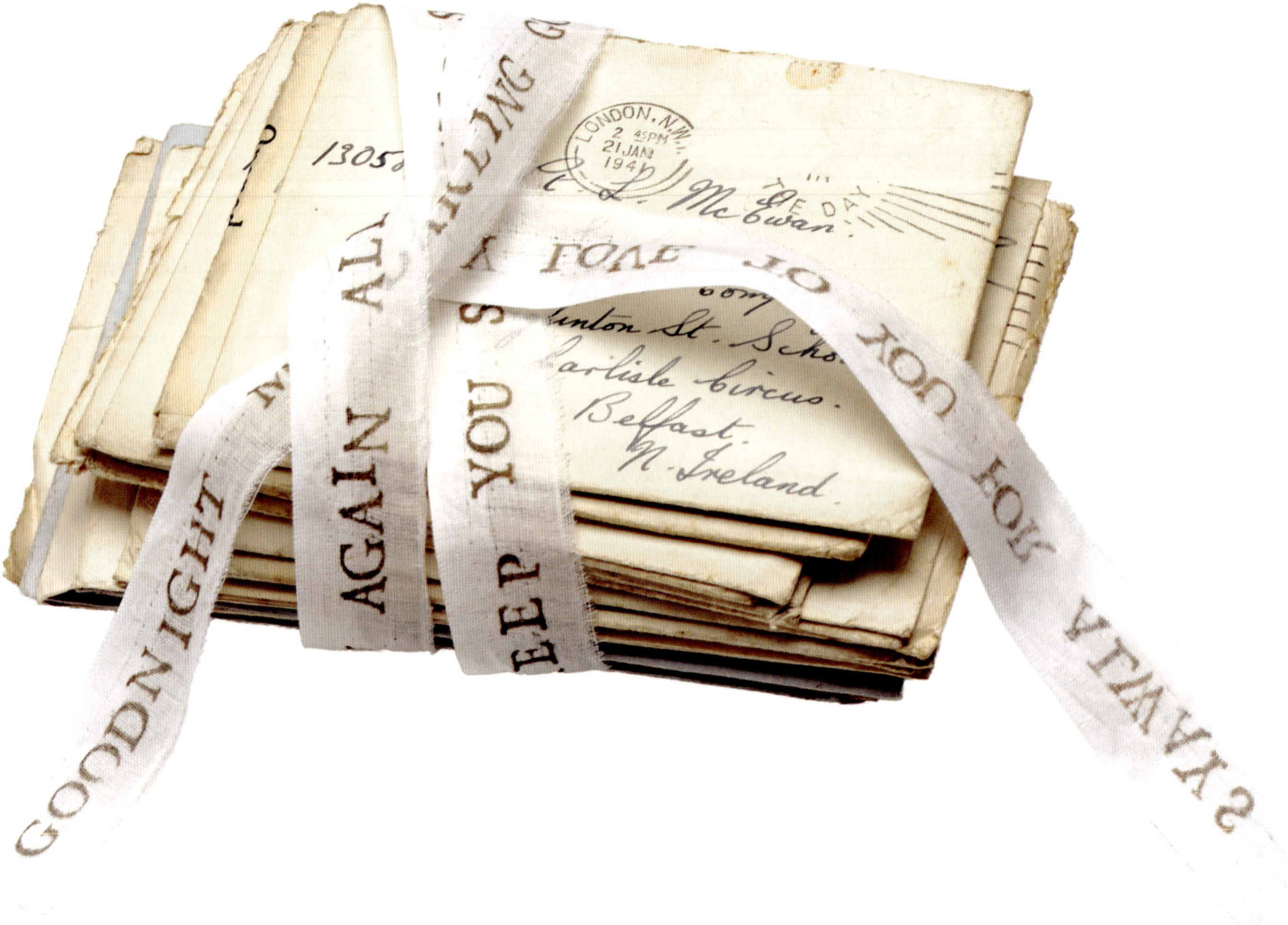

Bundles of letters

People often ask me what to do with bundles of precious letters. I seldom use the letters themselves to create art works; they feel too precious to repurpose and I feel a strong need to preserve them with their little peeks into other people's lives and the time they lived in. I mainly keep mine in boxes and tins, or in old wooden filing drawers that are the perfect width of an envelope, but sometimes the bundles themselves are too pretty to hide away.

Think about tying the bundles together with anything from simple brown twine to coloured silk ribbon. Perhaps you could write a sentence or two from one of the letters along the tie. Or think about wrapping them in fabric, furoshiki style, and consider the qualities of the fabric used:

- A piece of old quilt would suggest to me warmth, comfort and home – perfect to wrap the letters of a family member sent far from home.
- A soft silk suggests a wrapping that would be gently but strongly protective – perhaps for the letters of a mother written to her child.
- Intimate letters could perhaps be wrapped in silk or satin from an old petticoat or tied with a lace ribbon.
- Perhaps a man's letters could be bundled in tweed, a piece of shirting fabric or displayed with an old shirt collar wrapped around them.

ABOVE: A bundle of Ada's letters wrapped in a ribbon of silk organza stamped with the words she used to sign off ... 'Goodnight my darling God bless you and keep you safe and sound til I see you again, all my love to you for always'.

You could have a lot of fun thinking about what would relate to your collections, and perhaps even create a little ritual in the wrapping and the unwrapping as a way of acknowledging the little piece of someone's life that lies within the pages.

You could make a bag or a pouch to store your collection, or repurpose an old evening bag. I was inspired by the pockets worn by the fishwives under their aprons and made one to store my precious postcards. A line from one of the cards is couched down one side 'Mother we are in Greenock yet, a gale of wind ahead'. I've written more on pockets on pages 118–123

BELOW: *A Fishwife's Pocket*, 20 × 28cm (8 × 11in). Pocket made from antique Japanese cotton fabric, vintage ticking and feed sack scraps. Postcard inkjet printed onto fabric. Embellished with hand stitching.

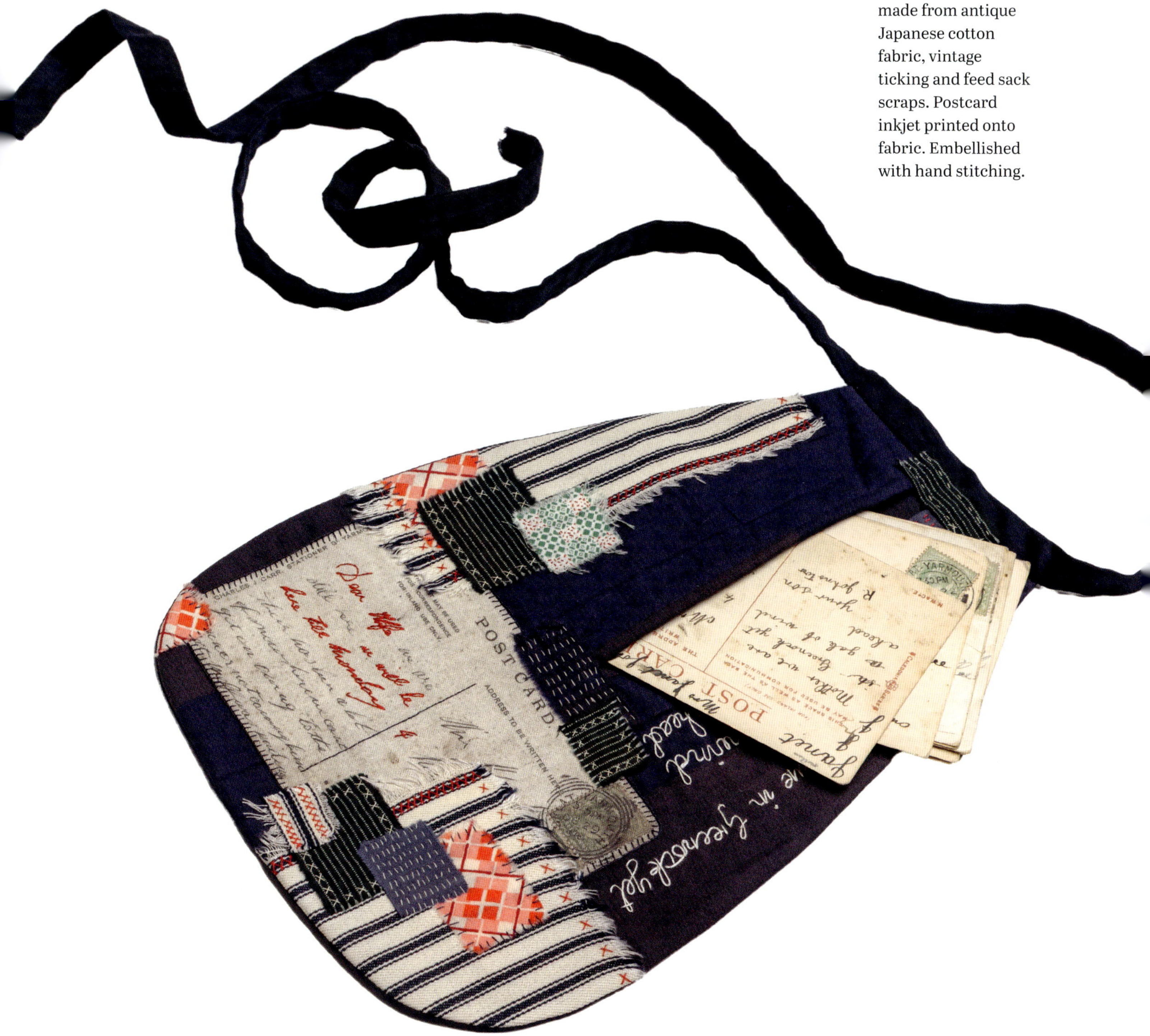

Old photographs

There's something compelling about old photographs. I treasure my box of old family photos, particularly the small, black and white or sepia ones that offer the tiniest glimpse into my mum's life as a young girl in the 1930s, growing up on a small croft in the north-east of Scotland.

BELOW: *A Mile in Your Shoes*. Photos of my mum (right) and her birth mother (left) printed onto fabric and glued inside a pair of old leather baby shoes which have been simply embellished with blanket stitch. Stitched as a reminder not to judge the actions of another.

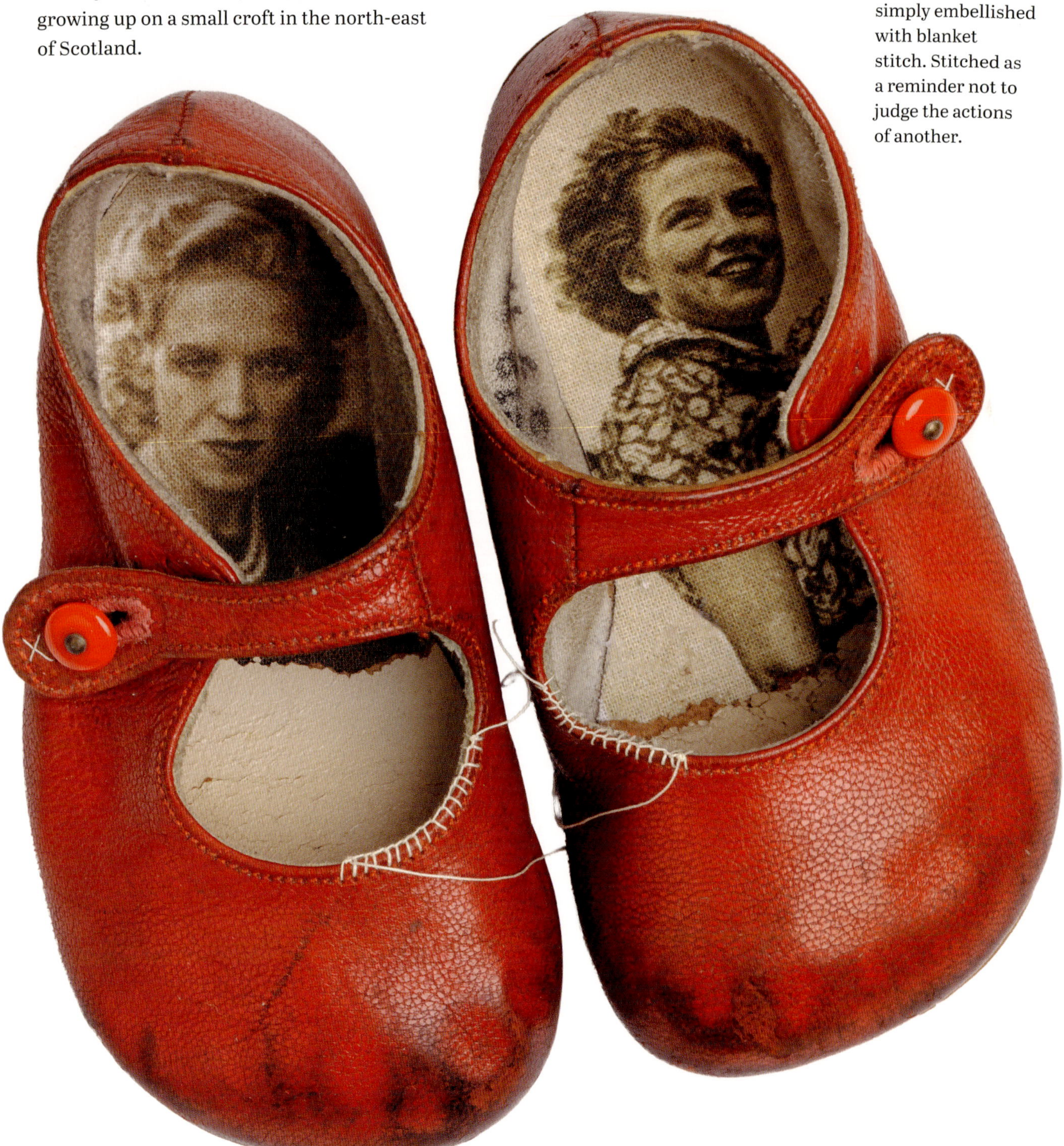

Sadly, there are only a few. One or two were taken in a photographer's studio in the local town, formal and stiff; they show people that I barely recognize as being my granny and grandad. The ones I treasure most, however, were taken on the croft showing my granny in her apron and my grandad looking 'couthie' (Scots for kind, warm or friendly).

I can't help but wonder who owned the camera. It would've been much too frivolous an item to have belonged to my granny or grandad, but perhaps it belonged to one of my mum's older brothers. I can imagine my granny protesting at the ridiculousness of it all while she discreetly smoothed down her pinny, and my grandad's unruly hair.

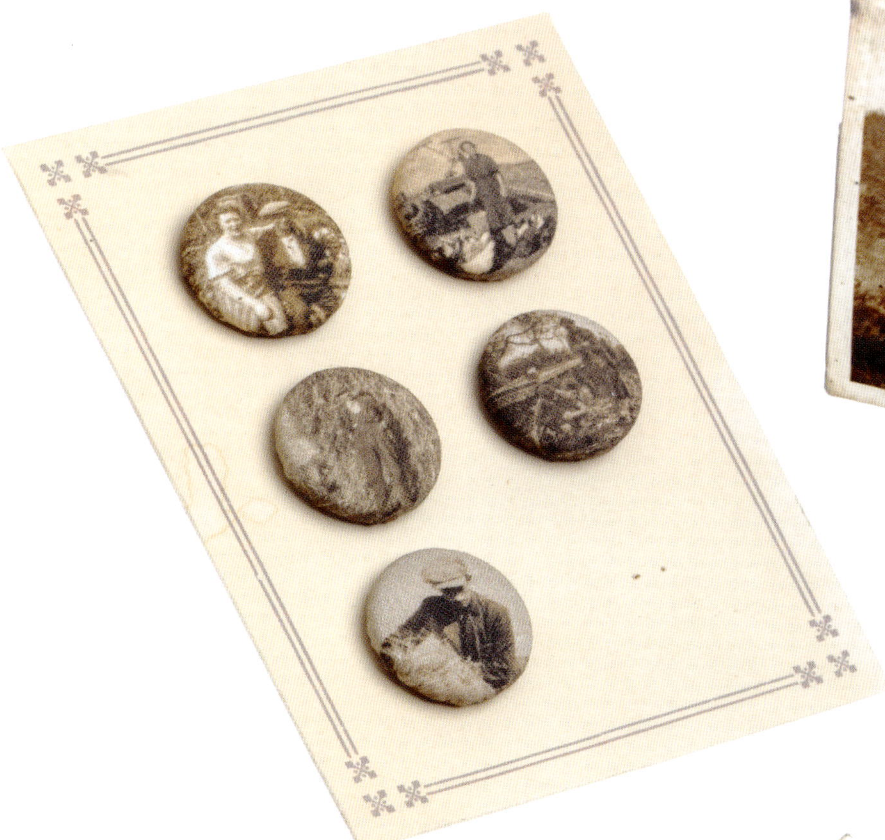

ABOVE: Take inspiration from everyday objects around you to come up with novel ways for using photos in your work. Here, family images are digitally printed onto cotton and made into covered buttons and mounted on a vintage button card.

BELOW: Collection of photographs of my mum's family on their croft in Aberdeenshire. Old photos like these can be improved significantly with computer software, however I try to be sparing in its use as I like to maintain the authenticity of the original.

Printing photos on fabric

Increasingly I'm having my photos commercially printed onto fabric. Companies will print as little as a fat quarter in a huge choice of materials. The quality of the print is good, and the resulting fabric is washable (depending on your choice).

I do, however, find my home inkjet printer invaluable for experimentation and printing small runs of photos, so here are some of my thoughts:

Commercial products: Paper-backed fabric sheets are straightforward to use and available in different fabric types. The downside is that they are expensive if you are simply experimenting.

Freezer paper: I prepare my own fabric sheets for printing by using a lightweight cotton or silk, and freezer paper sheets to stabilize for printing. Printers vary hugely, but I have great success using the following method:

1. Cut your fabric slightly larger than the freezer paper sheet and iron the shiny side of the paper onto your fabric until it sticks. Carefully trim the excess fabric and snip away any loose threads. Iron again, paying particular attention to the edges.

2. Place the fabric in your feed tray and then print. I use normal settings, but you may need to experiment. Peel the freezer paper away from the fabric and iron your print. The freezer paper can be used several times.

The resulting fabric is not washable and may smudge if you get it wet, but there are products that you can use to pre-soak and rinse your fabric sheets to make them permanent. I use Bubble Jet Set 2000 and Bubble Jet Rinse and follow the manufacturer's instructions.

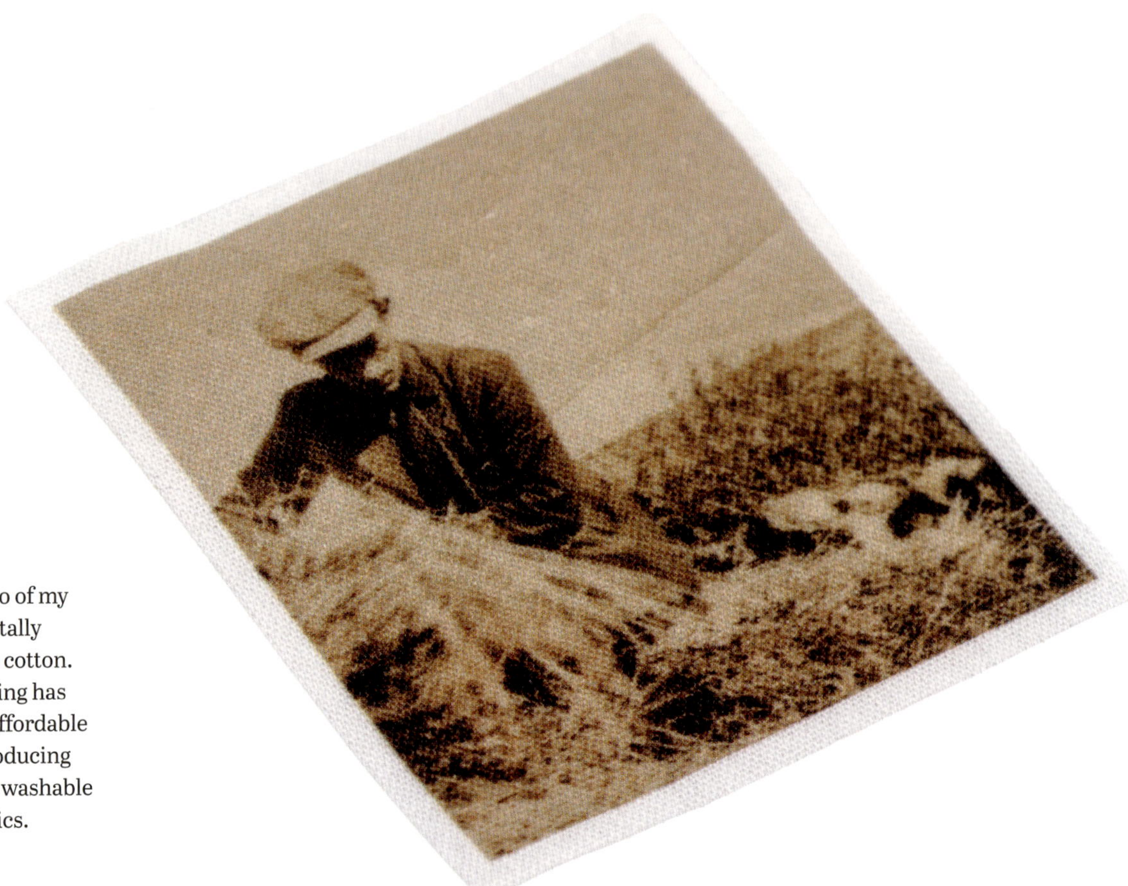

RIGHT: Photo of my grandad digitally printed onto cotton. Digital printing has become an affordable option in producing high quality, washable printed fabrics.

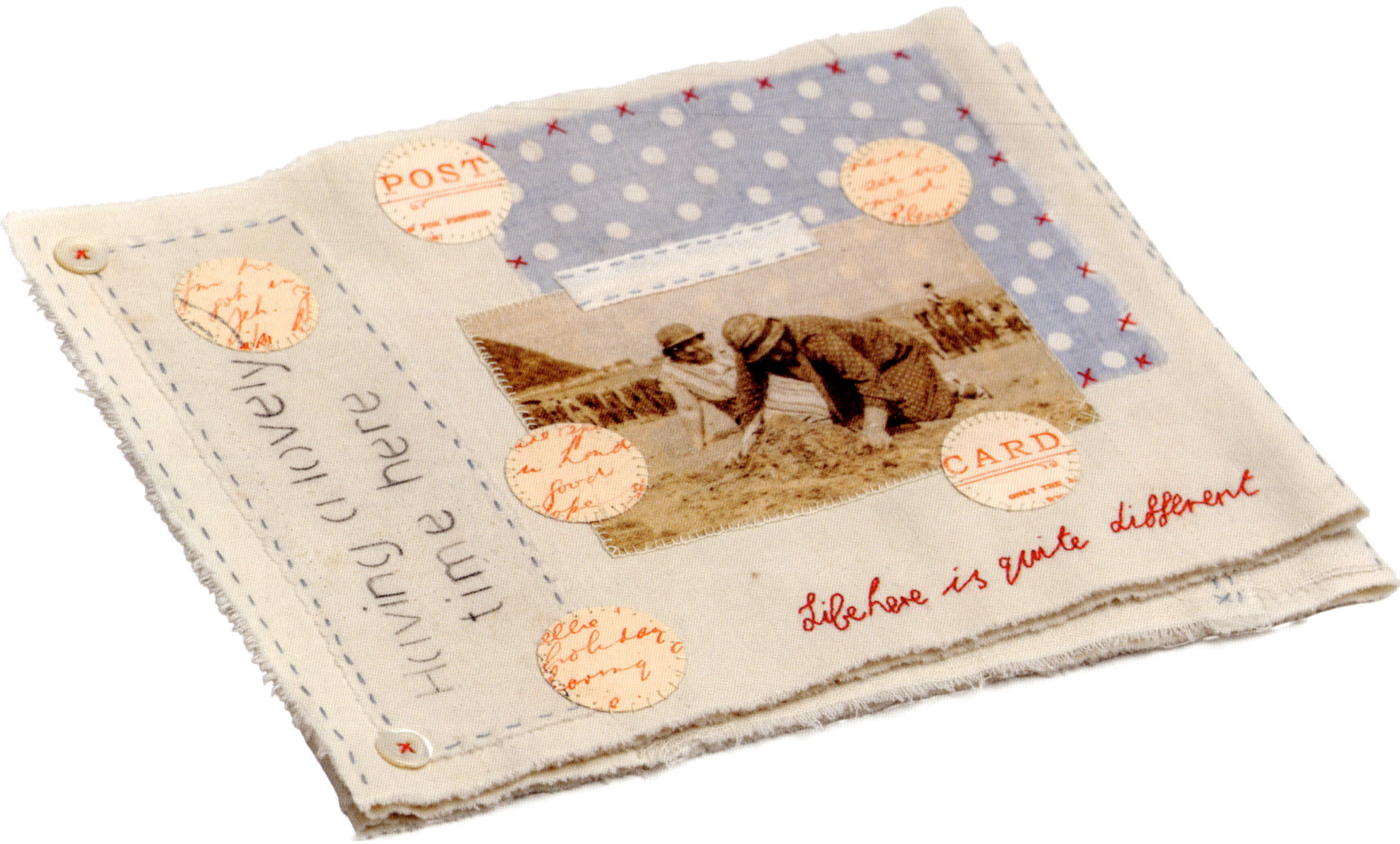

Found photos

I don't tend to collect 'found' photos, but there was something about a collection of seaside holiday snaps that I just couldn't resist.

CREATING A STORY

As I looked through the envelope full of old prints, little stories started to form in my mind; stories of factories closing their doors for a week in the summer – I can almost hear the sirens heralding the end of the working day and imagine people pouring out, laughing and chatting at the thought of a week's holiday. I can picture the women packing their best clothes into their suitcases while the men enjoy a pint at the pub. Then the next day, the hardworking couples board a train and escape for a week at the seaside.

I imagine days starting with bacon, eggs and toast with curly pats of butter washed down by a pot of tea, conversation muted and polite as they sit around a pristine white tablecloth, watched over by a stern-looking landlady. Then the same days ending with fish and chips, eaten out of newspaper while sitting on a bench watching the sun going down.

With these thoughts in mind, I selected five of my favourite photos to work with, and, inspired by the polka-dot dress worn by one of the women, I came up with the title *Polka Dots and Postcards*. This title then provided me with the further inspiration for this piece.

ABOVE: *Polka Dots and Postcards* (detail). On this page the polka dots are cut from an old postcard and words are added using a pencil and stencil.

Polka dots and postcards

The concertina book form was made from an old and patched piece of cotton sheeting. It wasn't quite firm enough to use on its own, so I backed it with another layer of the same. I like to leave raw edges, so I simply ripped it to size before pressing the folds in place and tacking front and back together. I printed my selected photos onto paper first so that I could play around with their layout and size, and then had them commercially printed onto cotton.

The words come from old postcards dating from the 1920s. They have no connection to the people in the photos, but were chosen purely because they made me smile. The layout of the pages is simple because I imagine Gladys, Joan, Reg and Bill as being down-to-earth kind of folks! I have no idea of their real names, but they became familiar to me as I spent my evenings stitching.

I worked on the book as a whole, moving between the pages adding colour here and balancing it there, spreading it out on my table every so often to allow me to see it with fresh eyes and to see what needed adding next, or changing.

I don't know how these pictures ended up in a flea market in Edinburgh, but I do know that 'Gladys' sat back in a deckchair and rested her weary legs on a beach in Rhyl one day, and she looks content. In a world where so-called celebrities are snapped in the most mundane of moments and emblazoned all over the media, I like to think that Gladys's little moment of peace also deserves to be acknowledged.

BELOW: *Polka Dots and Postcards*, accordion-style cloth book, 99 × 15cm (39 × 6in). Cotton sheeting, cotton shirting and dress fabric from an old quilt, postcards inkjet printed onto fabric, photos digitally printed onto cotton, tape typed with words from the postcards. Embellished with vintage buttons and hand stitching.

OPPOSITE: *Polka Dots and Postcards* (detail). It feels important to me to honour ordinary moments of everyday life. I've imagined the story but the 'moments' are real.

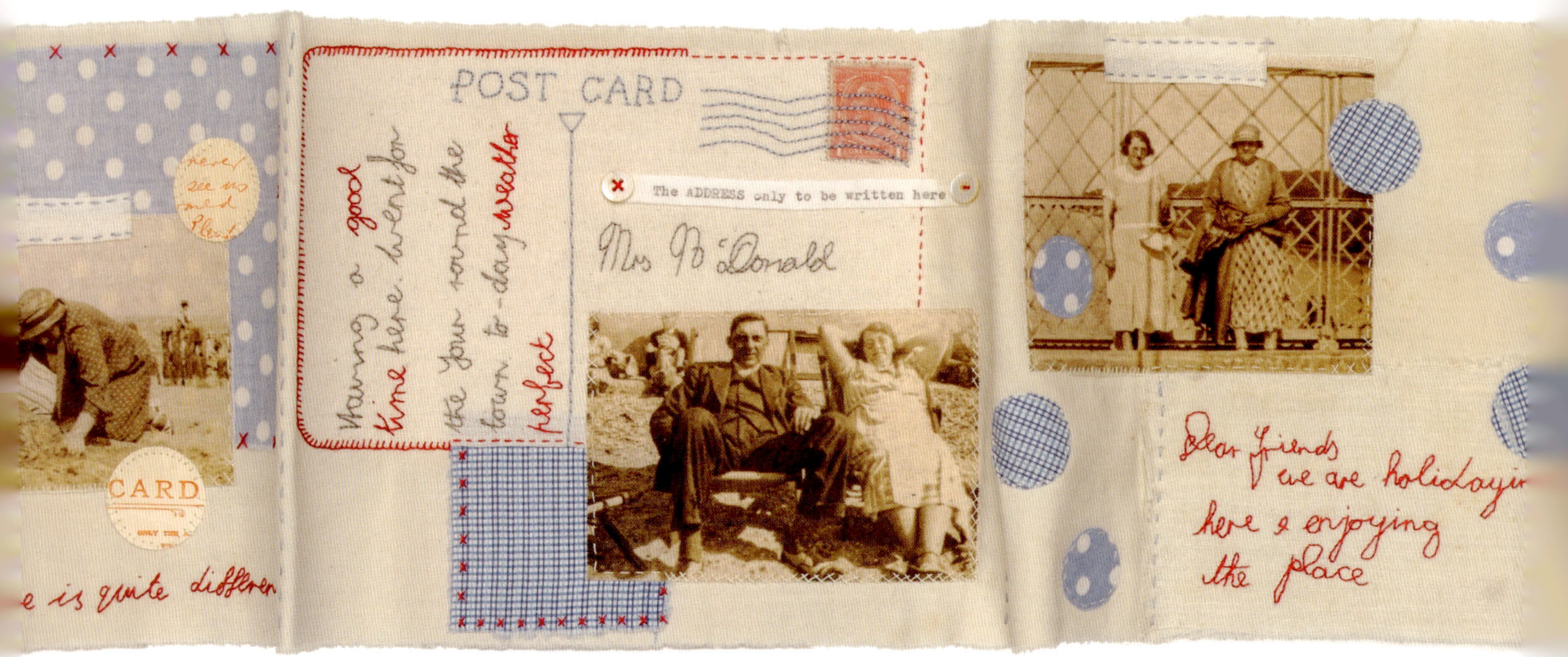

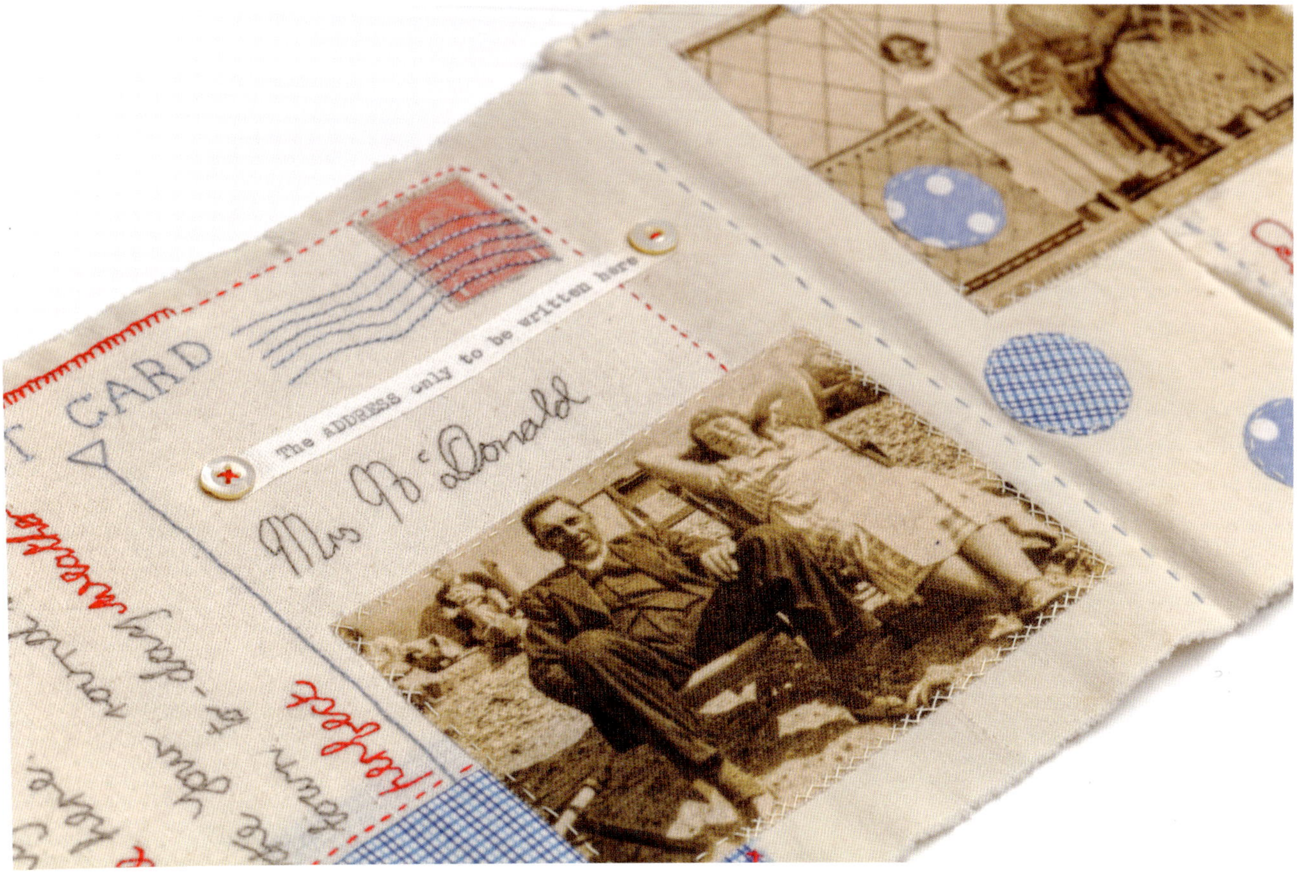
CARD
The ADDRESS only to be written here
Mrs McDonald

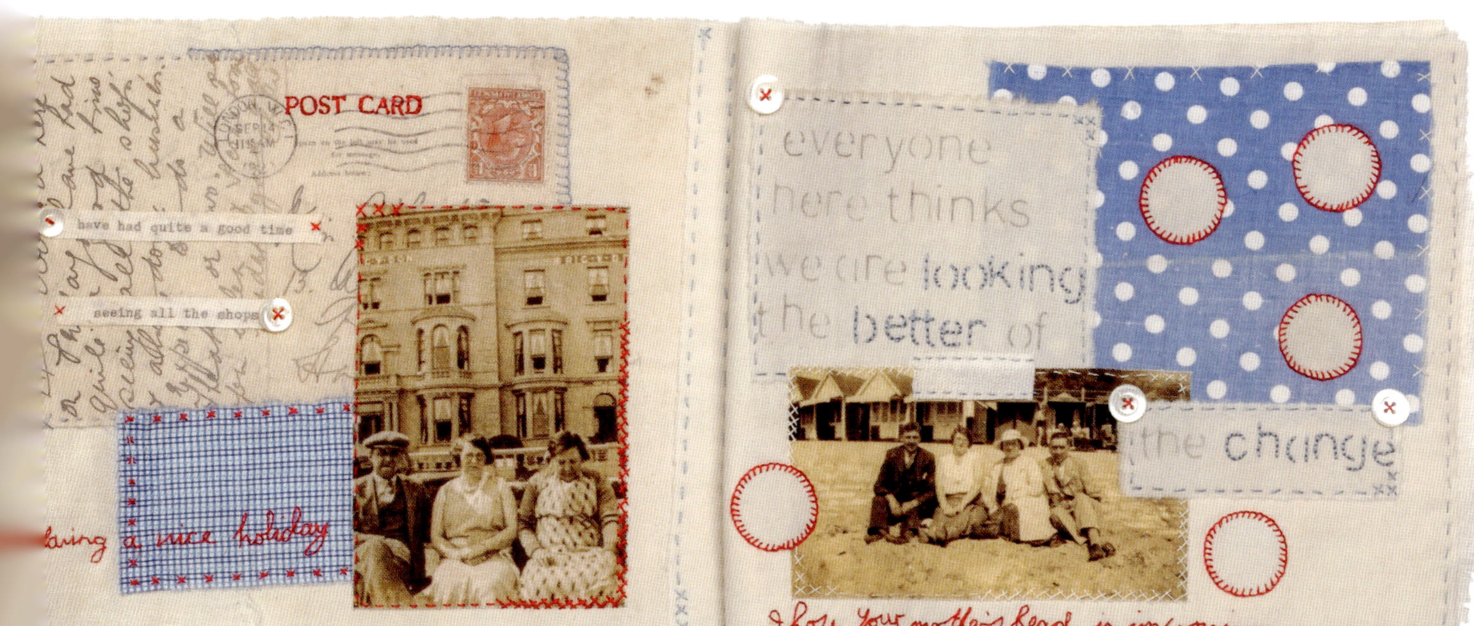
POST CARD
have had quite a good time
seeing all the shops
a nice holiday
everyone
here thinks
we are looking
the better of
the change
I hope your mother's head is improving

Victoria Merness

Victoria's autobiographical work is rooted in her family tree. It highlights feelings of belonging and loss and serves as a poignant reminder of the passing of time. Her work combines the traditional craft of stitch with family photographs from years gone by, evoking memories, and nostalgic themes around anemoia.

When Victoria's paternal grandfather passed, her family discovered a secret branch of the family tree. They were given a photo album containing photographs of the everyday lives of this unknown family. Victoria learned that her great-great-grandfather was a Spanish sea captain, explaining the glamorous photos of sea journeys between Argentina and England. Other photos were of her great-grandmother's family, taken when the family relocated to Blackpool, and later to the family's farm in Saddleworth. Victoria explains:

From a very early age, I holidayed with my parents in popular tourist spots in Wales and the north-west of England, such as Llandudno, Blackpool and Southport. It was the realization that this unknown family album contained very similar memories to the photos taken by my father on his Kodak Brownie in the late 1960s and 1970s, that inspired this autobiographical project. In the photo album, there were two photos showing the Minana-Merness family on Blackpool beach, just as my dad had photographed me as a small child several decades later.

This inspired my series of stitched artworks. I enlarged the small original photos and printed them onto linen and then imagined the black and white images into coloured thread. The act of bringing life to the unknown family was a way of connecting with the past and providing resolution. The stitched photographs happily sit side by side in my studio, with no apparent lapse in time, or lack of connection.

Victoria's studio, Little House of Victoria, is based in Woodend Mill in Mossley, just two miles from the farm in Uppermill, Saddleworth, where her great-grandmother Florence lived. Victoria describes moving into her studio as 'homecoming'.

BELOW: *Great Grandmother Florence*, 80cm × 40cm (31½ × 15¾in). Black and white photograph digitally printed onto linen with hand stitching.

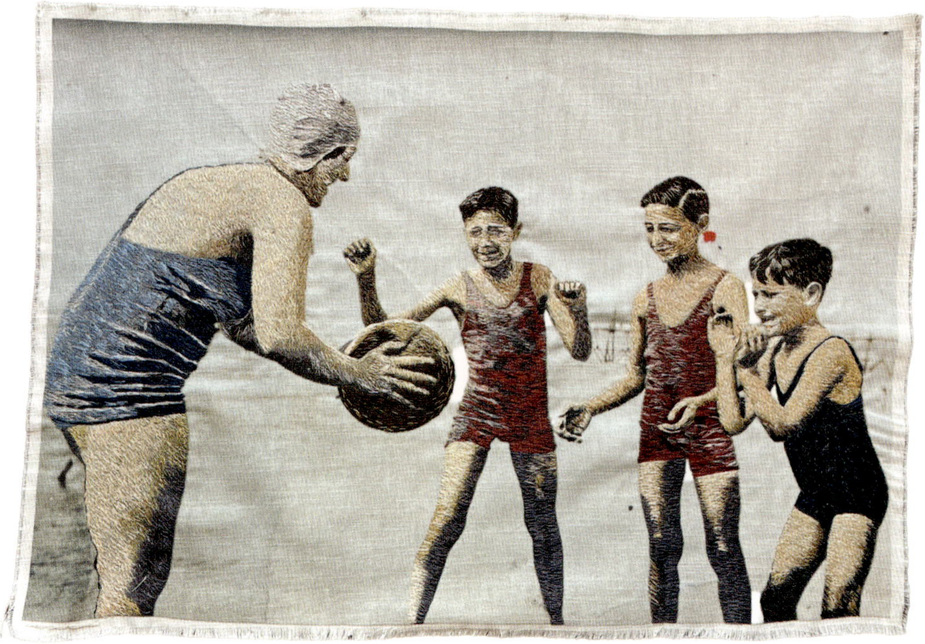

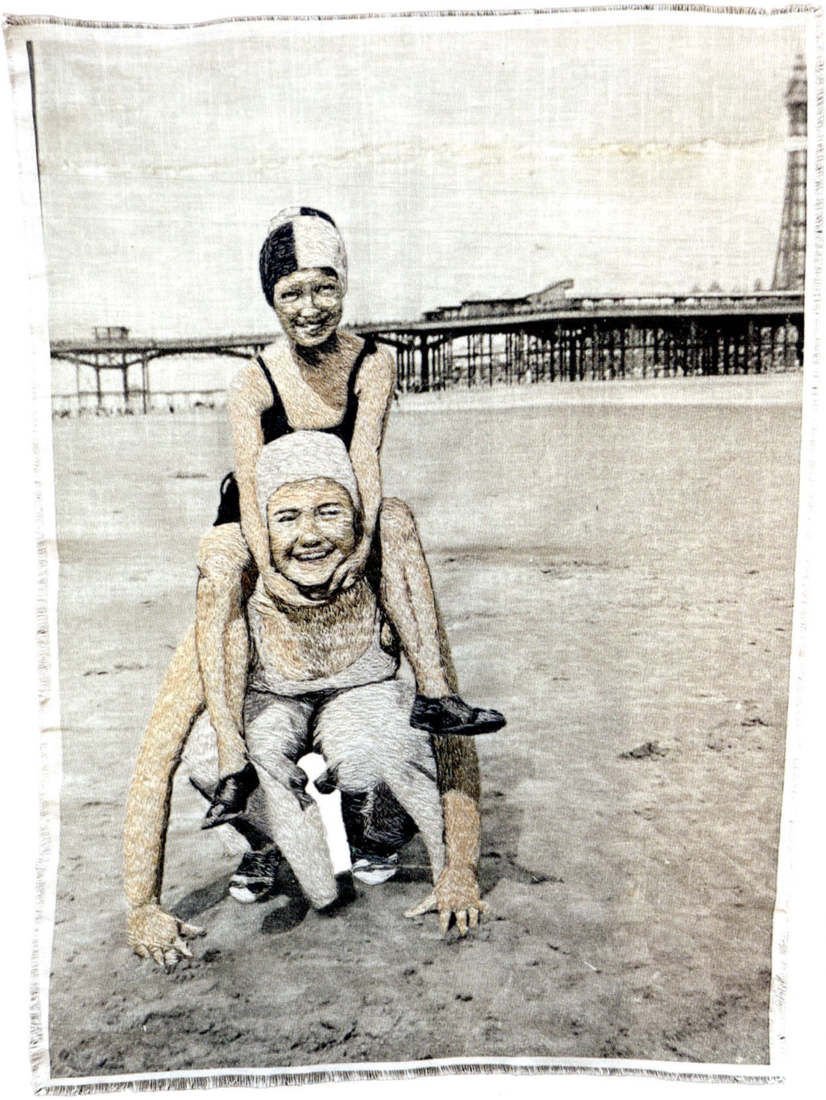

LEFT: *Great Aunt Pauline*, 40 × 80cm (15¾ × 31½in). Black and white photograph digitally printed onto linen with hand stitching.

RIGHT: *Father & Daughter*, 60cm × 60cm (23½ × 23½in). Black and white photograph taken by the artist's father, digitally printed onto linen with hand stitching.

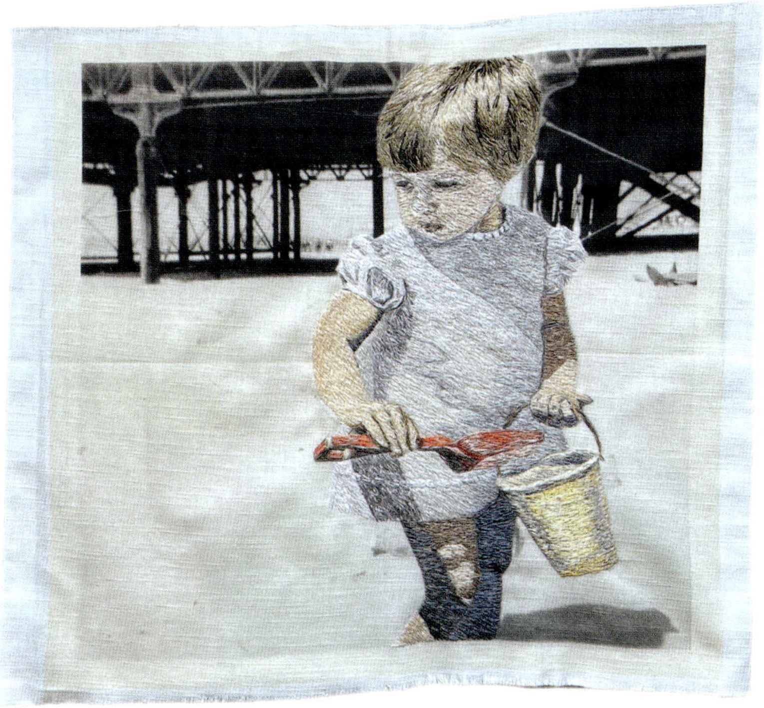

Working samples: Lest we forget

These pieces were inspired by a large bundle of photographs that belonged to my dad. I think they were mostly taken in Belgium, but I don't know anything about the men pictured, other than assuming that they were friends of his during his war service. My dad looks young and very handsome. He never spoke of these years, and I do rather wish that I had asked more questions when I had the chance to do so. I can't get over the thought that these young men were all somebody's son. They were husbands, sweethearts, brothers, nephews, uncles and grandsons too, of course, but it's the mother in me that the photographs speak to.

My mum often talks about her childhood during World War II. It was one of her stories about falling bombs, blackouts and blackout curtains that got me thinking about using the photos to make a small tribute to my dad, to his generation and to the mothers who watched their boys leave home into the unknown. As I write that last sentence, I feel my chest fill with overwhelming emotion and I am very much reminded that this is the everyday reality of so many people in the world today.

BELOW: *Working sample 1.* Photos inkjet printed onto silk organza, patched together and stitched in simple running stitch with vintage cream thread.

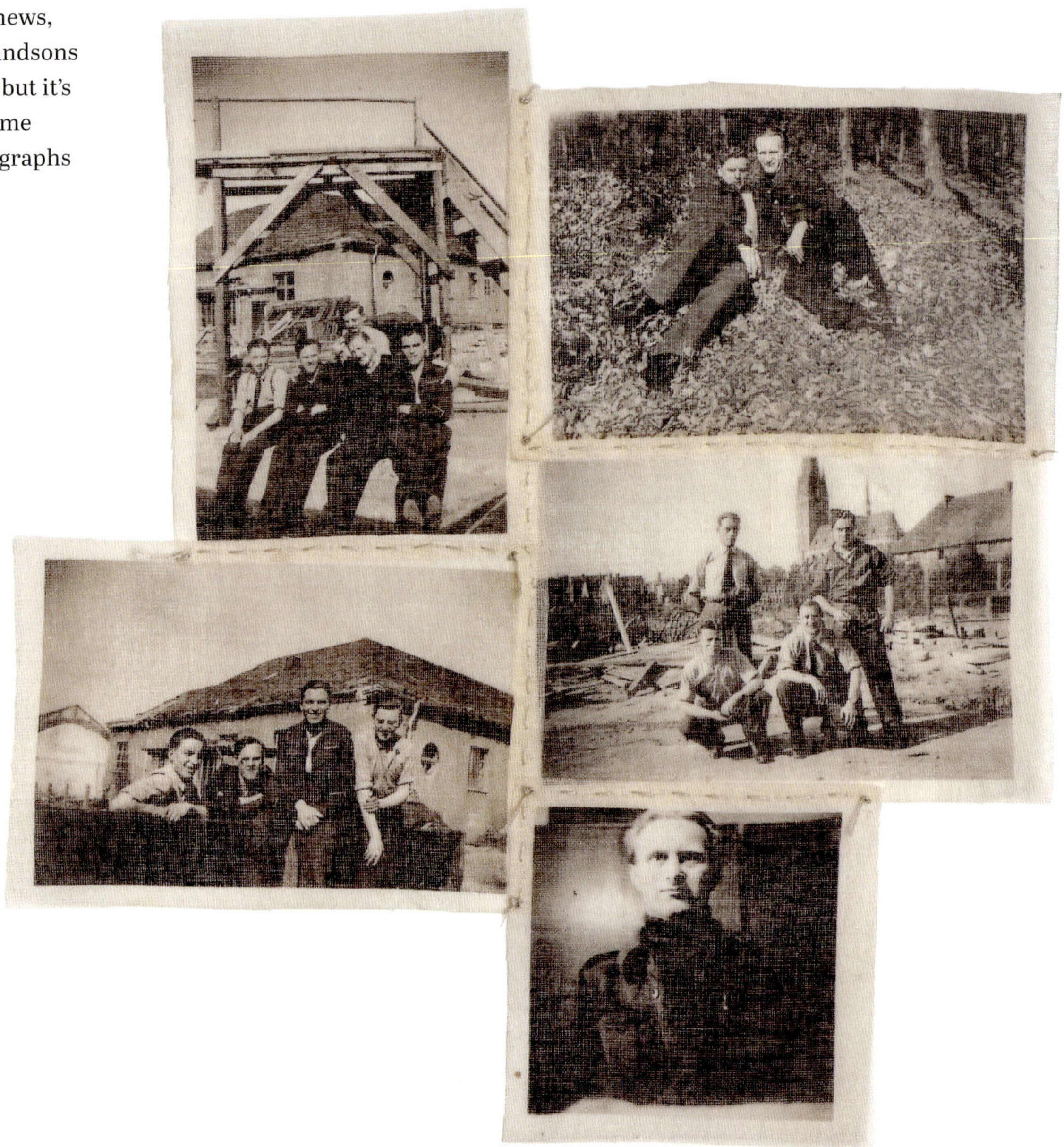

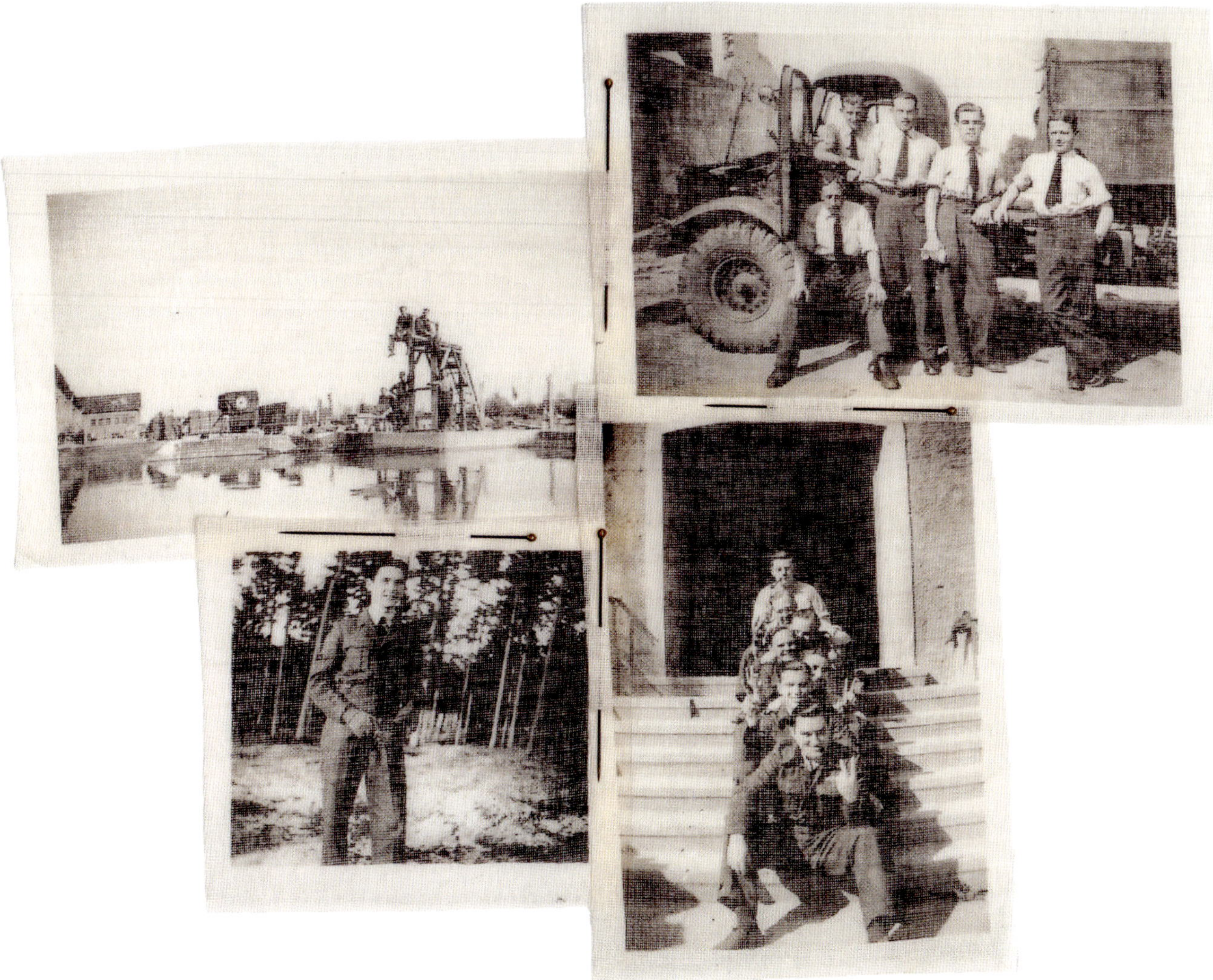

A vague idea

I thought about making a small curtain but instead of a blackout curtain, whose purpose is to block out the light, I wanted to create transparency (something that feels sadly lacking within the political world today) to allow the light to shine through. My idea was vague, so I decided to work on a few samples to see where they would lead me. I started by printing a few photos onto silk organza using my inkjet printer and freezer paper. I then played with different ideas for joining them together, from pinning them to using simple stitching in different colours.

I immediately liked the transparency of the organza and the fragility of the resulting pieces. They waft in the breeze when hanging. They suggested to me the fragility of the world and the feeling that it is holding together merely by a thread. I considered including words from some wartime airmail letters to represent the connection between the men and home; however, I opted instead to make a collection of organza envelopes, each containing a photo (see page 45).

ABOVE: *Working sample 2*. Photos inkjet printed onto silk organza, patched together and pinned with black entomology pins to represent fragility.

BELOW: *Working sample 3*. Photos inkjet printed onto silk organza, patched together and stitched in simple running stitch with vintage Turkey Red thread.

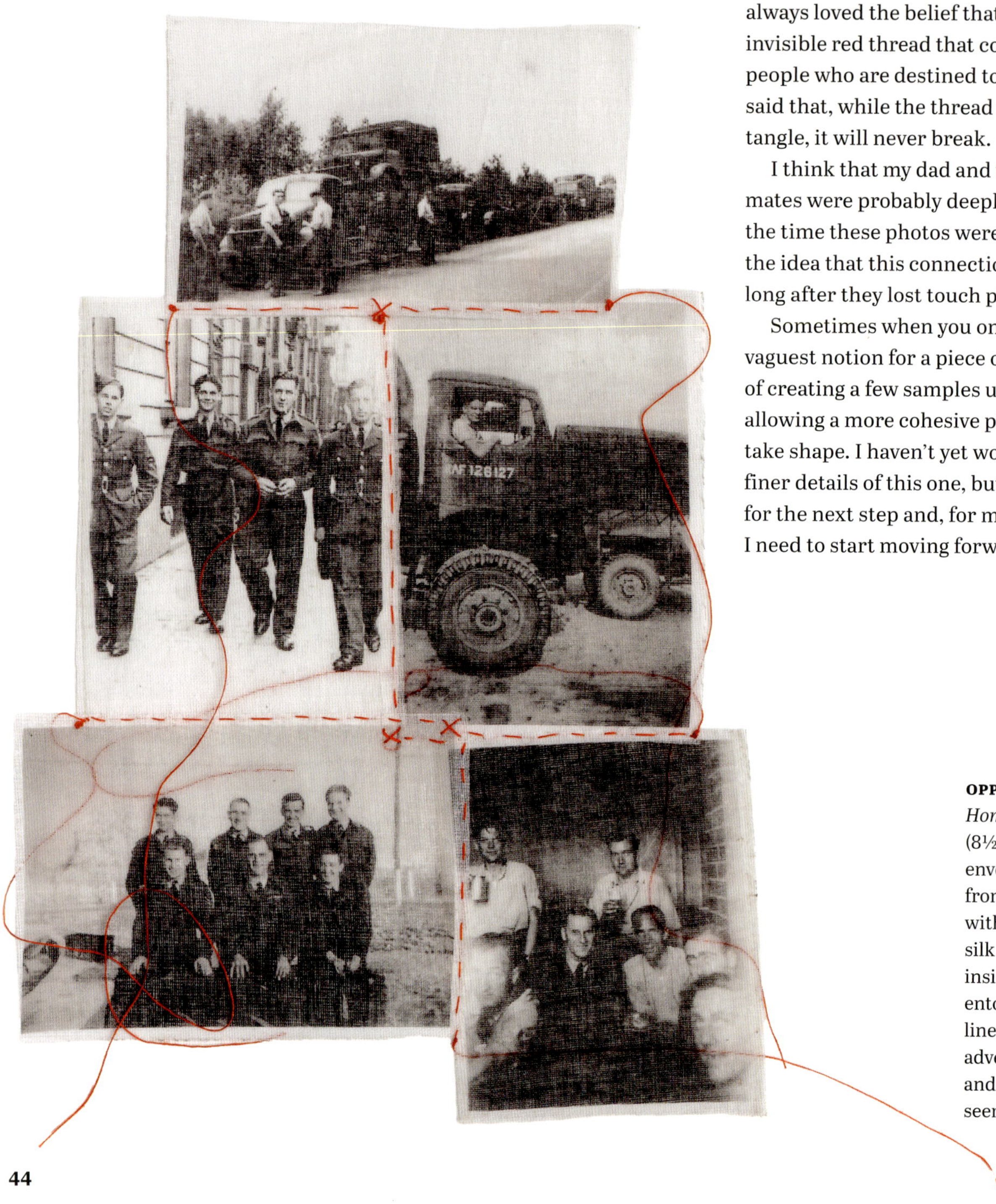

How I will take this forward

Having worked on a few samples, my intention now is to create a bigger piece. I will have the images digitally printed onto silk organza and then join them together with red stitching to make my curtain.

I'll leave the loose ends dangling, as in my sample. There are many superstitions and beliefs around red threads. In some cultures, red string is worn around the wrist as a symbol of protection, and I've always loved the belief that there is an invisible red thread that connects two people who are destined to be together. It is said that, while the thread may stretch and tangle, it will never break.

I think that my dad and this group of mates were probably deeply connected at the time these photos were taken, and I like the idea that this connection continued long after they lost touch physically.

Sometimes when you only have the vaguest notion for a piece of work, the act of creating a few samples unlocks ideas, allowing a more cohesive plan to start to take shape. I haven't yet worked out the finer details of this one, but I have a plan for the next step and, for me, that's often all I need to start moving forwards.

OPPOSITE: *Letters Home*, 22 × 30cm (8½ × 12in). Stitched envelopes made from silk organza with inkjet printed silk photo pinned inside each one with entomology pin. The linen buttons were advertised as 'strong and durable' which seemed appropriate.

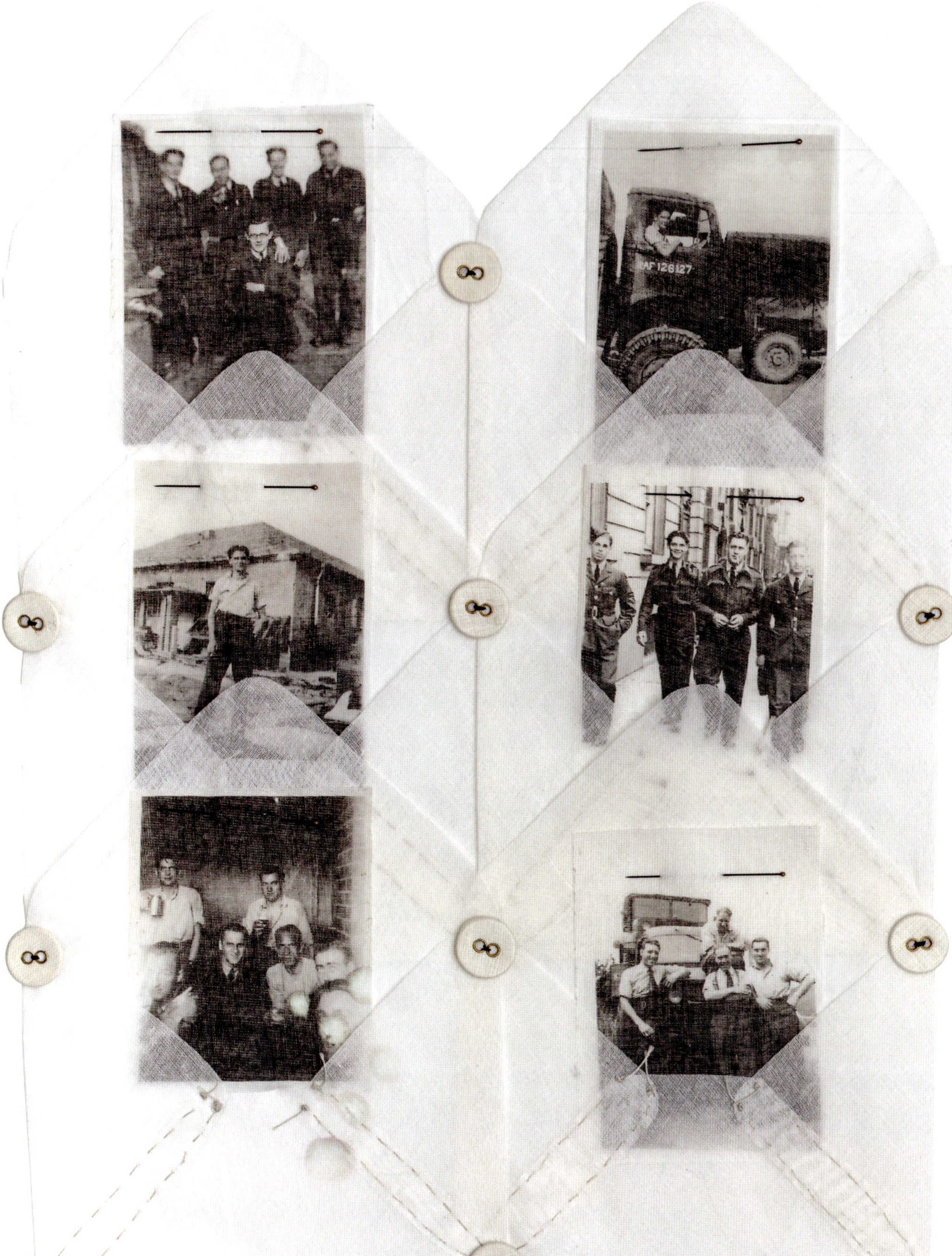
AF 126127

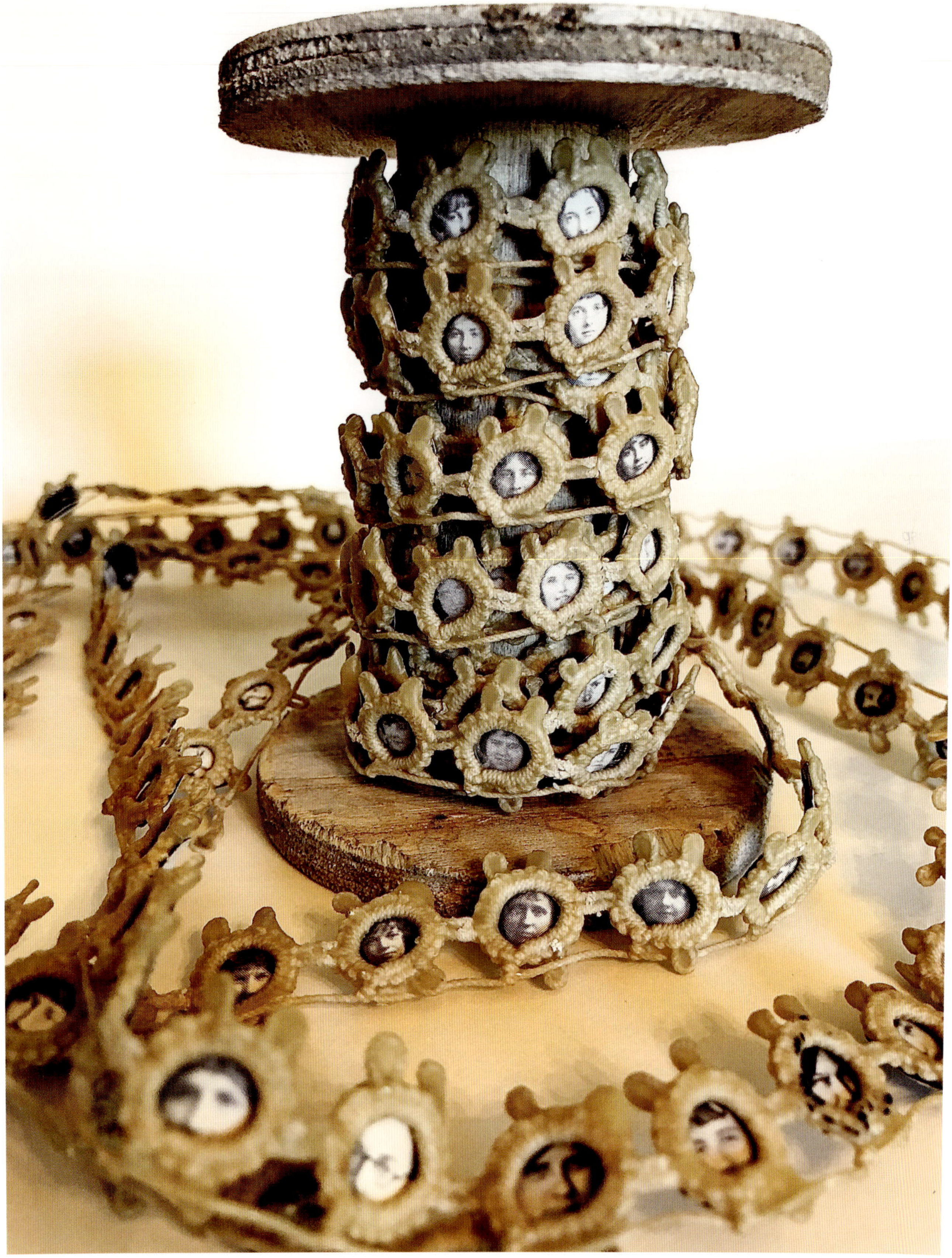

Karla Fuller

Raised in a family of artists and travellers, Karla showed an interest in the visual arts and wanderlust at an early age. Her intimate pieces combine scavenged ephemera along with found objects and unique vintage elements. Karla works from her home studio and resides in Oconomowoc, Wisconsin, with her husband and children. Karla says:

> *I have always had a penchant for collecting the unusual and interesting. Objects with mystery and the evidence of being genuinely timeworn are especially alluring to me. With their beguiling and enigmatic qualities, old photographs found at flea markets and antique shops are always part of the search. This is especially true for anonymous old photos and their bewitching patinas. Who were these people and what history did they leave upon this world? As a collage and assemblage artist with these questions, I often frame the person's untold history and develop a small glimpse of their biography by creating an inventive narrative.*

To create her wonderful narratives, Karla combines these old photographs with found objects and collected vintage ephemera such as dictionary words, faded thread, cancelled stamps, tattered textiles, weathered maps and handwritten letters.

> *In my studio I explore the veiled connections between the old photographs and my collections of unusual ephemera and interpret the intimate dialogue between them. It is my hope that the viewer may discover a serendipitous connection, or have a subtle memory evoked by a peculiar detail within the final storied artwork. This is my version of authoring historical fiction, but through a visual artistic method.*
>
> *In my piece* Unravelling, *225 hand-cut 1920s university yearbook photos compose the courageous sisterhood of intellectual women, bound together in the dichotomy of domestic craft. Preserved in pure melted beeswax, their portraits are tucked inside vintage tatted lace rings, and unravel from an old spool like stories of bravery passed down by generations of strong women.*
>
> *In* Thread Heads, *the two assemblage portraits signify the daring leap made by young women who sought intellectual opportunity in the early 1900s. They tell a story of the pursuit of both domestic craft and scholarly knowledge.*

BELOW: *Thread Heads*, 8 × 8 × 4cm (3 × 3 × 1½in). 1920s yearbook photos, vintage thread spools, old porcelain doll arms, found beach shells and aquatic vertebrae.

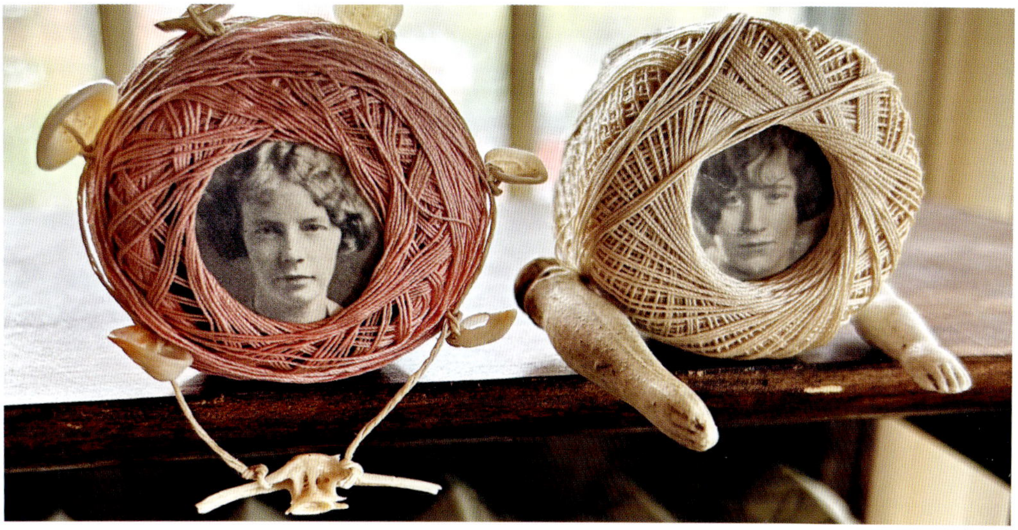

OPPOSITE: *Unravelling*, 8 × 8 × 10cm (3 × 3 × 4 in). 1920s university yearbook photos, beeswax and vintage tatted lace rings unravelling from an old spool.

Vintage magazines: A snapshot of time

There's something very pleasing about magazines, particularly women's magazines, that date back to the 1960s and earlier. The paper itself is generally soft, almost fabric-like, and the pages, often discolouring through age, cry out to be turned.

Then there is the content: beauty and fashion features, short stories, a letters page, a problem page, horoscopes and patterns for making just about everything from a simple egg cosy to a fully lined winter coat. And then, of course, there are the adverts, often my favourite part of any old magazine. I get lost among the pages, each offering a little glimpse into the domestic worlds of busy, working families and women of the time.

Beats as it sweeps as it cleans

This is the first of a series of aprons continuing my exploration of ordinary domestic lives.

I started by gathering my materials – in this case, paper from old magazine advertisements – and then made a pattern by taking measurements from a very simple 1950s apron. As the paper is fragile to work with, I cut my apron pieces from a medium-weight iron-on interfacing and bonded the papers onto it. At this point my 'fabric' was stiff and I wanted it to be much softer and worn in appearance, so I decided to knead the paper to make it more supple and cloth-like.

Great care must be taken when kneading old papers, as some are very soft and will start to go into holes quite quickly. I worked some hand cream into my hands and then slowly and gently started crumpling the paper, releasing it and then crumpling again, until I was happy with the feel and appearance. There are several tears – after all, some of the papers are 100 years old – but I don't mind that.

BELOW: Two adverts cut from the same vintage magazine. The top one has been gently kneaded and then ironed to create a soft, 'fabric-like' appearance.

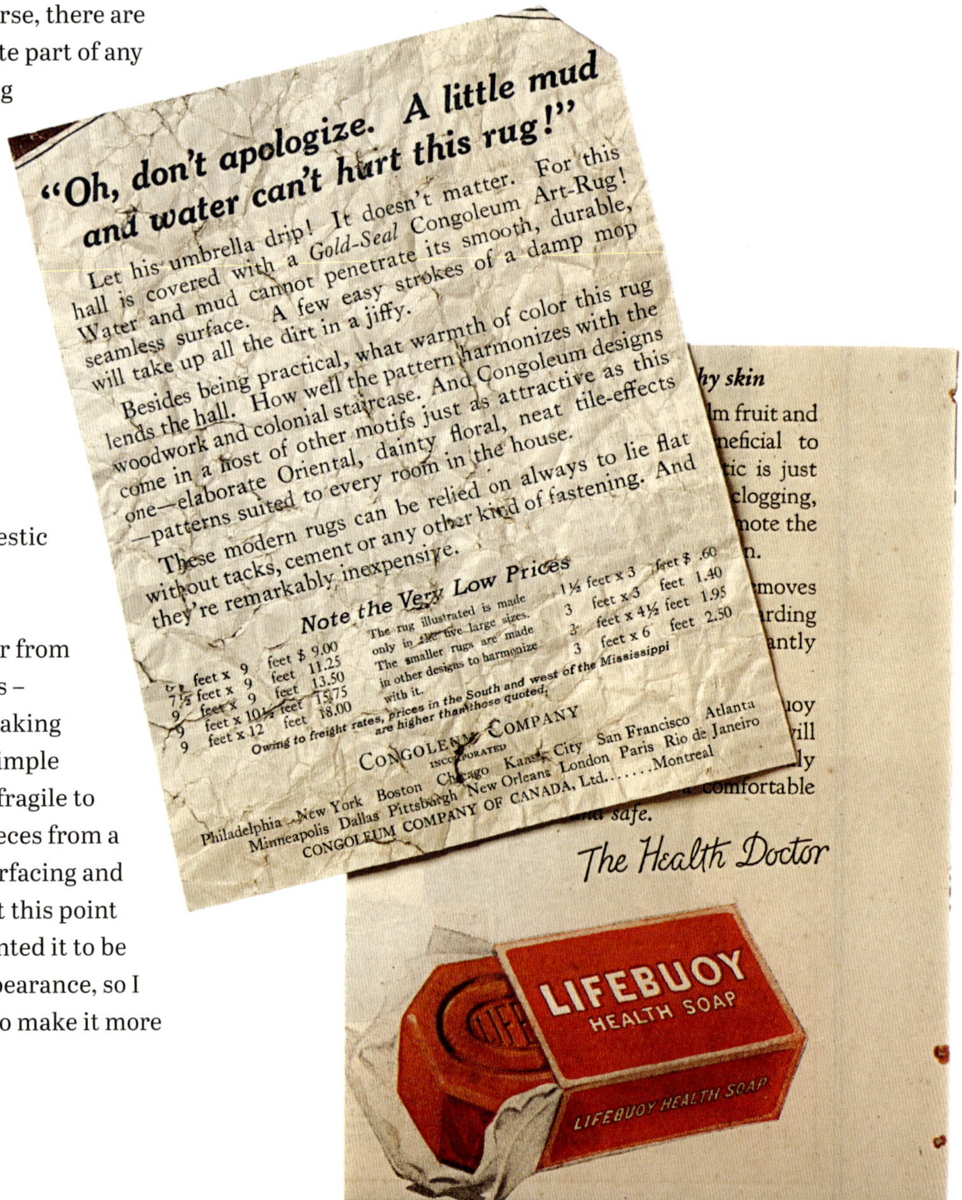

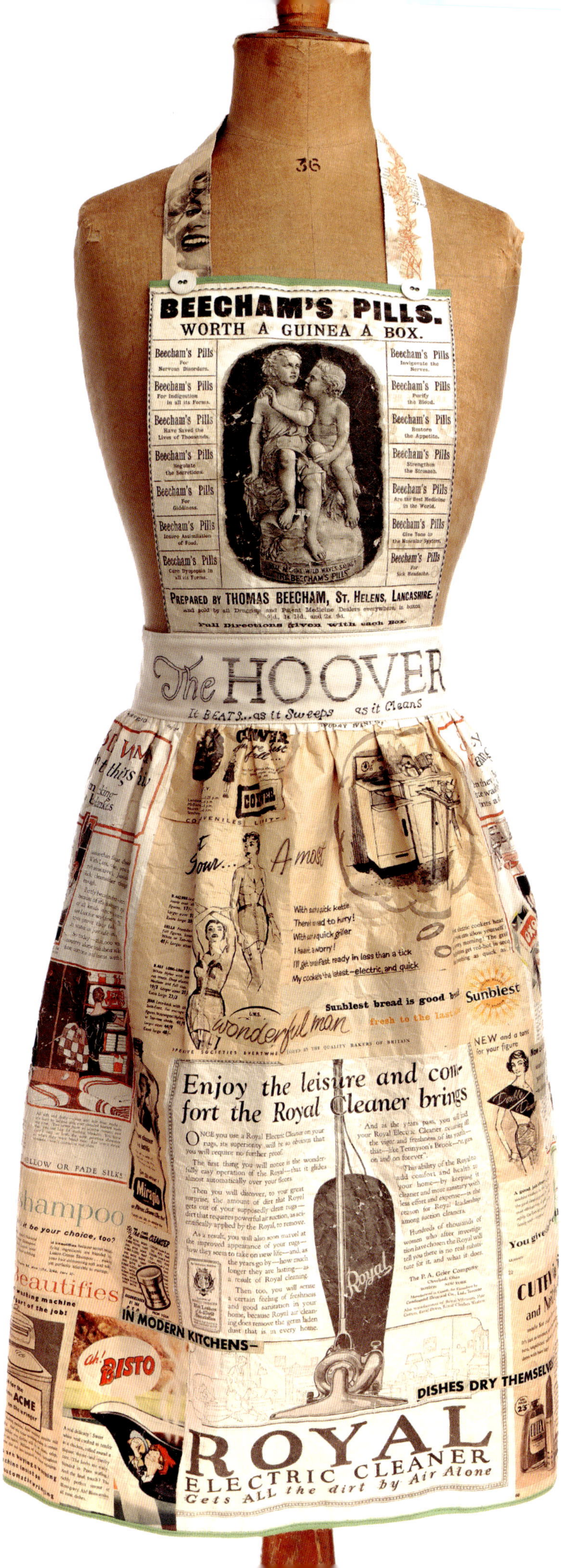

I stitched the typeface of a 1920s Hoover advertisement onto a fabric waistband and then gathered and stitched the skirt to the apron bodice by machine. I bound the skirt edges and the top of the bodice with a lovely vintage bias tape, as so many old aprons were bound in this way. I then added the strap round the neck and the ties.

LEFT: *Beats as it Sweeps as it Cleans*. Life-sized apron constructed from old magazine paper. The adverts were chosen to illustrate some of the expected domestic roles of post-war women in the UK.

How I won first prize at the WI

'I feel I must tell you,' writes Mrs M. Fawbert, 'that last night I entered a cake competition for the W.I. and won 1st prize.'

I often tell the story of this collage at my workshops, and as soon as I start talking, I feel a smile start to form. For me, emotion is an essential ingredient in creating personal artwork. It is inspired by an advert from one of my 1950s *Woman* magazines. The heading 'How I won first prize at the W.I.' reminded me of my mum's stories of teaching craft classes at the local Women's Institutes dotted around Angus in Scotland.

In Scotland at the time the Women's Institute was called 'the rural' and it was well named. Mum drove her old car all over the countryside, venturing up into the Angus glens in the most wintery of conditions. She tells the story of one snowy night when she drove as far as she dared into the hills, before being met by a farmer who then took her the rest of the way to the village hall on the back of his tractor.

The items made during her classes were proudly entered into the crafts category of the local flower shows until complaints were made that my mum's pupils always swept the board of prizes. From then on, anything made at 'Betty's class' was banned from entry and, as you can imagine, my mum proudly told this story – often!

This cloth collage is stitched on an old woollen blanket, and I've chosen a small selection of homely materials to layer and patch onto this. I printed one of my late mother-in-law's handwritten recipes onto calico and stitched the drawing in the advert as my motif. The cake is stitched on the backing fabric of an old quilt, and I love that the original stitching lines are still visible.

I stitched the words from the advert onto a patch of tablecloth and layered this over an old postcard printed onto calico. I've added a simple appliqué teaspoon made from fabric cut from an old apron, and typed some more ingredients onto old cotton tape. More recipe ingredients were highlighted with red back stitching and, of course, I just had to score out the words 'butter' and 'lard' and replace them with 'Kraft Superfine margarine'.

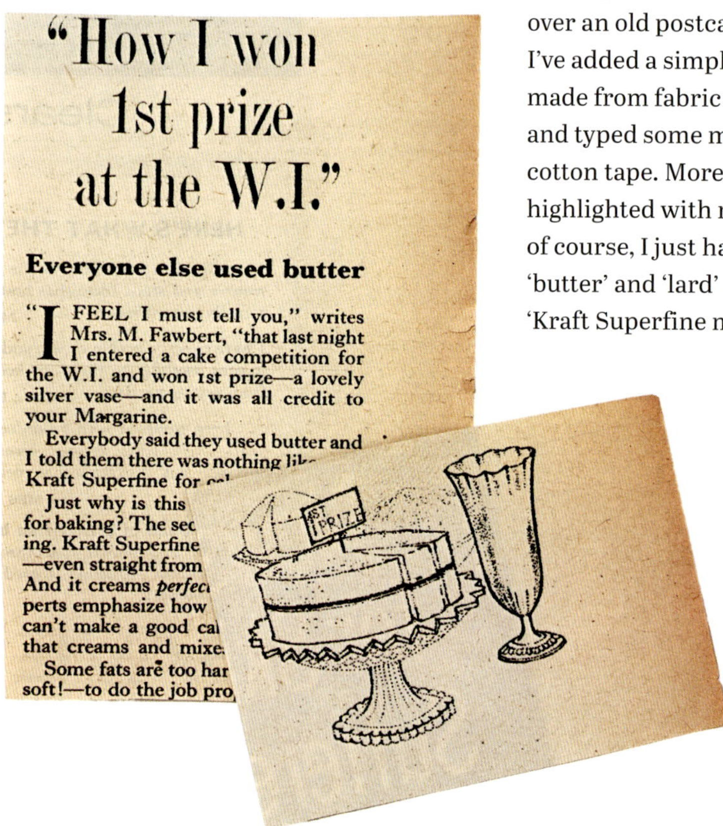

OPPOSITE: *Everyone Else Used Butter*, 26 × 36cm (10 × 14in). Cloth collage using vintage and feed sack cottons, vintage table linen, old quilt backing, inkjet printed calico, typed cotton tapes and vintage buttons hand stitched onto a woollen blanket backing.

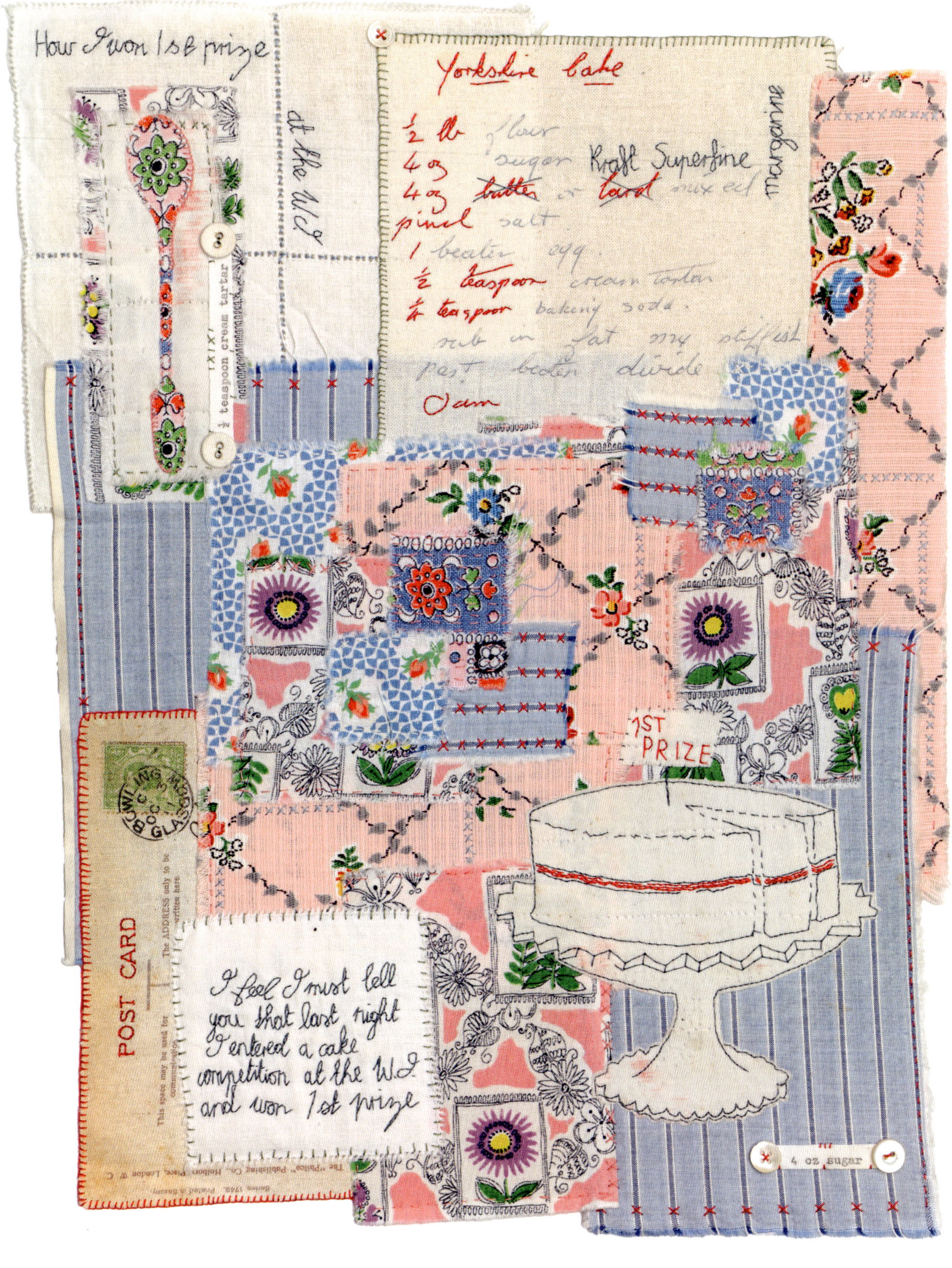
How I won 1st prize
at the W.I.
¼ teaspoon cream tartar
Yorkshire Cake
½ lb flour
4 oz sugar Kraft Superfine
4 oz butter or lard mixed
margarine
pinch salt
1 beaten egg
½ teaspoon cream tartar
¼ teaspoon baking soda
Jam
1ST PRIZE
POST CARD
GLASGOW
The ADDRESS only to be written here
This space may be used for communication
I feel I must tell you that last night I entered a cake competition at the W.I. and won 1st prize
4 oz sugar

Darren Ball

Having personally spent so many hours poring over copies of vintage magazines, I can't help but be attracted to the beautifully illustrative work of artist Darren Ball. I particularly love how his sensitive use of materials and textural stitching bring the models pictured on the magazine pages alive. He transforms a knitting pattern illustration into a character whose story I want to know more of.

Darren originally trained in fashion textiles, specializing in hand knitting. He then taught himself free machine embroidery while teaching art and textiles in school and college. He brings this strong fashion background into his textile work using appliqué and machine embroidery to illustrate personal narratives or ideas, inspired by memorabilia and images from his collection of vintage *Stitchcraft* magazines.

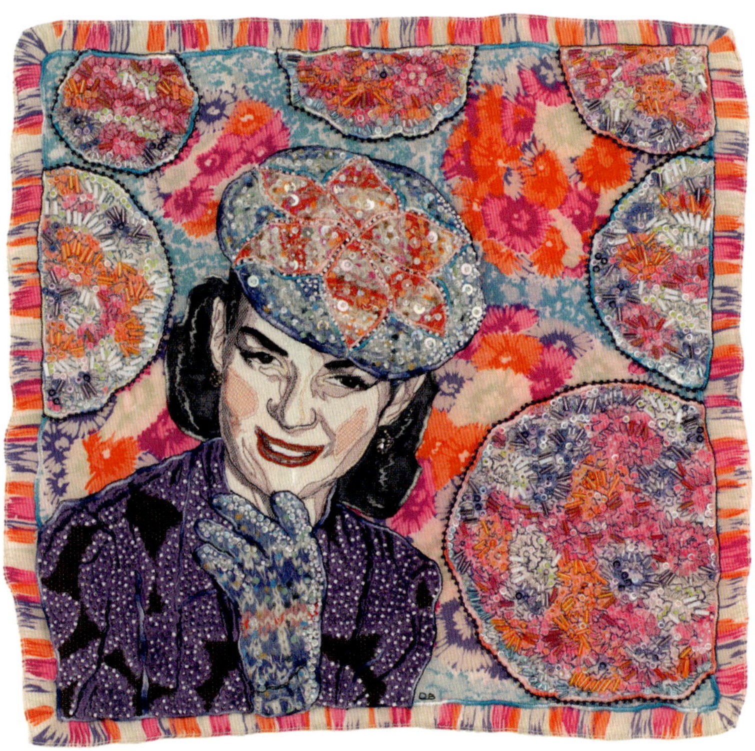

BELOW: *Louisa May*, 42 × 42cm (16½ × 16½in), framed. Made with hand-knitted Shetland wool and found fabrics. Appliquéd and machine embroidered using a domestic sewing machine onto a vintage handkerchief and embellished with beads and sequins.

Darren combines his knitting skills with the use of vintage and repurposed fabrics such as old handkerchiefs, pieces of domestic embroidery, wools, satins, beads and sequins to create his unique pieces of work. He says:

> *My aim is to make contemporary embroideries that reference and celebrate the domestic life and craftsmanship of the past, repurposing vintage fabrics for a new audience to be enjoyed now and in the future.*

The starting point for Darren's embroidery *Cultivation* is an image of a sleeveless sweater that was featured on the cover of the September 1947 issue of *Stitchcraft* magazine.

> *The piece focuses on the restorative powers of gardening and cultivation. It is embroidered onto a vintage handkerchief, which is edged with images of garden borders representing gardens of the 1940s. The handkerchief reflects the domestic nature of the garden, which is seen as an idyllic place of escape. The gardener, still in his tie and pinstripe trousers, is purged of the stresses of the working day as he gardens.*
>
> *Pieces of found embroidery from the period add examples of domestic stitch. The sweater is hand-knitted and sequined using a floral palette. Floral transfer designs from the December 1931 issue of* Good Needlework *magazine add stylized floral imagery to contrast against the more representational figure and to link the creativity of embroidery and gardening.*

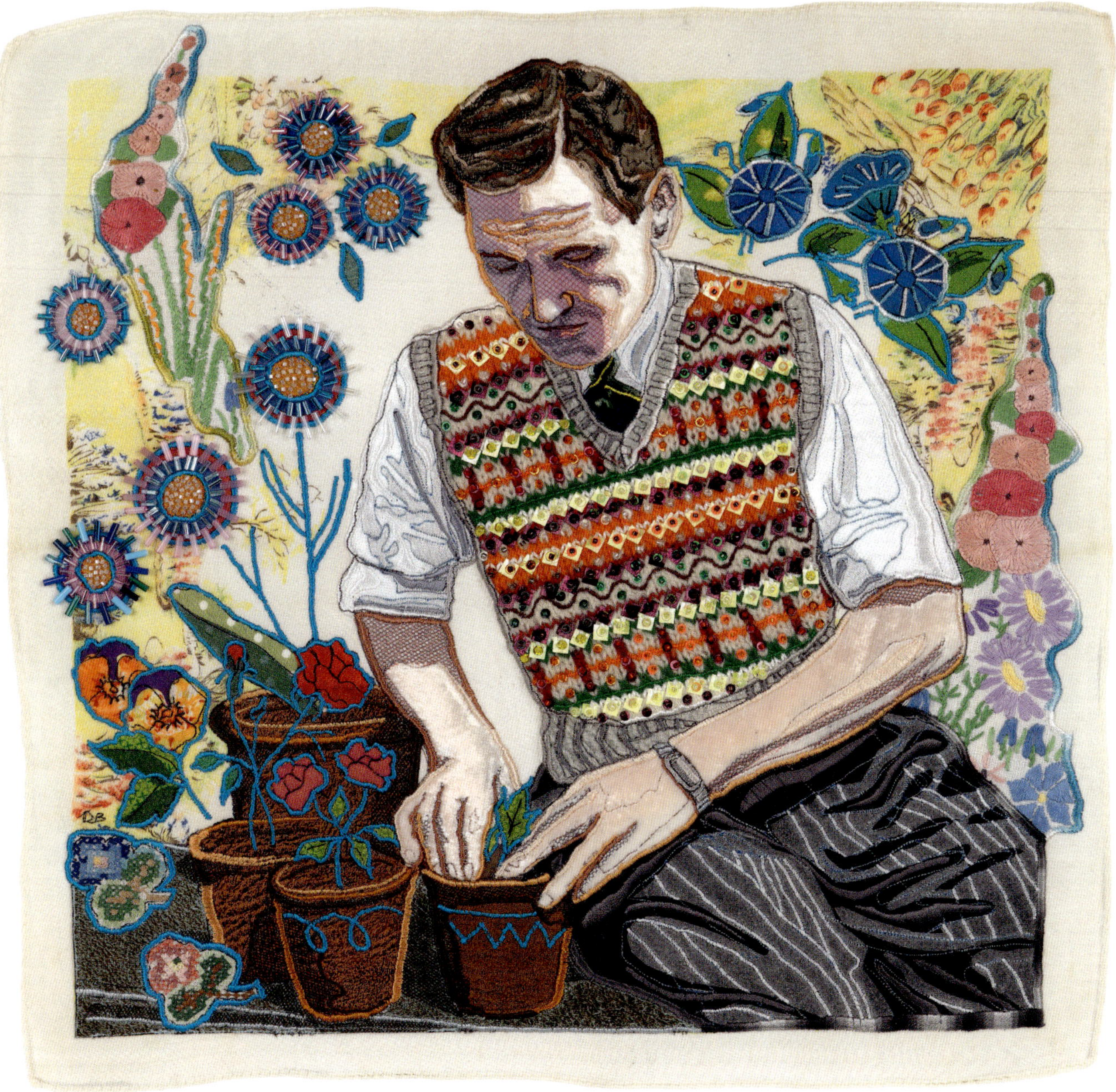

ABOVE: *Cultivation*, 46 × 46cm (18 × 18in), framed. Made with hand-knitted Shetland wool and found fabrics. Appliquéd and machine embroidered using a domestic sewing machine onto a vintage handkerchief and embellished with beads and sequins.

Sewing paraphernalia

So many of us stitchers and cloth lovers share a love for collecting haberdashery, along with the tools and various trinkets associated with our crafts. I am always attracted by stalls with vintage haberdashery at flea markets and can't resist the packaging of old button cards, cardboard strips of hooks and eyes, scissors and tape measures – especially those made from cloth, where the fabric has softened and faded over years of use. The tapes may have stretched and distorted, rendering them useless for measuring, but the font of the numbers and the uniformity of the lines make them beautiful materials to use. I should add to this that I only use tape measures with inches, as I don't find centimetres nearly as pleasing!

I often bring a selection of vintage haberdashery items along to workshops, where participants are drawn to them like magnets, as they handle and explain their use to others while remembering long-forgotten stories of making. I find sewing paraphernalia to be a constant source of inspiration in my work because of the stories they conjure up and the beauty of using them as 'meaningful materials' in themselves.

OPPOSITE: *No Need to Languish*, 27 × 38cm (10½ × 15in). Cloth collage with words from an old school jotter digitally printed onto cotton, words from a post-war needlework magazine typed onto cotton tape, vintage cottons, a corner of a family tablecloth, paper pattern, tape measure and vintage buttons. Hand stitched motifs.

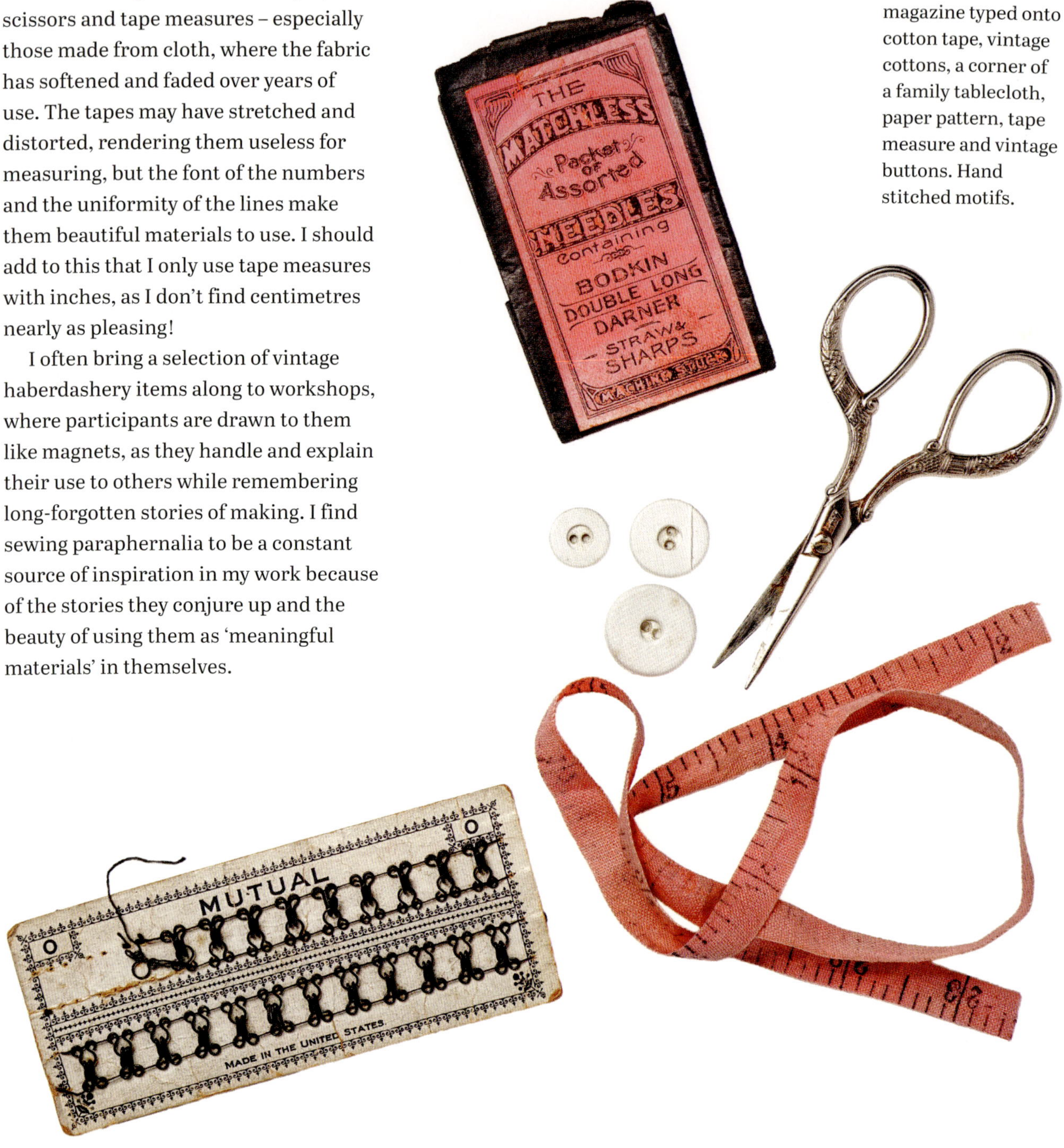

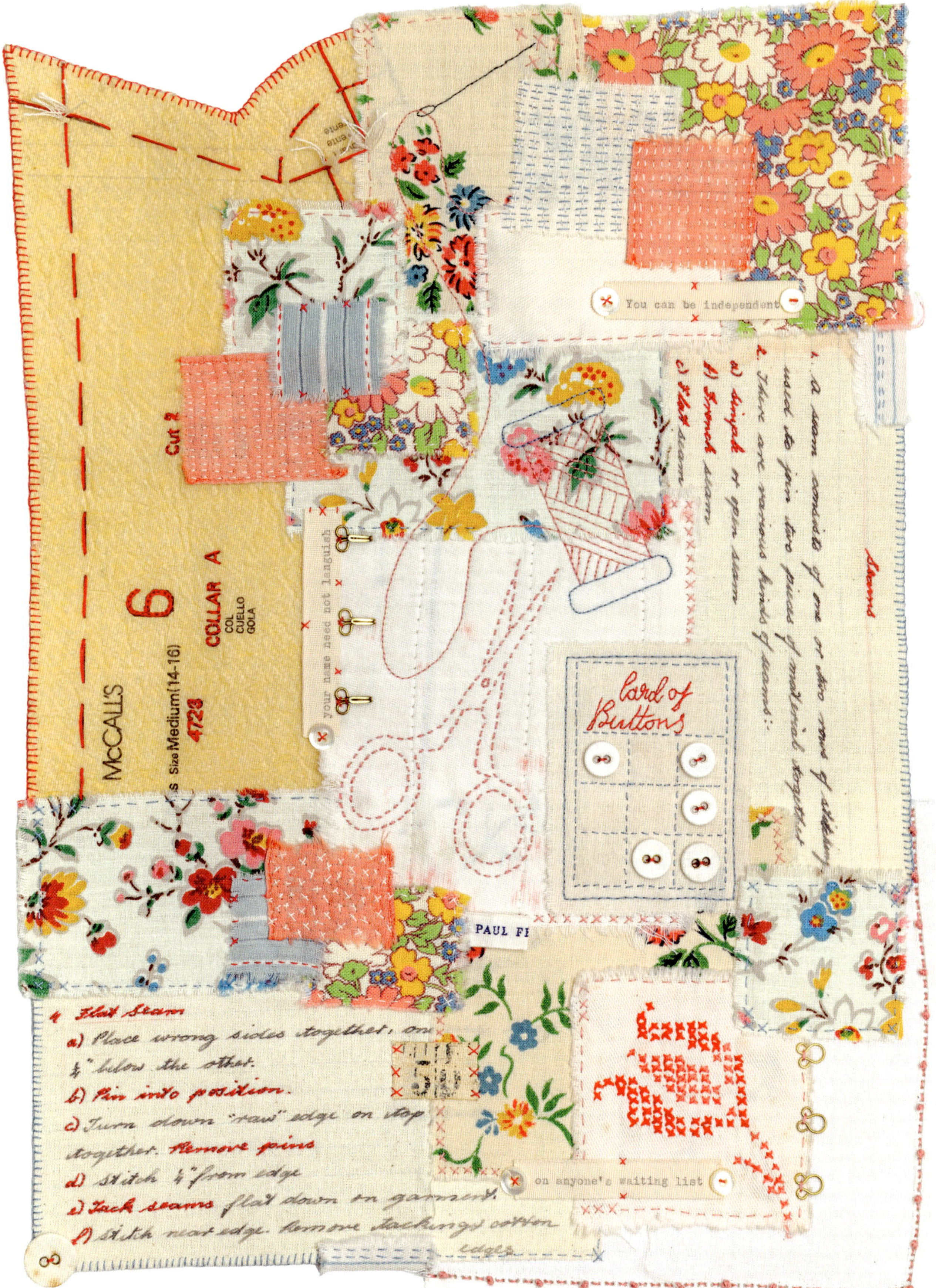

You can be independent
your name need not languish
on anyone's waiting list
Cut 2
6
COLLAR A
COL
CUELLO
GOLA
McCALL'S
Size Medium (14-16)
4723
Card of Buttons
PAUL F
1 Flat Seam
a) Place wrong sides together, one
¼" below the other.
b) Pin into position.
c) Turn down "raw" edge on top
together. Remove pins
d) Stitch ¼" from edge
e) Tack seams flat down on garment.
f) Stitch near edge. Remove tackings cotton
edges.

Ideas

Here are some ideas for your own stitching:

Dressmaking patterns: these are full of interesting shapes, lines and other markings. Instantly familiar to anyone who dressmakes, they bring back memories of garments made, and occasions worn. You can use the pattern paper in cloth collages. I attach it to the background with Bondaweb. Try stitching some of the markings on the top of the patterns and add tailor tacks to create texture and interest. You can also trace and stitch the outlines from pattern pieces. Alter the size and scale by enlarging or reducing on a photocopier/printer.

Button cards and cards of hooks and eyes: these can be used in collages if they are a suitable colour and scale, but I prefer to use the packaging as inspiration to stitch outlines. I photocopy the card and enlarge or reduce as necessary before tracing off a simplified outline for stitching. Scissors also make lovely outlines for stitching, as do spools of thread, pincushions, needle packets and so on.

Buttons, hooks and eyes, pieces of tape measure, small buckles, old needle packets and other bits and pieces: these can be stitched onto your work. My caution would be to use these sparingly and to make sure that the item you are adding doesn't dominate your piece.

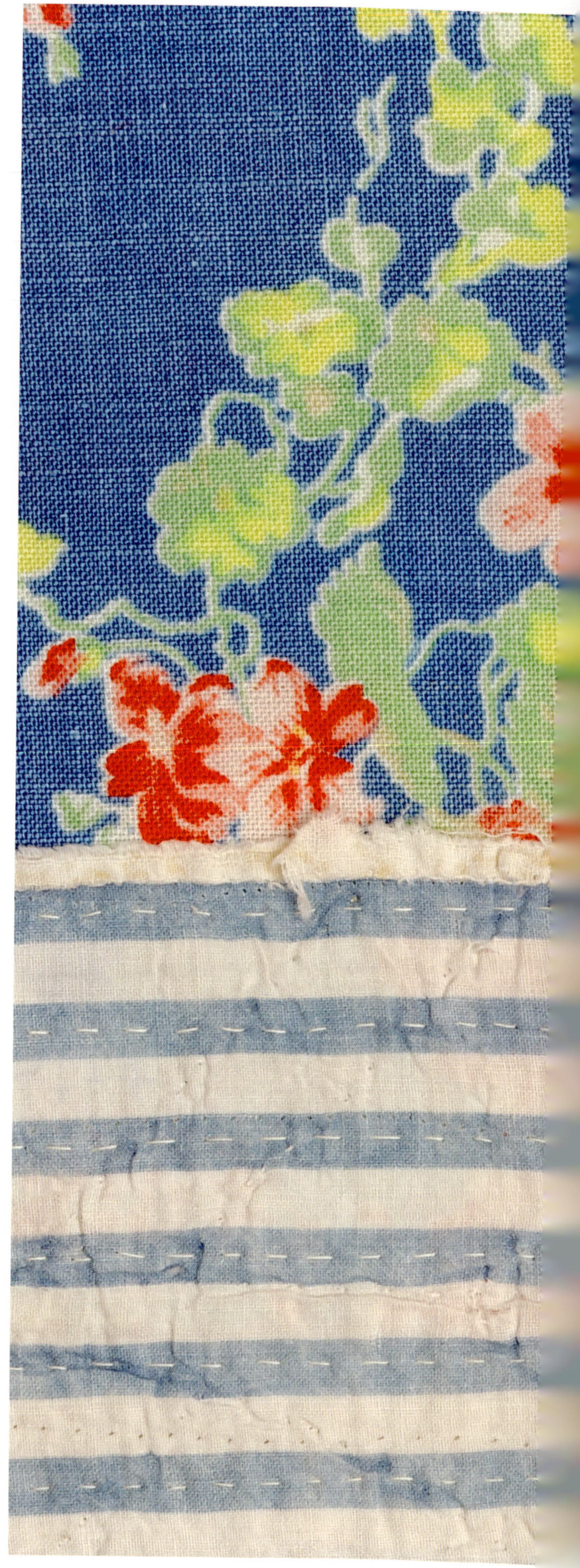

RIGHT: *If Their Fingers Were Busy* (detail). I like to use paper patterns with interesting shapes and detail. I add colour and texture to the paper by stitching in some of the markings.

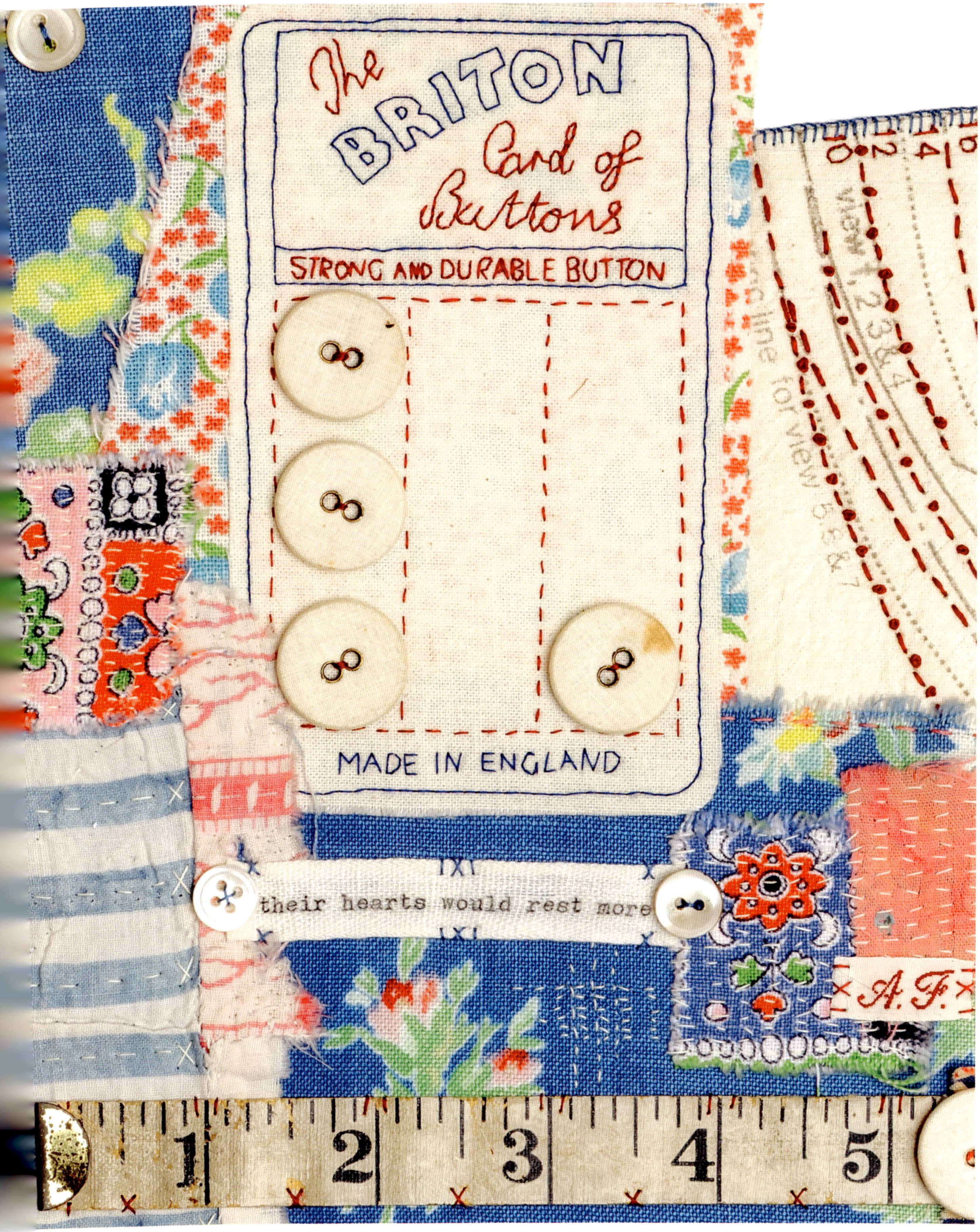
The BRITON Card of Buttons
STRONG AND DURABLE BUTTON
MADE IN ENGLAND
their hearts would rest more
A. F.
1 2 3 4 5

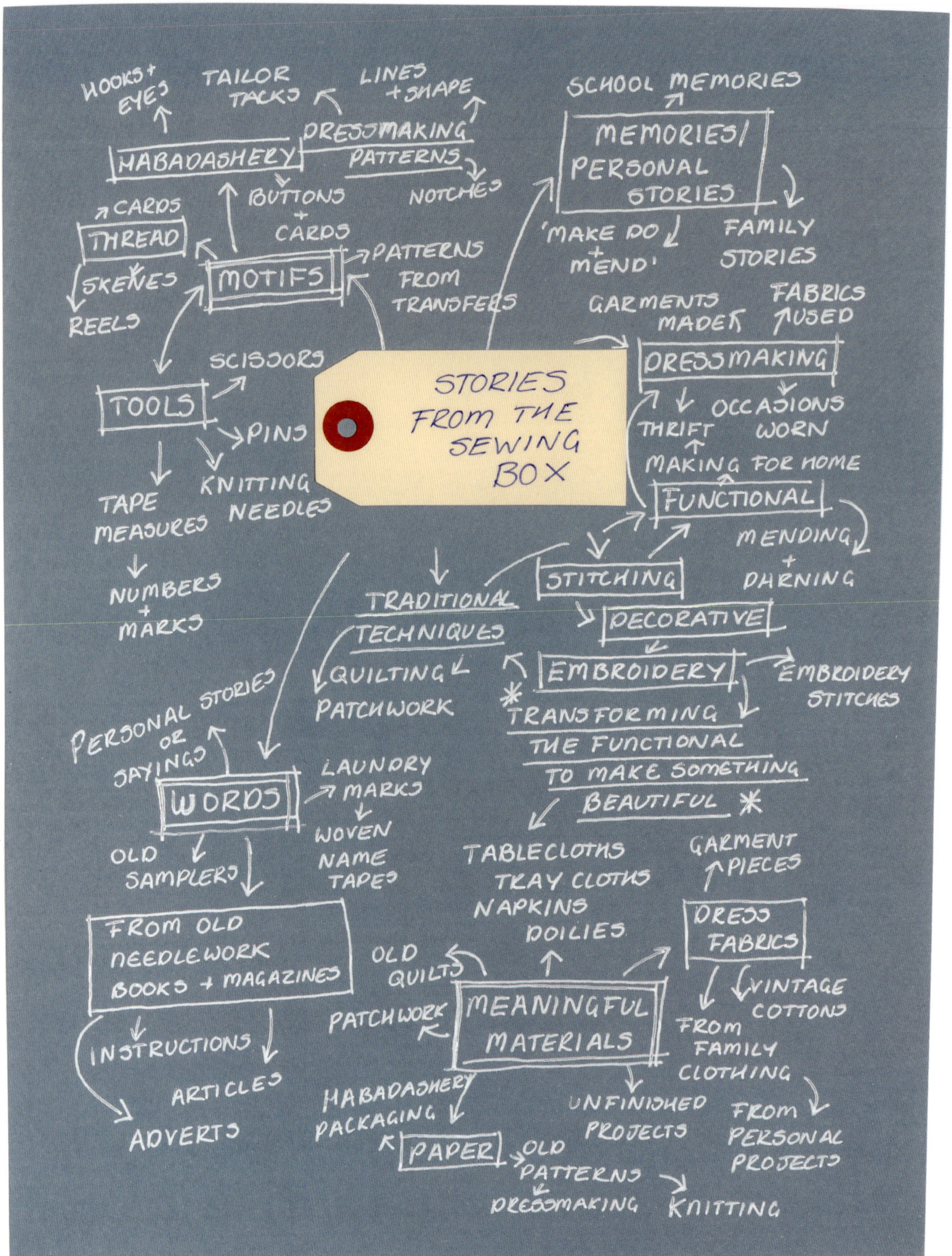
STORIES FROM THE SEWING BOX
HOOKS + EYES
TAILOR TACKS
LINES + SHAPE
DRESSMAKING PATTERNS
HABADASHERY
BUTTONS + CARDS
NOTCHES
CARDS
THREAD
SKEINES
REELS
MOTIFS
PATTERNS FROM TRANSFERS
SCHOOL MEMORIES
MEMORIES/ PERSONAL STORIES
'MAKE DO + MEND'
FAMILY STORIES
GARMENTS MADE
FABRICS USED
DRESSMAKING
THRIFT
OCCASIONS WORN
MAKING FOR HOME
FUNCTIONAL
MENDING + DARNING
STITCHING
DECORATIVE
EMBROIDERY
EMBROIDERY STITCHES
TRANSFORMING THE FUNCTIONAL TO MAKE SOMETHING BEAUTIFUL
SCISSORS
TOOLS
PINS
TAPE MEASURES
KNITTING NEEDLES
NUMBERS + MARKS
TRADITIONAL TECHNIQUES
QUILTING
PATCHWORK
PERSONAL STORIES OR SAYINGS
WORDS
LAUNDRY MARKS
WOVEN NAME TAPES
OLD SAMPLERS
FROM OLD NEEDLEWORK BOOKS + MAGAZINES
INSTRUCTIONS
ARTICLES
ADVERTS
TABLECLOTHS
TRAY CLOTHS
NAPKINS
DOILIES
GARMENT PIECES
DRESS FABRICS
OLD QUILTS
PATCHWORK
MEANINGFUL MATERIALS
VINTAGE COTTONS
FROM FAMILY CLOTHING
HABADASHERY PACKAGING
UNFINISHED PROJECTS
FROM PERSONAL PROJECTS
PAPER
OLD PATTERNS
DRESSMAKING
KNITTING

A process of working: Six Sewing Box Studies

You will need:

- A neutral-coloured fabric for your background. A linen or medium-weight cotton is perfect. I've used an old linen tablecloth.
- A selection of small cotton fabric scraps – include some cream or white fabrics.
- Threads for stitching and possibly a collection of small haberdashery items such as hooks and eyes, and buttons.

1. Start by ripping or cutting six pieces from your background fabric approximately 15cm (6in) square. I always rip fabric wherever I can, as I love the scrappy edge that it creates and the way that it distorts the cloth. Some linen tablecloths are almost impossible to tear, however, so you may need to cut your squares. By leaving the edges unfinished they will start to unravel and fray – embrace this!

2. Create your *threads of thought* around sewing and stitching. Reading through mine might help you get started. Allow one thought to lead to another and, as you write, memories and stories will start to emerge. Once you have lots written down, take a step back and highlight the things that particularly interest you.

3. Decide on your theme for each study, or follow mine. I chose:
   - Hooks and eyes
   - Buttons and buttonholes
   - Embroidery and stitches
   - Mending and darning
   - Dressmaking
   - Cross stitch and embroidery

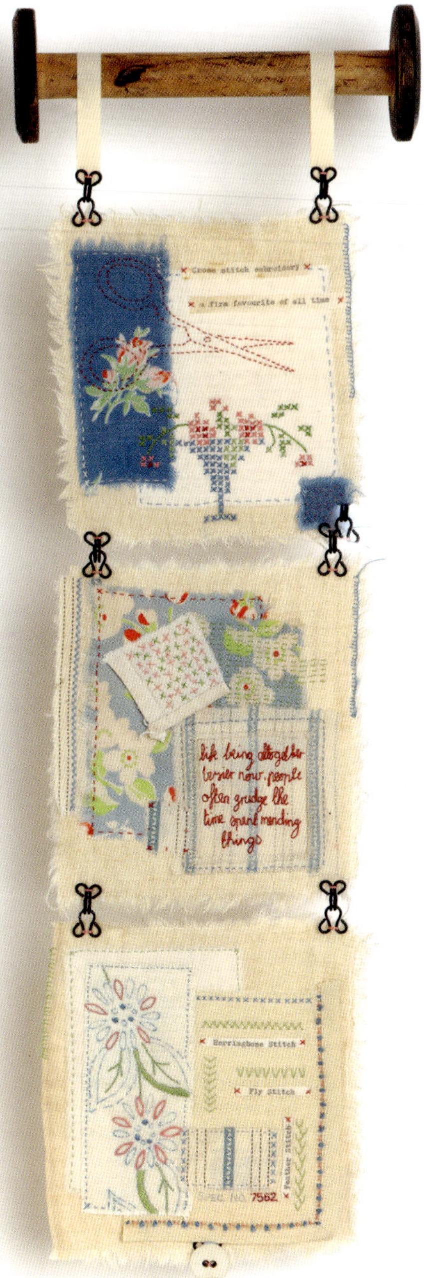

OPPOSITE: Creating your own *threads of thought* at the start of any project will help you to uncover personal memories and stories as well as highlighting areas of interest that you might want to explore further.

ABOVE: Three of my studies pictured overleaf are displayed hanging from an old weaving bobbin. Hooks and eyes make a perfect means of hanging, further illustrating my sewing box story.

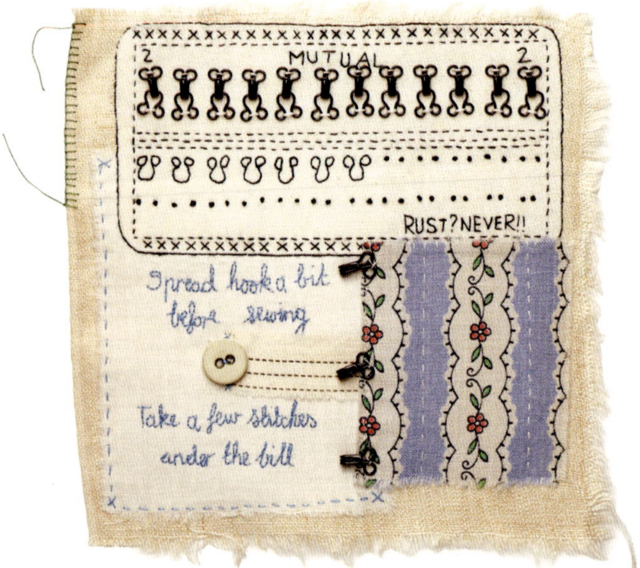
MUTUAL
RUST?NEVER!!
Spread hooks a bit before sewing
Take a few stitches under the bill
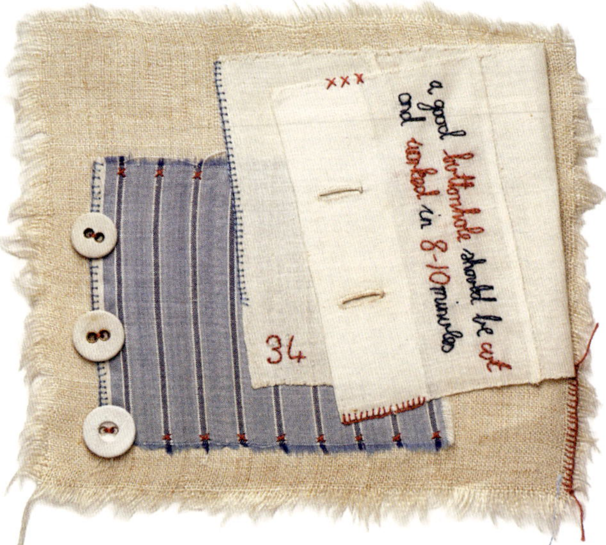
a good buttonhole should be cut and worked in 8-10 minutes
34
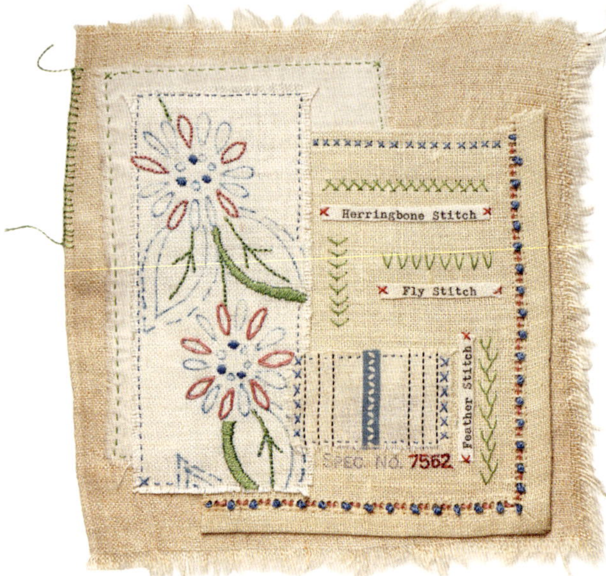
Herringbone Stitch
Fly Stitch
Feather Stitch
SPEC. NO. 7562
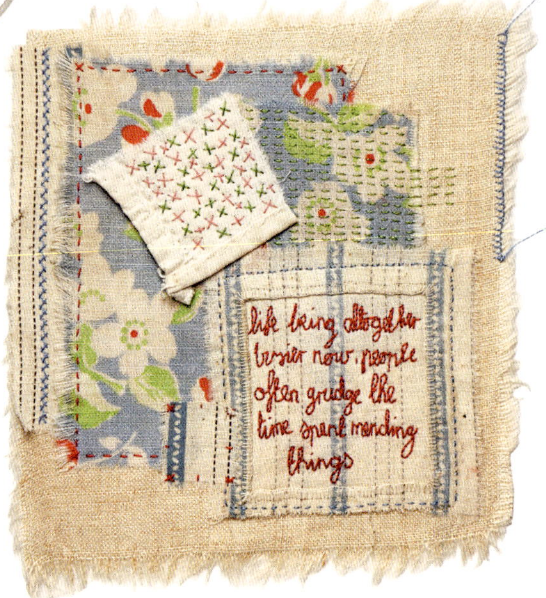
life being altogether busier now, people often grudge the time spent mending things
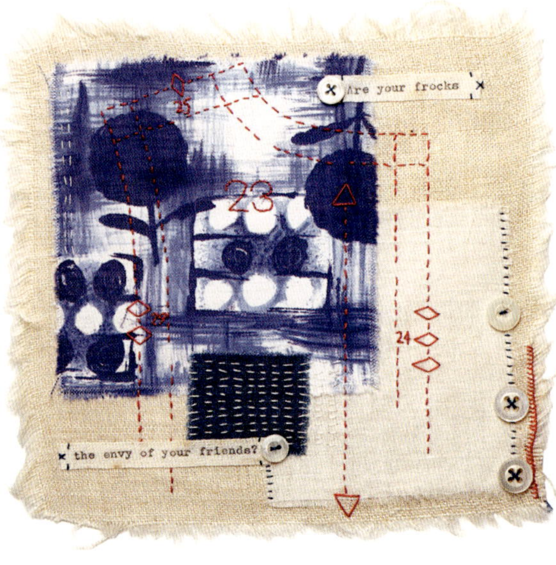
Are your frocks
23
24
the envy of your friends?
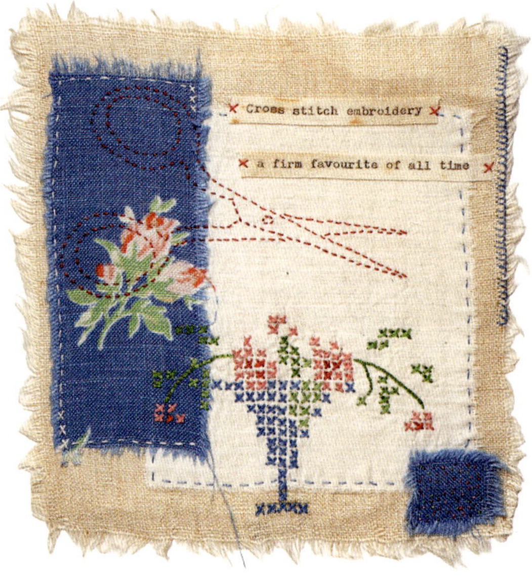
Cross stitch embroidery
a firm favourite of all time

It's useful to write each heading on scraps of paper and pin them onto each of your backgrounds.

4. Go back to your gathered fabrics and select six pieces that you would like to use, one for each of your studies. Remember that, although each is an individual study, you want them to display together as a group, so choose colours that sit well together. Place each of your chosen fabrics onto a different background piece.

5. Hunt out words that will help tell each story. I turned to my collections of words from my old sewing magazines and books, but of course, it would be lovely to use your own words from your own stitching story. Add the words to your study notes.

6. Gather motifs that will help illustrate each study. Again, either write down your motif idea on each study note, or place any gathered items onto their backgrounds.

7. You now have lots of ideas gathered and are ready to start arranging each collage. Because each individual study is so small, it's best to keep the design for each one simple.

8. Start by choosing one of your studies and select something to be your main focal point.

OPPOSITE: *Six Sewing Box Studies*, each piece 15 × 15cm (6 × 6in). Clockwise from top left: Hooks and eyes; Buttons and buttonholes; Mending and darning; Cross stitch and embroidery; Dressmaking; Embroidery stitches. All hand stitched on linen.

RIGHT: Buttons and buttonholes. I've noted my heading, chosen my focal fabric and gathered my words. These words come from the instructions in an old needlework book.

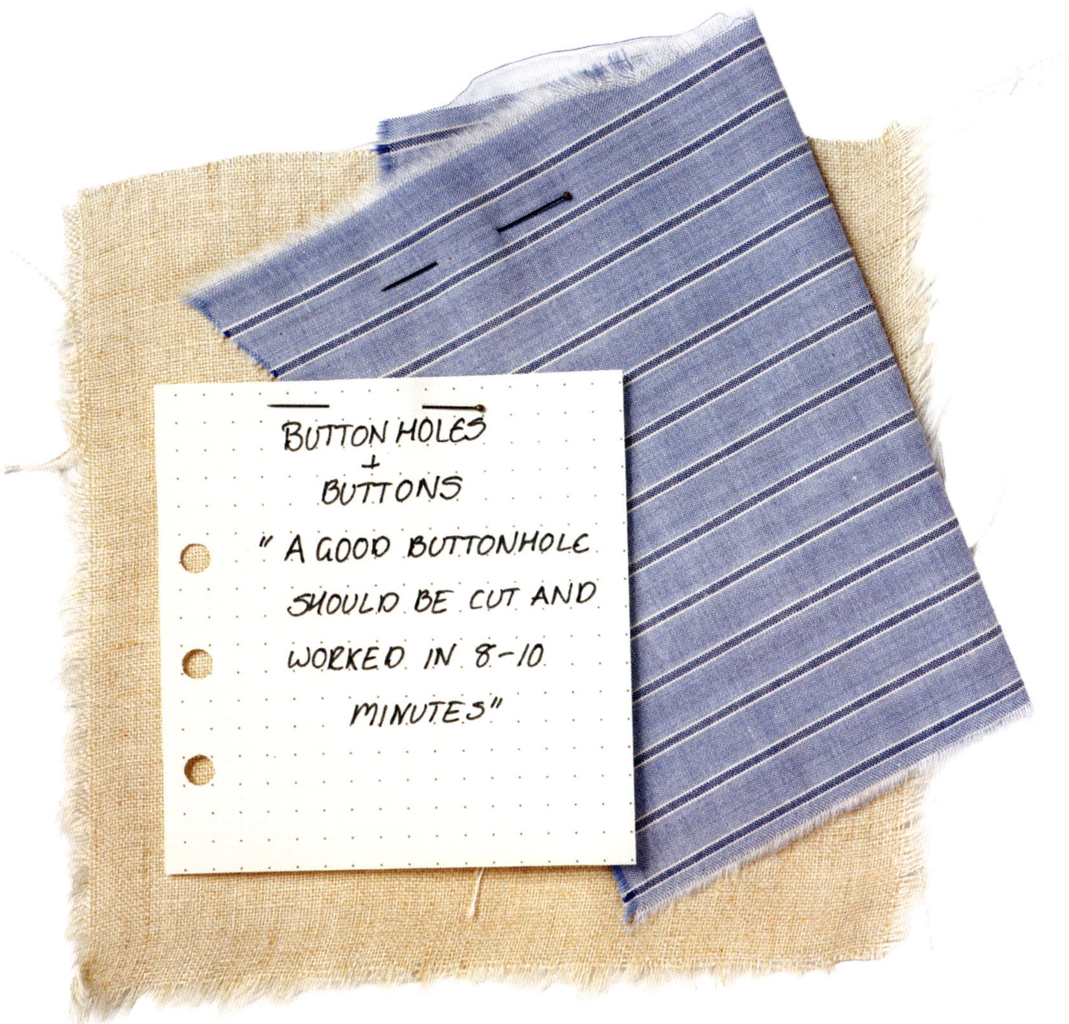

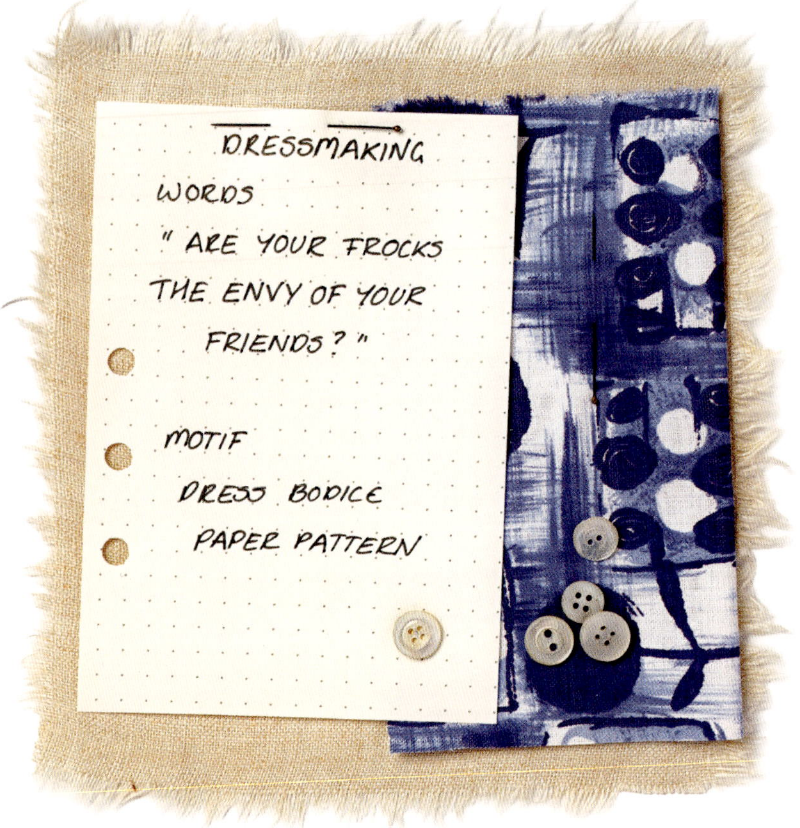

For my dressmakers study, I chose this 1940s print to be the focal point, balanced with a piece of off-white cotton. I reduced the size of a paper pattern bodice from a child's dress on my printer and then traced it onto tissue paper. I then played with their placement while also considering where my words would go. I typed these words onto old cotton tape using my typewriter; you'll find more information on this and other ways of creating text in the next chapter (see pages 72–91). I then added a small patch breaking up the lines of the two main ones, and added buttons to give a bit of depth and texture.

ABOVE: Dressmaking. I've noted my idea for my stitched motif and gathered a selection of mother-of-pearl buttons to help illustrate my dressmaking story. The words come from a 1960s *Vogue* magazine and the fabric is a beautiful scrap of 1940s cotton.

RIGHT: Tracing your motifs and words onto vellum allows you to play around with their placement. By gathering everything together in this way, you create your vision for each piece, enabling you to see how they sit together as a collection.

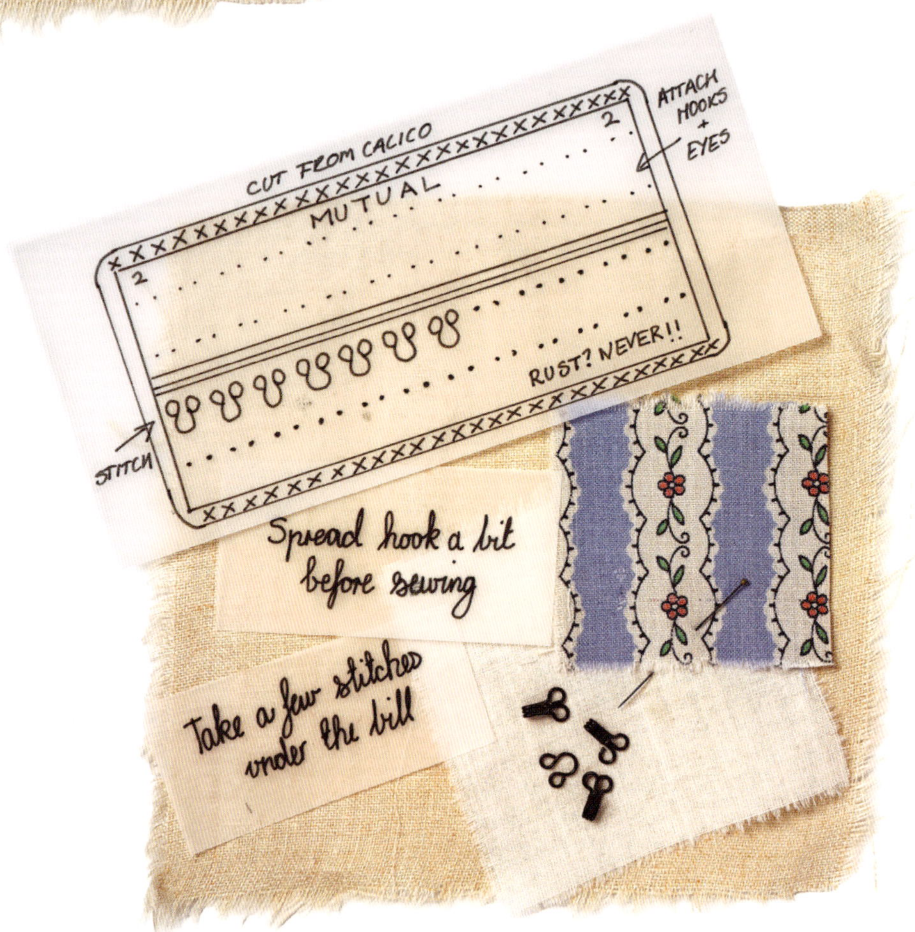

1. Pin or simply lay your fabrics in place, set your study to one side and start on the next one. Take photos of your layouts as you go along.

2. Once all six studies are planned, attach your main fabrics to the background. I used fusible web on some of my larger patches, but others were simply pinned ready for stitching.

3. Choose a small selection of threads to use across each of your studies.

4. If you don't know where to start, choose one of your patches and sew round it with a running stitch – maybe add a cross or three in one of the corners! As you do this you will get an idea for what to do next. Work intuitively, adding simple stitching patterns, doodling with your thread and letting your fabrics tell you what they would like.

5. I traced my hooks and eye card onto calico using a light pencil line. I ironed fusible web onto the back before cutting out my shape. This gives a sharp cut line which won't readily fray.

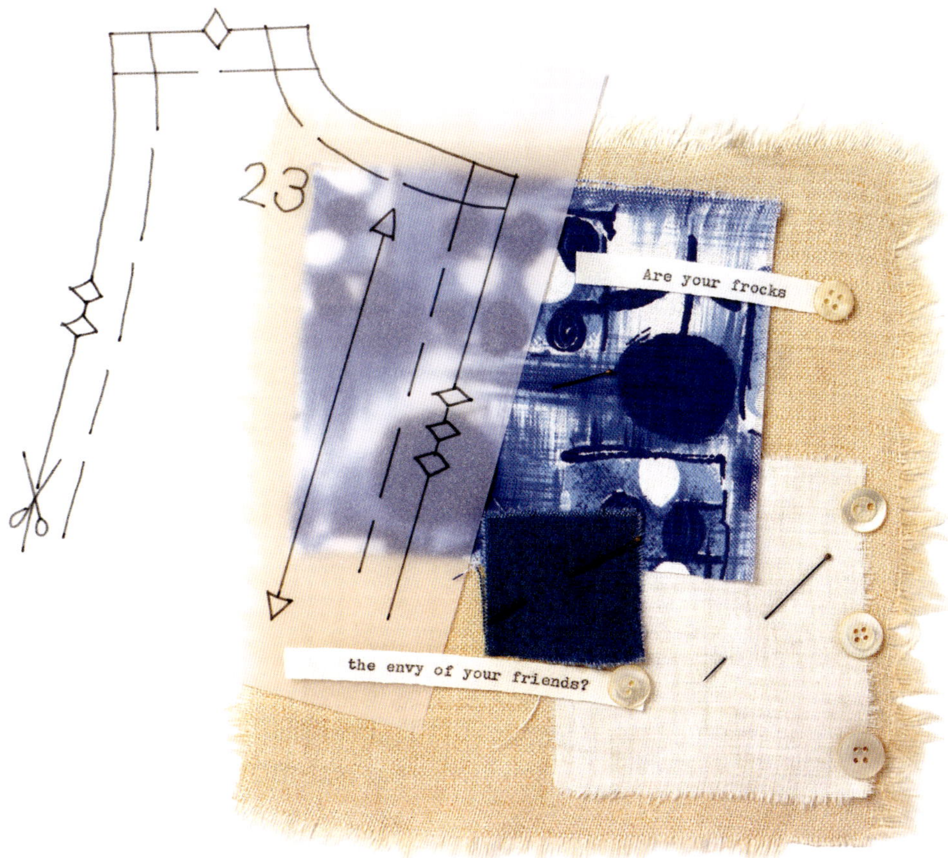

LEFT: Once each study is planned, fabrics are pinned in place ready for stitching. The motif will be traced onto tissue paper before stitching, following the method outlined on page 21.

RIGHT: *Stories from the Sewing Box* (detail). A cloth book is a beautifully tactile way of presenting small collages using meaningful materials, words and motifs. The simplicity of the layouts allows the beauty of the materials to take centre stage.

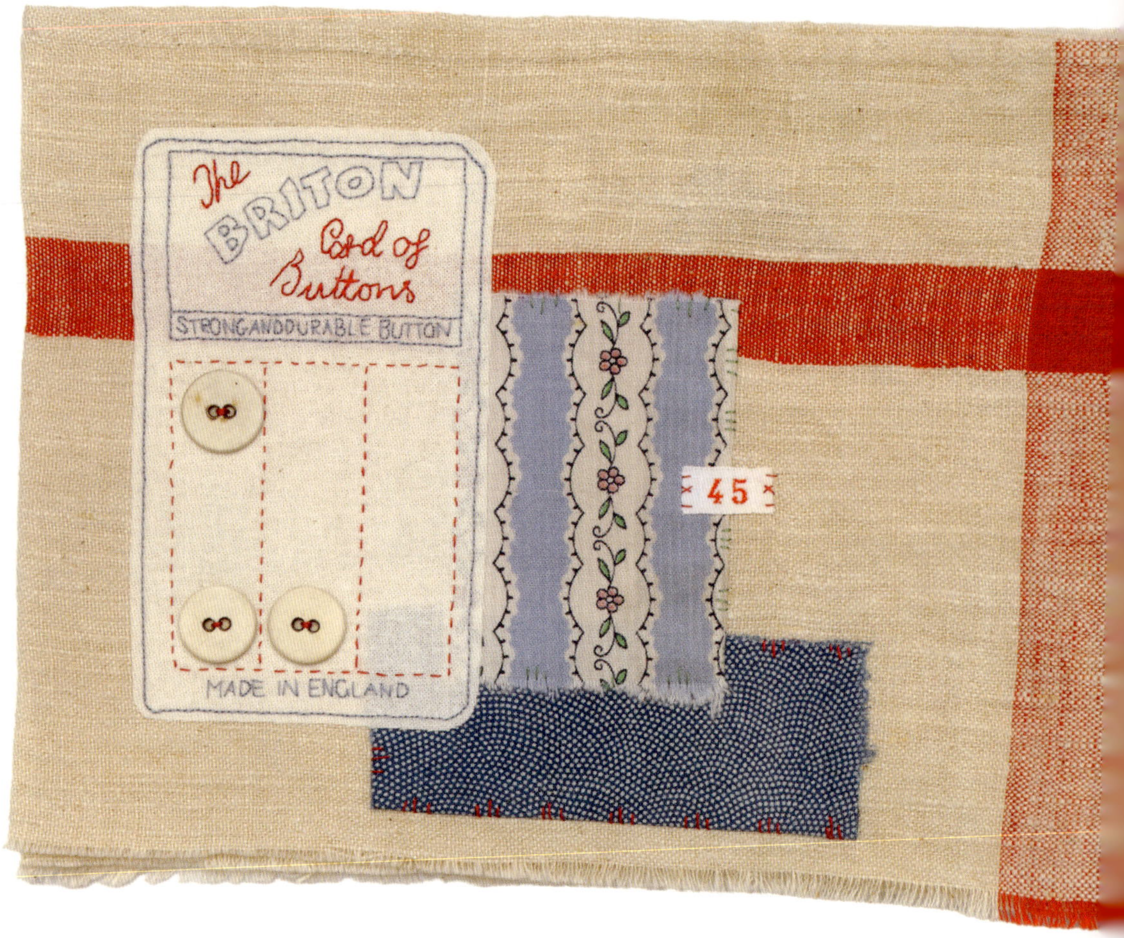

Cloth book

I decided to extend the idea from the sewing studies into making a cloth book. There's just something very tactile about a book made from fabric. My book is made up of six double pages. I used two old French torchons, made from soft linen. You'll need a fabric that has a bit of body to it, but feels soft to handle.

Rip or cut six pieces roughly 56 x 18cm (22 x 7in). Fold each piece of fabric in half widthwise and press down the fold. The book will be formed by the folded pieces of fabric sitting one on top of the other. The fold is at the right edge and the raw edges are at the left (where the pages will be joined to form the spine). It's held together with three buttons stitched through the layers.

Approach the planning and making of each page in the same way as the sewing studies. It's useful to start with your pages one on top of the other and your written notes pinned onto each page. In this way you'll mark the front and back covers and what will go in each of the double pages.

Open each individual page out to work on it, but remember that the two pages on the same piece of cloth will not sit next to each other in the book. This is why your written notes are important. Creating the pages in this way means that the back of your work will be hidden when you come to construct the book.

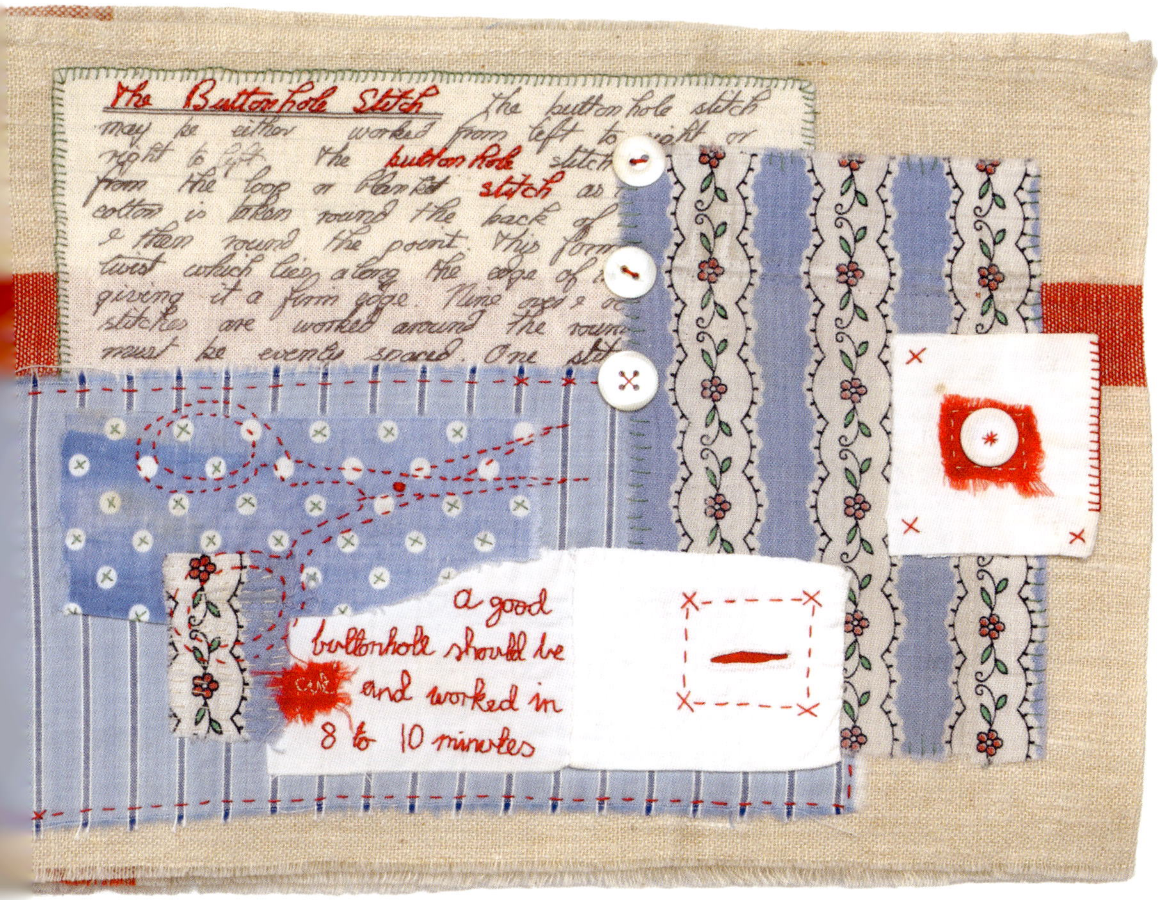

BELOW: *Stories from the Sewing Box*, 28 × 18cm (11 × 7in). Cloth book inspired by the previous sewing studies. The pages are made from an old French torchon with large mother-of-pearl buttons holding them together at the spine.

When planning your page layout, remember to leave a margin along your joining edge where the buttons will go. I left a margin of 3.5cm (1½in).

Once you've completed all your stitching, construct your book by:

1. Pressing the pages, particularly along the fold line.
2. Laying them in order with the raw edges lined up. It's useful to hold the left hand (joining) edges together with clips.
3. Stitching a button through all the pages in the centre of the spine and then another top and bottom. Use a long, strong needle such as a long darner. I used a double thread to stitch and left a tail when starting so that I could tie off the two ends on completion.

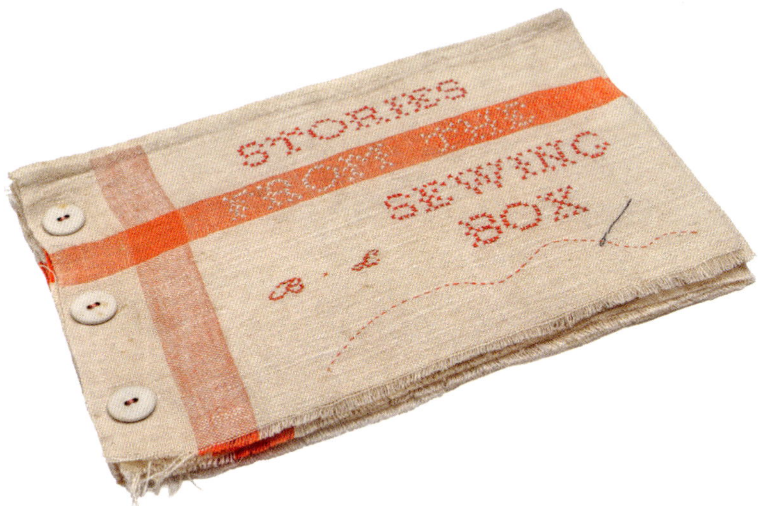

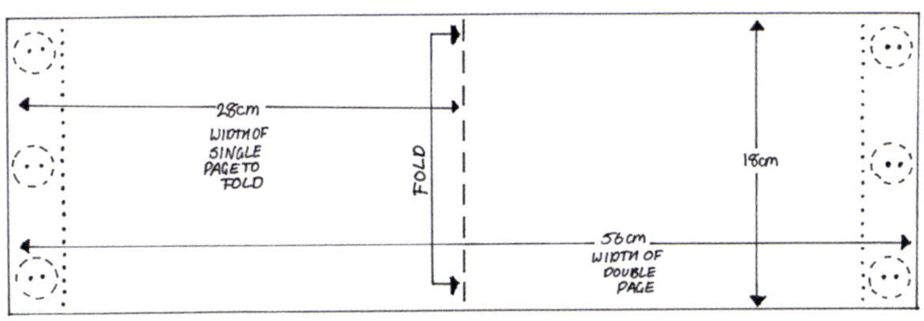

Capturing (hi)stories and memories

This can be a wonderful way of displaying some special pieces of fabric that you have in your collection. They may be special because of what they are, or simply because of what they mean to you. I've included such items as an old school needlework sample of a flannel patch – the stitcher, D. Gray, is unknown to me, but I treasure it all the same. I've used an old piece of fabric, faded and darned, that was gifted to me on a teaching trip in New Zealand. Every time I turn to this page, I am reminded of the wonderful friends I made there.

I've also used a scrap of old hand-stitched quilt where I've carefully unpicked the layers and then worked my own lines of stitching in the holes left by the previous maker. There's something quite poignant about displaying and valuing an everyday household item – handmade by someone and then used, washed and worn through many times over, with a new layer of cloth added each time.

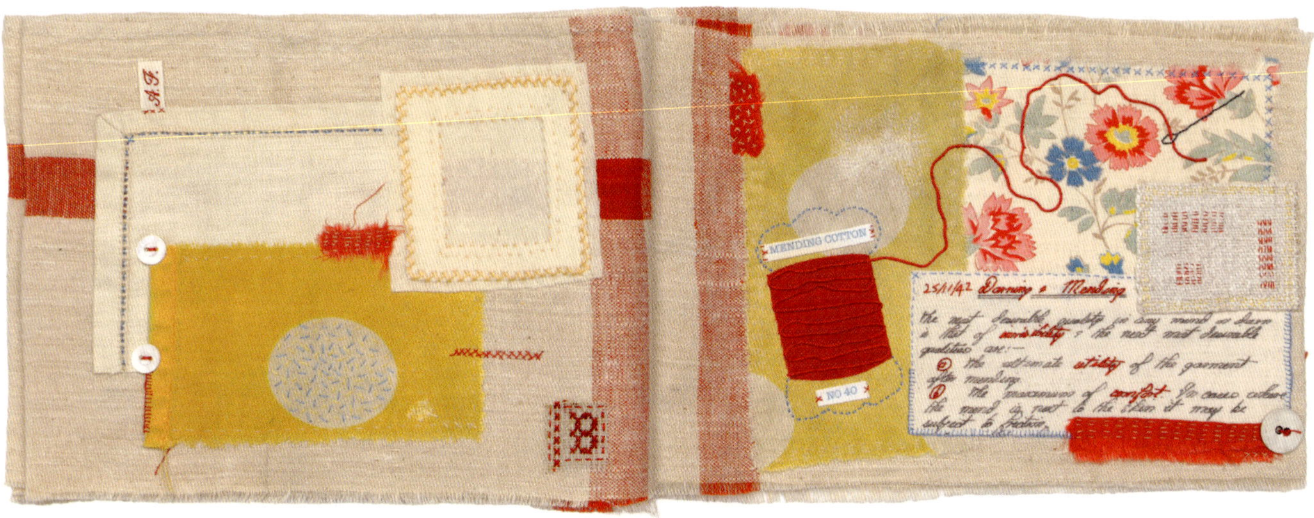

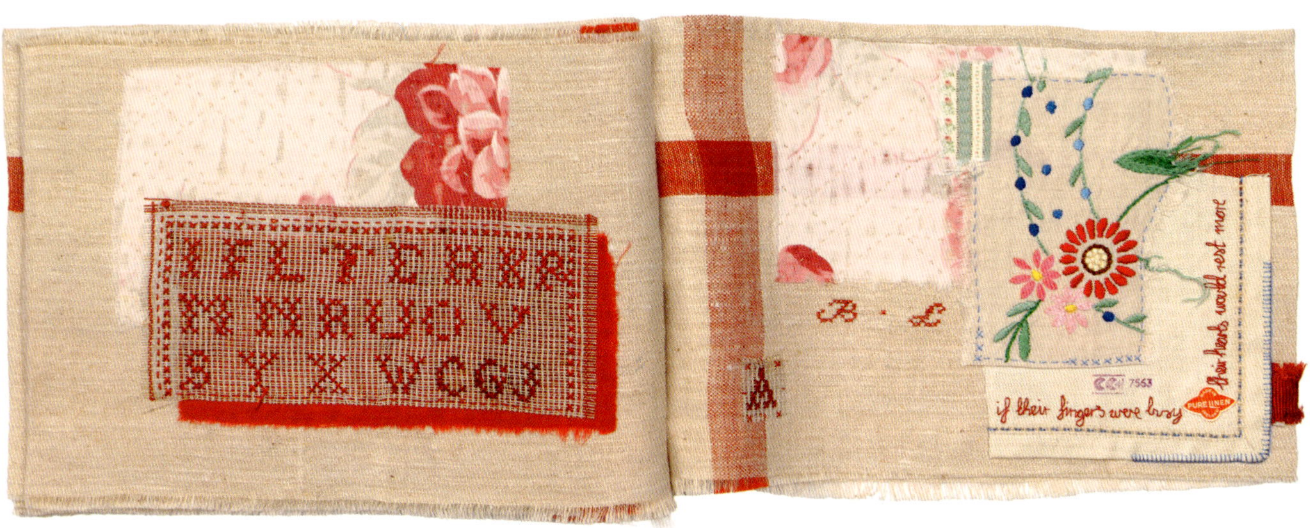

BELOW: *Stories from the Sewing Box* (detail). Simple compositions made from old table linens, gifted fabric from friends across the globe, old school needlework samples and old quilts, embellished with vintage buttons and hand stitching.

I've included a fragment from a very simple sampler, not particularly well stitched, by quite a young child I assume, and I rather like to think that it was stitched grudgingly when there was much more fun to be had outside! I love how stories start to form in your mind as you work with these old pieces – wildly inaccurate, I'm sure, but the real story is hidden in there somewhere and, of course, I'm adding a bit of my own with every stitch that I make.

Many of my off-white scraps come from the lining of an antique skirt. I've shown the wrong side with the stitched seams showing as part of the design and part of the hidden history, now sitting among the pages in my book. I wonder where it has been, who it has met and what they got up to – secrets hidden forever, yet still present within my pages.

I created my own printed fabric from pages of old needlework school notes. I scanned the text, and had it professionally digitally printed, but you can easily print your own fabric using a home inkjet printer and the process with freezer paper outlined earlier in the chapter.

BELOW: A cloth book is a wonderful way of displaying found treasures such this child's stitching sampler.

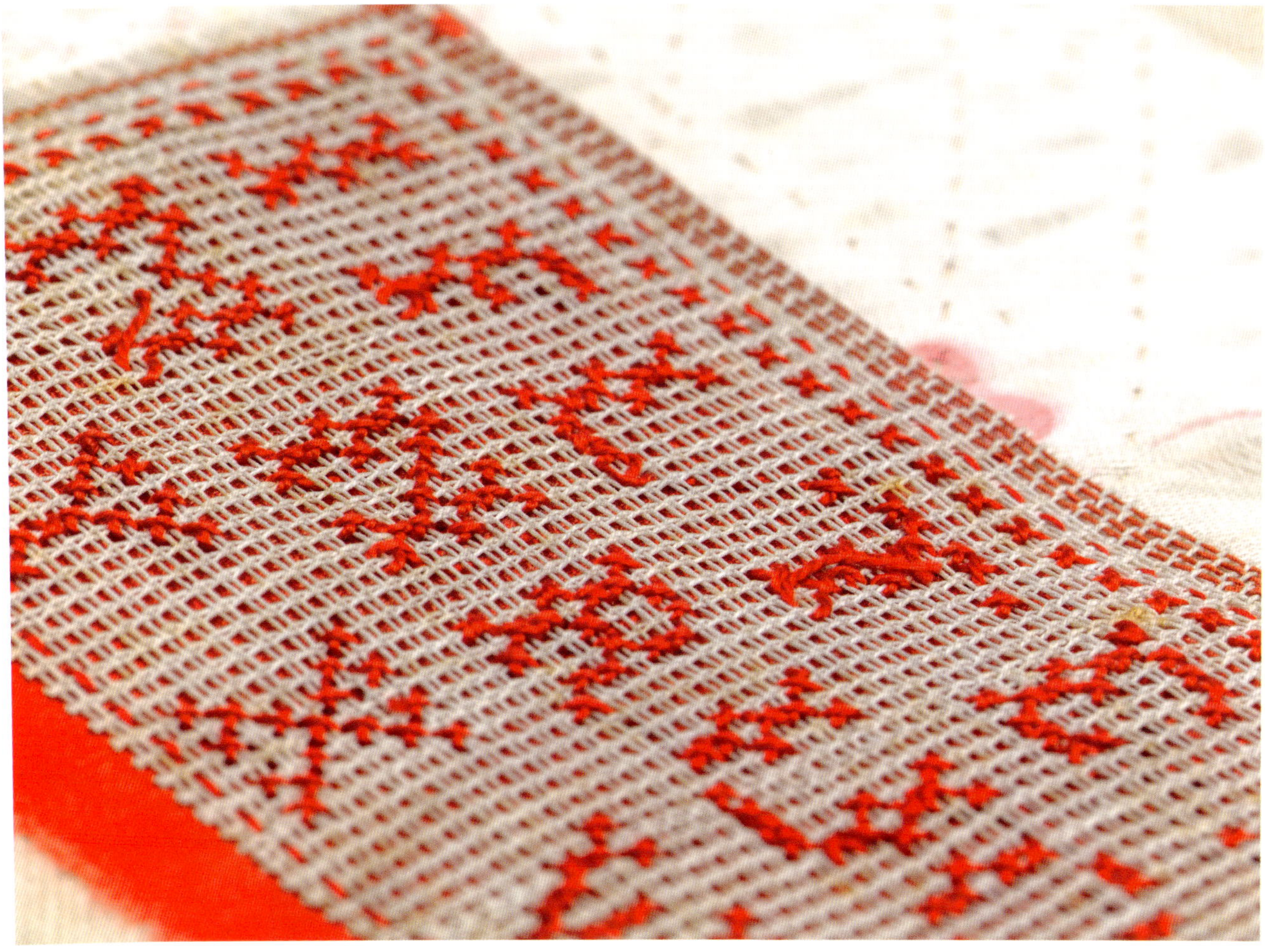

Fran Buxton

Inspired by heritage hand stitching

Fran is one of the resident artists at Unit Twelve, a beautiful contemporary textile studio and gallery in the village of Hixon, West Midlands. She combines her love of collecting with traditional hand-stitching techniques to make the most covetable pieces. She says:

> *I adapt heritage hand-stitch techniques, predominantly needle lace and needle weaving, to work around a found or vintage object. The stitches are often mistaken for crochet or tatting (which are on my list to learn!) but predominantly involve just a spool of perle cotton, a needle and some patience.*
>
> *Alongside my love of stitch is an inherent desire to collect "treasures" – some of these may have monetary value, while others are found on the ground. My house and studio contain clusters of both curated and mismatched temporary installations. Some objects I collect with a thought about how I will utilize them – scissors, for example, provide a perfect viewfinder or recess to stitch into. Others can wait for years until inspiration strikes.*
>
> *I am drawn to notions with signs of use: the thimble that is worn and pitted, the darning mushroom with flaky paint, the tatty mending kit. Similarly, I am drawn to the nostalgia, the warm, almost grandmotherly familiarity. I think a lot of people can find a connection to sewing notions, whether personal or through generations before.*
>
> *With this nostalgic connection comes a fabulous opportunity to create artwork that either saves things from landfill or saves heirlooms from languishing in drawers. They also generate creative challenges – my most recent being to see how small I can stitch. So far, it's onto a sequin pin!*
>
> *I pair objects together in a storytelling way; think of a needle left poised on an old wooden cotton reel. While fixed as a sculpture, it hints to an owner, returning to resume the task. I also feel a wonderful serendipity or almost humour about me hand stitching onto a sewing needle.*

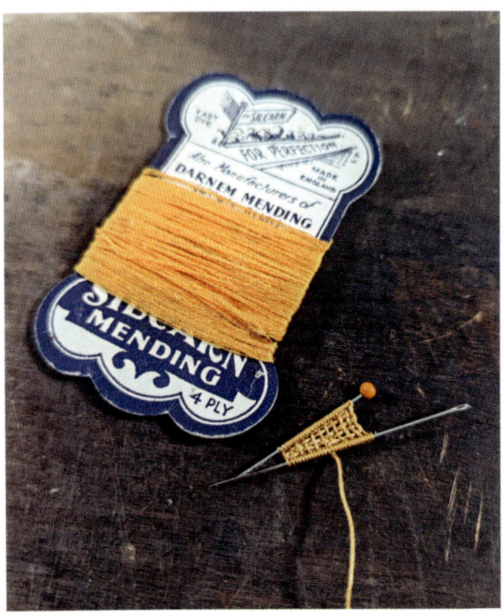

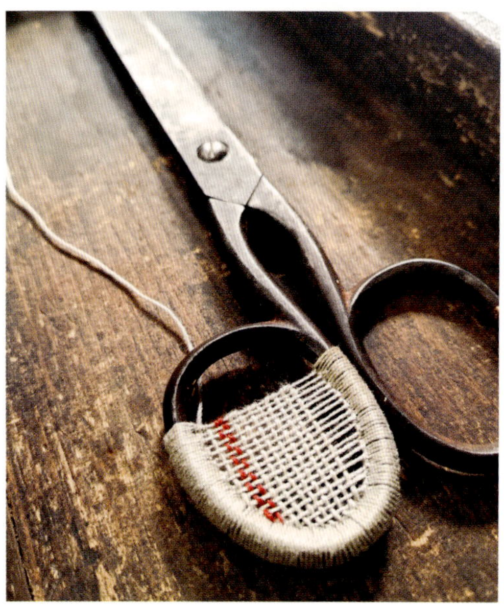

FAR LEFT: *Mending*. Vintage card of mending thread alongside pin and needle with hand stitched needleweaving in matching thread.

LEFT: *Scissors* (detail). Close up detail of vintage scissors with hand stitched needleweaving (part of a larger composition).

OPPOSITE: *Components*. Vintage key, pin and safety pin with hand stitched needlelace and needleweaving.

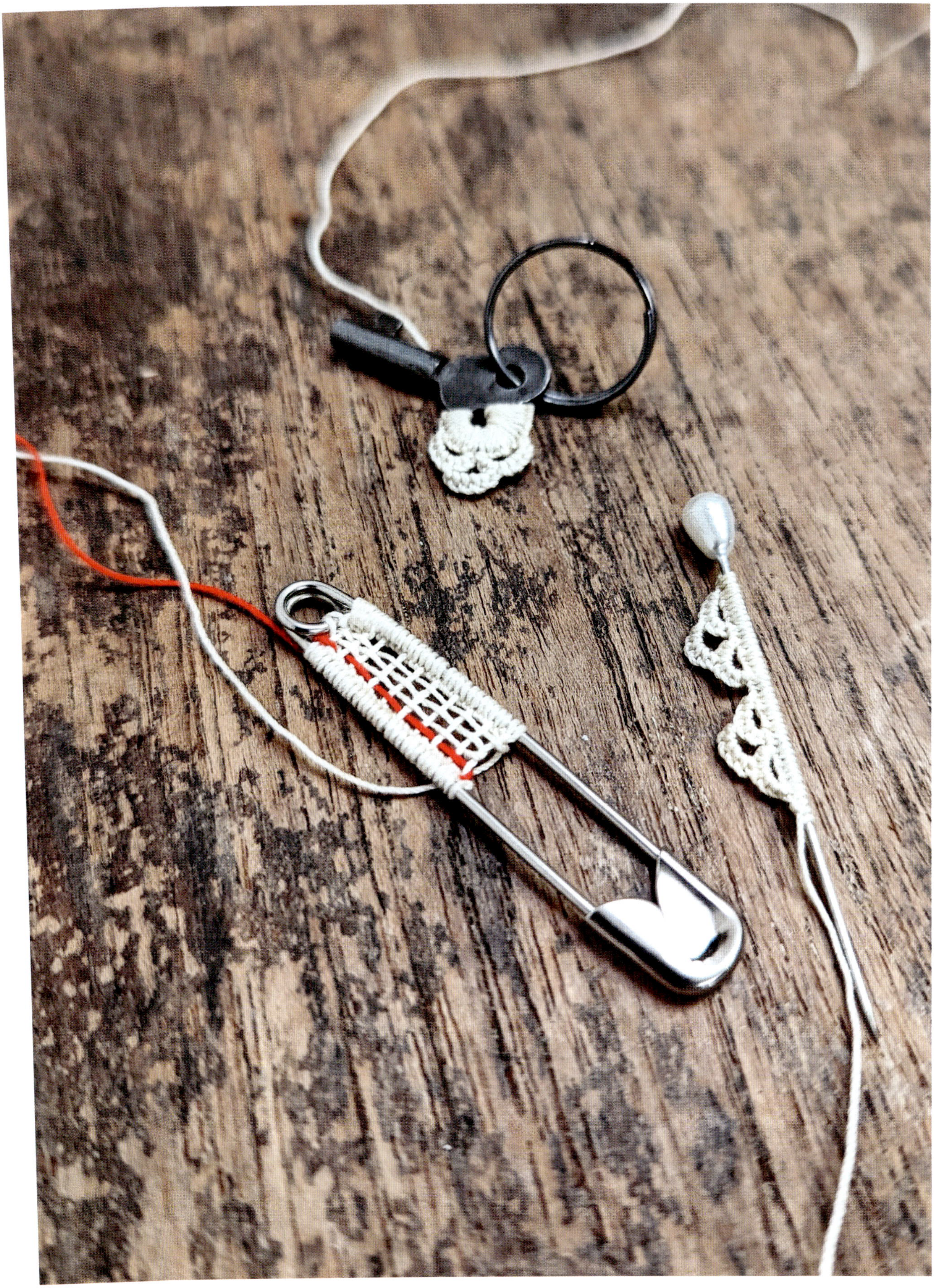

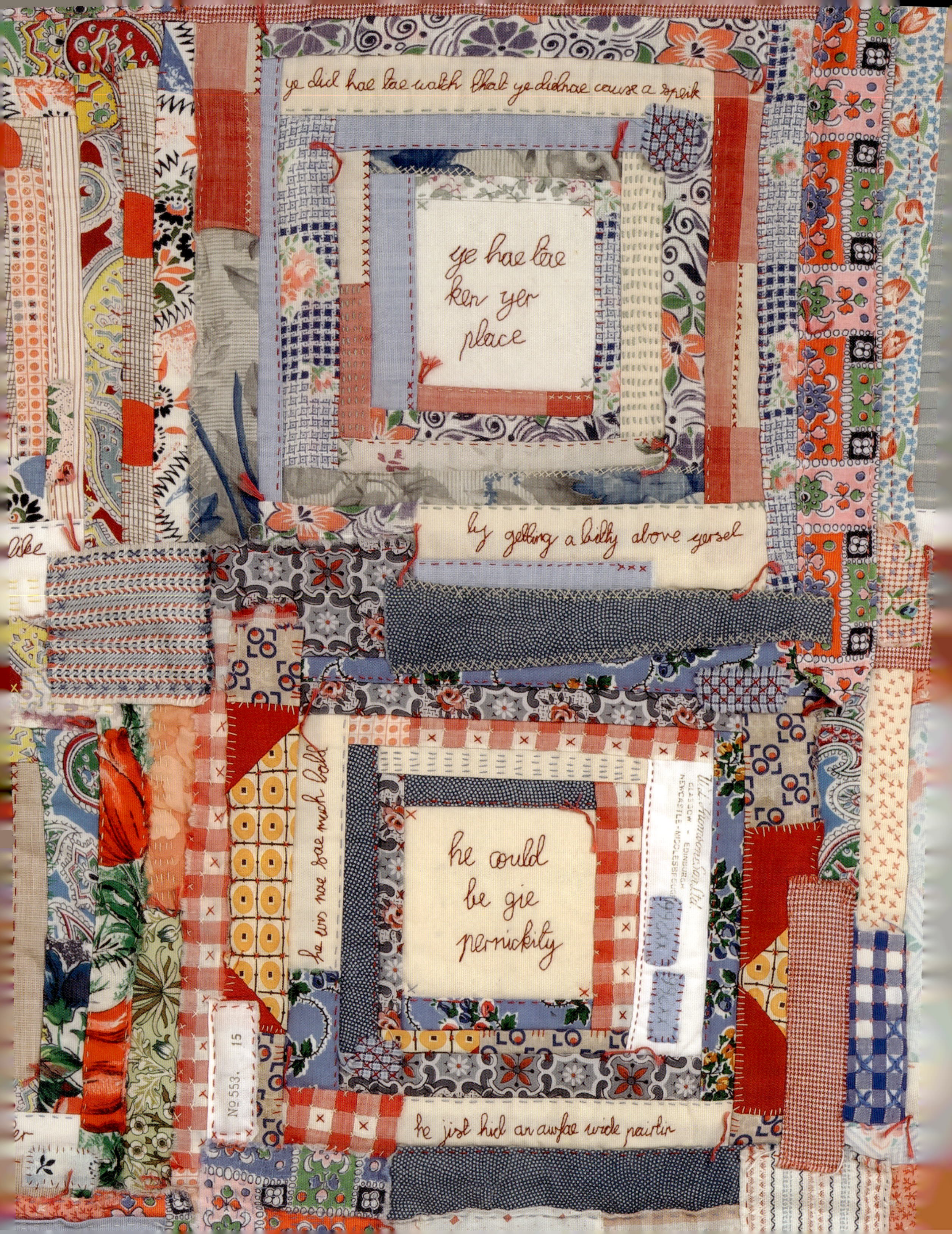
ye did hae tae watch that ye didnae cause a speik
ye hae tae ken yer place
by getting a bitty above yersel
he wis nae sae much bald
he could be gie pernickity
GLASGOW - EDINBURGH
NEWCASTLE - MIDDLESBROUGH
№ 553. 15
he jist hid an awfae wide pairtin

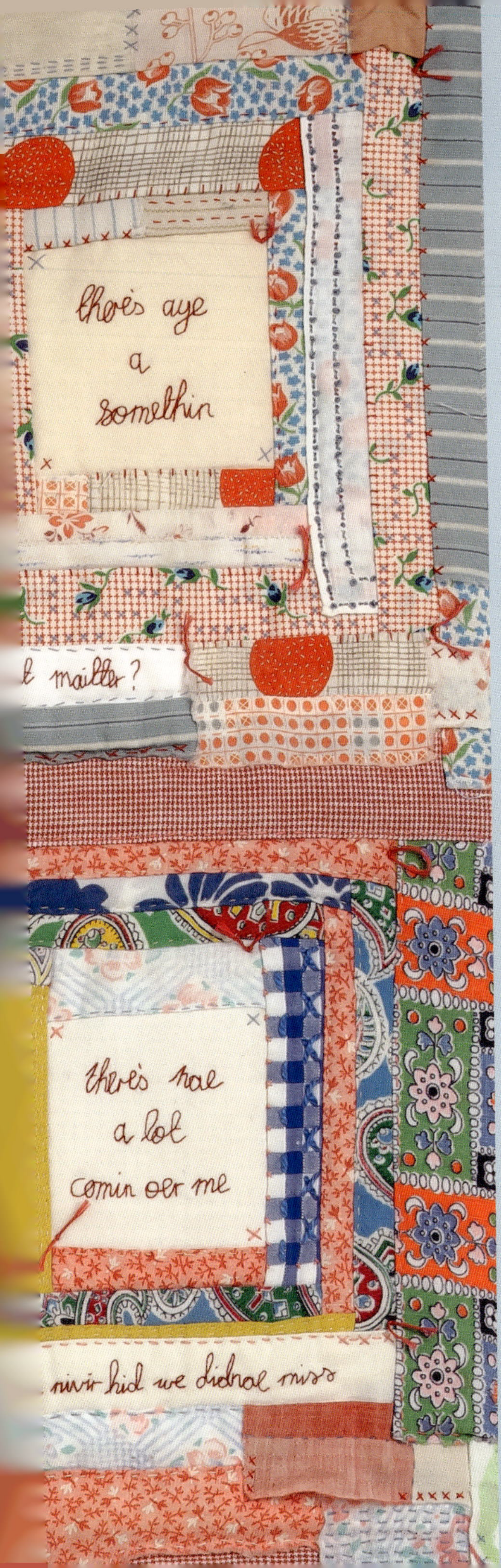

Words and stuff

Words play a pivotal role in my storytelling – not only the stitched and printed words that are visible in most of my work, but also those that remain hidden.

For example, three little words heard quite by chance many years ago sparked a line of thought that remains with me today. While working in my studio and half-listening to the radio, something caught my attention and I wrote down the phrase 'Locard's Exchange Principle'. Months later I came across the note and looked it up.

Developed in the early 20th century by French criminologist Dr Edmond Locard, this is a familiar concept to anyone who has ever watched crime drama on TV. It can be summarised by the statement 'every contact leaves a trace'.

In other words, wherever we go, whatever and whoever we touch, we will not only leave something of ourselves behind but also take something away with us. I love to explore this idea in my work, along with my *knowing* that cloth holds within its fibres the stories of everything that has come before.

Hand stitching words

I feel that hand stitching is a very special way of recreating words. It's a huge investment in time and patience and I like to think that it gives value to even the most mundane of phrases.

Take time to experiment with the type and thickness of thread you are using and, of course, the stitch. Chain stitch works well when working on a larger scale, stem stitch looks great as does couching, where a line of thread is laid to form the shape of your letters over the surface of your fabric, and then held in place with tiny stitches in a finer thread.

I mostly stitch life-sized handwriting, so I work with one strand of embroidery cotton or fine silk, a size 9 embroidery needle and a tiny back stitch. I'm not particular about the length of each stitch having to be even, but I'm sure the authors of my old needlework books would not approve of this. Using tiny stitches to recreate handwritten text takes practice, but keep at it and you will start to develop your own style – whether that's neat and precise, or wild and unruly, this will add a bit of your personality into the work you are creating.

BELOW: Sample showing words stitched in chain stitch, stem stitch, couching and back stitch.

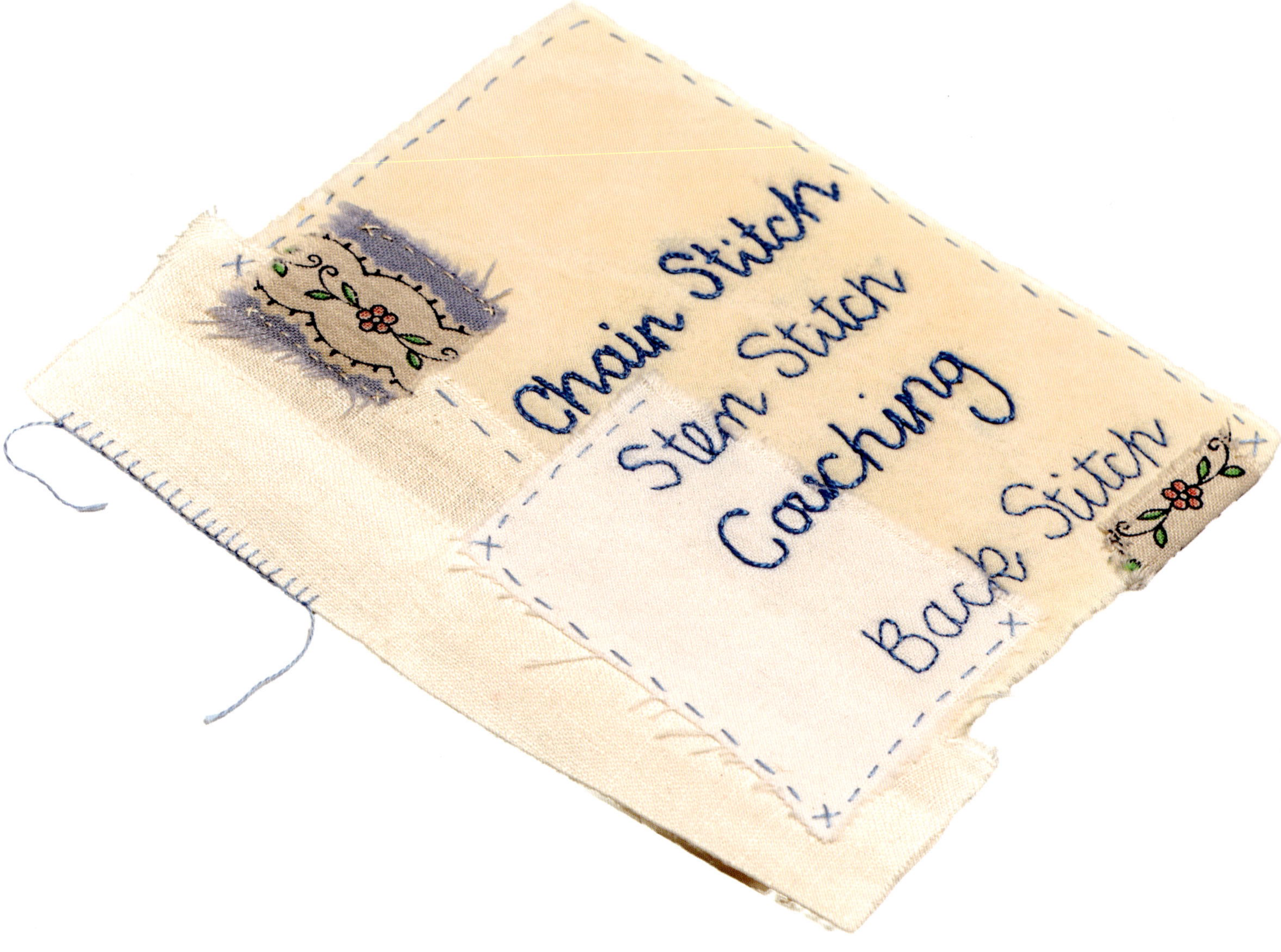

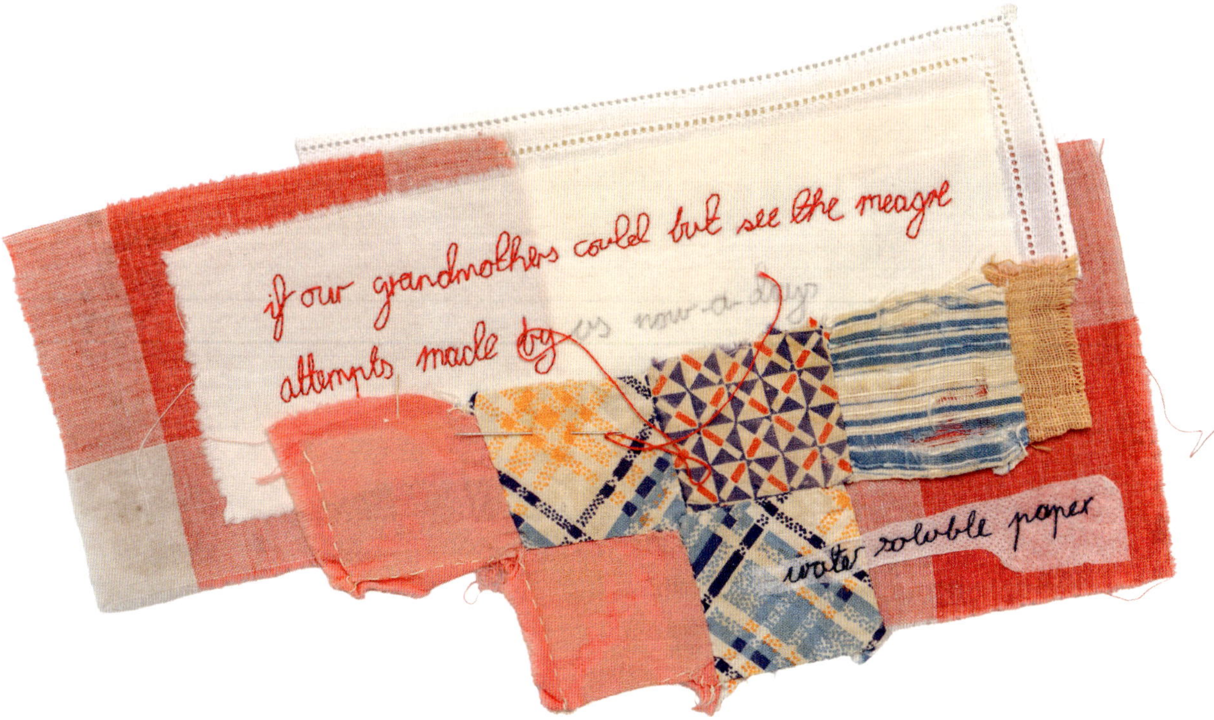

Once again, I turn to my vintage books for inspiration, but also look at the initials stitched in the corners of old handkerchiefs, tea towels, table linens and pillowslips. I particularly love the cross stitch initials beautifully stitched, often as simple laundry markers, on old French linens.

I tend to work on lightweight, light-coloured fabrics. I write my words on vellum and, working over a lightbox, I hold my fabric taut and trace using a light hand and sharp pencil.

Wonky cross stitch lettering

I use a cross stitch chart from an old needlework book called *Needlework for Student Teachers*, written by Amy K. Smith in 1897, as reference for my lettering. You can find many different styles of cross stitch lettering in embroidery books. My preference is for old books and magazines, but charts are also available online, or you could design your own lettering on graph paper. You could also use old stitch samplers as reference.

ABOVE: At the top of the sample the words were traced onto the fabric in pencil before being attached to the background and water-soluble paper was used for the text at the bottom. The words are stitched in a tiny back stitch.

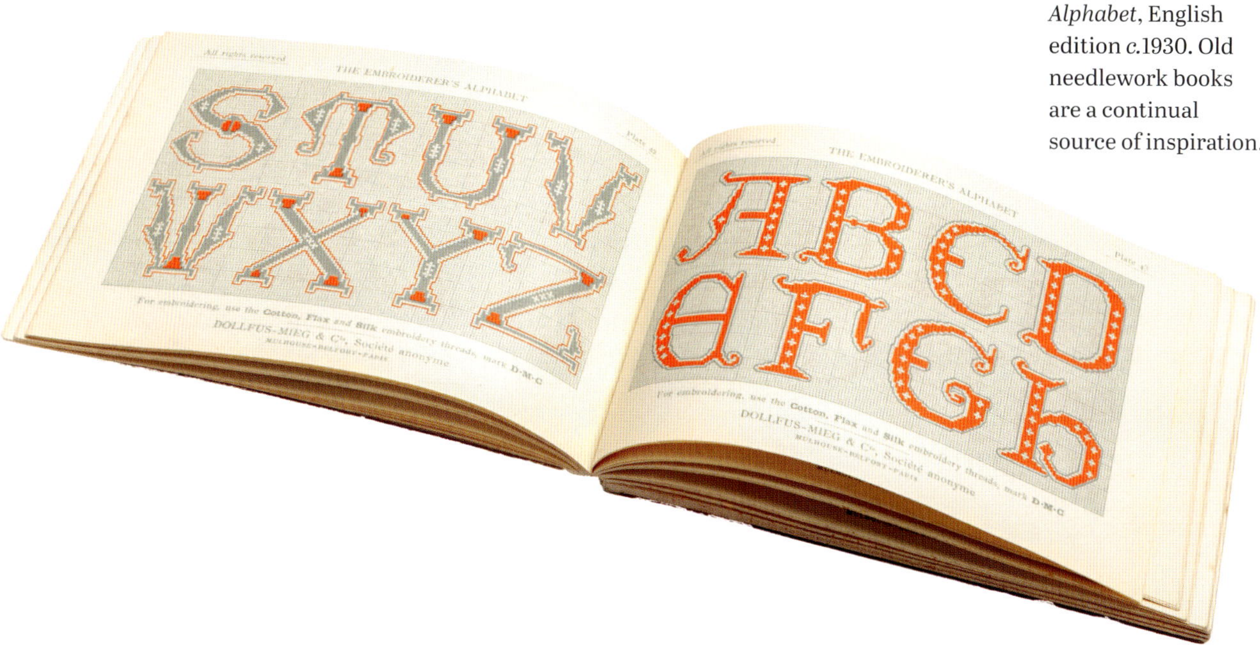

BELOW: Pages from *The Embroiderer's Alphabet*, English edition *c.*1930. Old needlework books are a continual source of inspiration.

AN EASY METHOD

You will need sticky, water-soluble embroidery stabilizer sheets, vellum and graph paper. Note: This is only suitable for projects that can be immersed in water.

1. Draw your cross stitch lettering onto a piece of graph paper and then trace onto vellum.

2. Place your vellum on a light box and trace your pattern onto the water-soluble paper using a sharp pencil.

3. Cut out and peel away the backing paper.

4. Position and stick it onto your fabric and then you're ready to stitch.

5. Once stitching is complete, wash away the stabilizer with warm water.

I call this process 'wonky' cross stitch lettering because I'm not always accurate in drawing my crosses, so I must sometimes alter their size when stitching to make them align!

Sticky, water-soluble sheets with a grid printed on them are also available, but these are expensive. I sometimes print my design onto the water-soluble sheets with my inkjet printer. I recommend creating a sample first to test that the ink washes away without leaving any trace.

These sheets are also useful to transfer handwritten text or motif outlines onto your fabric if your project can be immersed in water.

BELOW: Sample showing the different stages of cross stitch lettering made with water-soluble embroidery paper. The 'S' shows the result when the paper has been washed away. It is stitched with a single strand of silk.

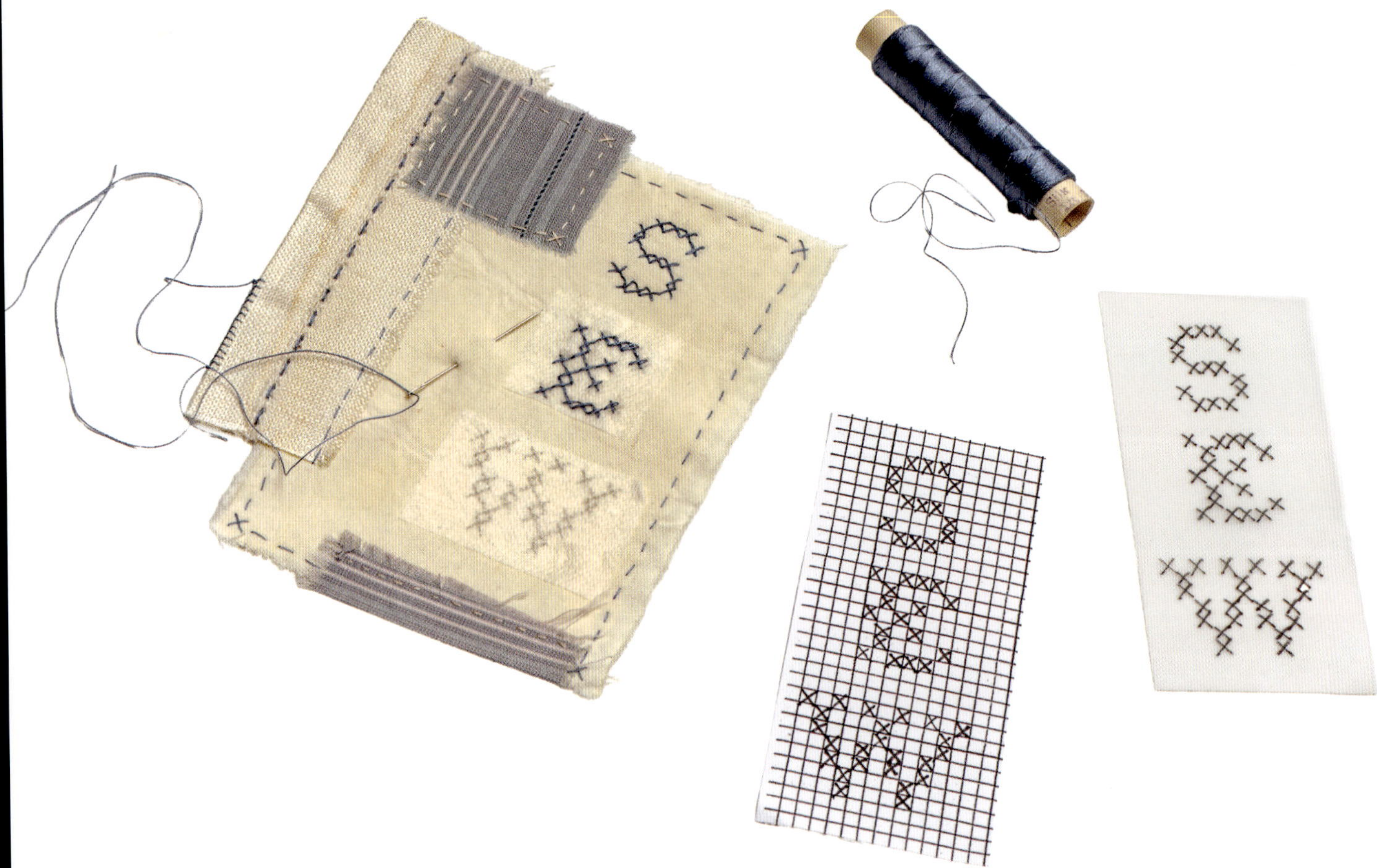

More ways of creating text on fabric

Depending on the project, there are several other quick and easy ways of creating text on fabric. I suggest that you try out any technique on a scrap of similar fabric first, before working on your actual piece. These methods are not washable.

Printing small pieces of fabric using a computer and inkjet printer

This method works for printing onto a small patch of fabric, or onto cotton tape or ribbon. You will need a lightweight, cotton fabric.

Type your text on your screen, in the middle of your page. You want the paper to feed normally through your printer, so leave a good space at the top. It may be helpful to create a text box in your document and type into this. Print this onto a sheet of paper.

Place your patch of fabric (right side up) over the printed words and attach with masking tape along the top edge. Do this over a lightbox or hold your paper up to the window so that you can see the position of your words. Carefully smooth the fabric and stick more tape over the bottom edge. Remove any loose threads. If you've used a text box with a line round it, then turn off the outline, return the paper to the printer and print your document again.

You can, of course, change the appearance by varying the font, size and colour.

Typewriter

If you have an old typewriter, you can simply use masking tape to attach a patch of fabric, top and bottom, to a piece of paper and then feed this into your typewriter.

You can type onto cotton tape by sticking a piece of double-sided tape across a sheet of paper – draw a straight line on the paper first to act as a guide. Feed the paper into your typewriter, remove the backing strip, and stick your fabric tape along the bottom edge. Adjust the typewriter so that it types across the middle of the tape.

Old typewriters can sometimes be found in charity or thrift shops as well as online, and more modern ones are often reasonably priced. Check that you can source a ribbon for it before buying.

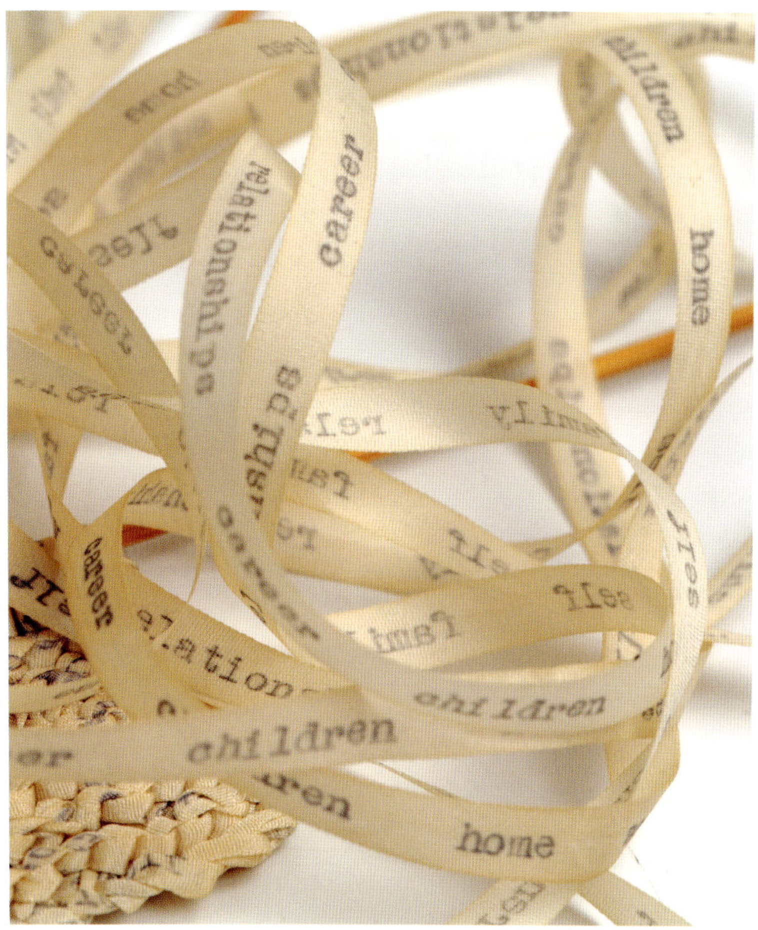

BELOW: Words typed along several metres of coffee-stained silk ribbon.

Pencil and stencil

You can simply write with pencil on fabric either by using a stencil or your own handwriting. For best results you'll need a smooth, fine-weave fabric and you will need to hold the fabric taut as you write. You could also tape your fabric down onto a smooth surface. You may wish to spray your text afterwards with a fixative to prevent smudging. Fabric pens are also readily available.

'Ransom note' lettering

This is great fun for some projects. I use letters cut from vintage magazines with their soft, muted brown paper. Cut the letters from different headlines so that you vary the font, colour and size.

I use a very fine paintbrush to apply matte medium to the reverse of the cutout, and then use a clean rag to press it down onto the fabric surface.

Rubber stamps and ink

Alphabet stamps come in a variety of fonts and sizes, as do beautiful old letterpress wooden printing blocks. I use them with an inkpad, although you can also use paints. I wipe any excess ink off the edges of my stamp blocks with a soft rag before stamping and I work on a padded surface.

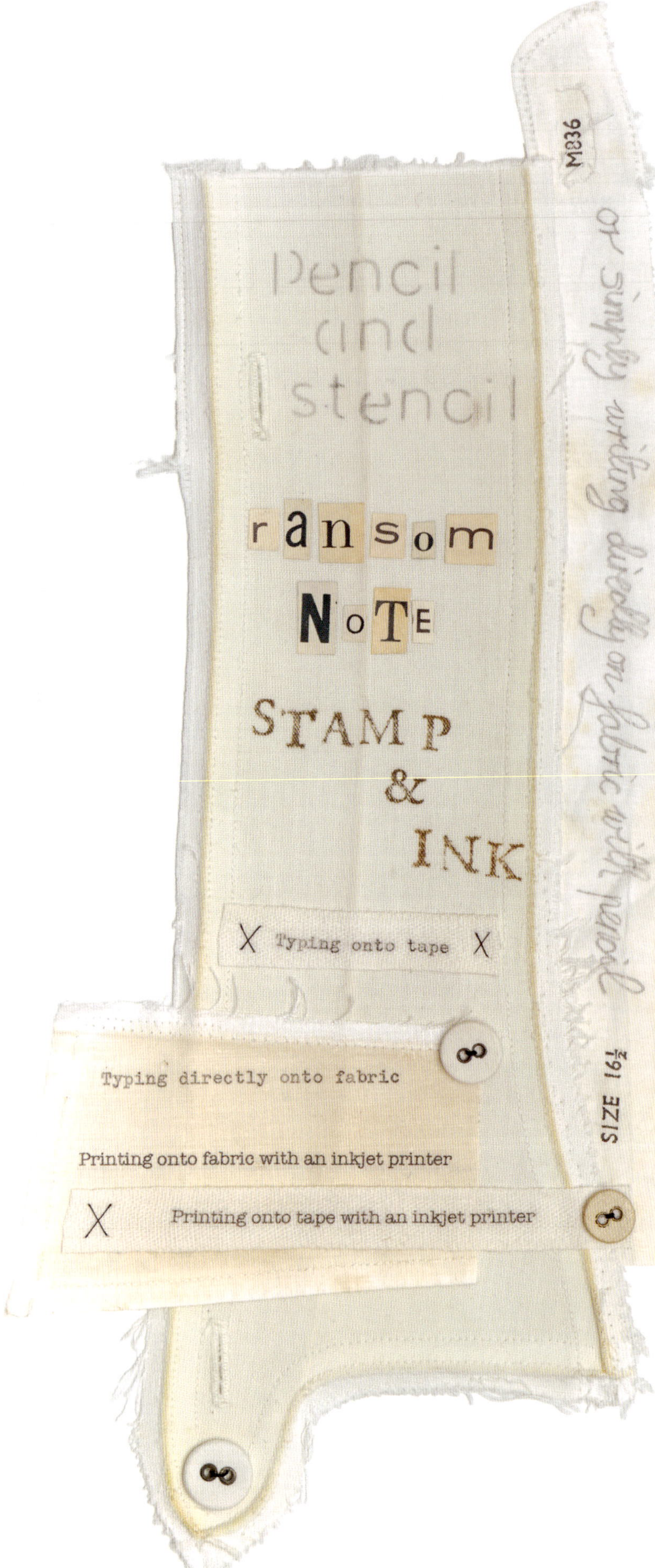

RIGHT: Sample showing different ways of creating text on fabric. I keep all my samples for future reference and therefore love them to be inspiring in themselves. The one shown here is made from an old detachable shirt collar.

Rusting powder

This product works by sprinkling the rusting powder over glue and shaking off the excess before spritzing with water. Follow manufacturer's instructions for your product (and see page 120). Be prepared for a lot of experimentation as I've found that results can be variable, but it is worth persisting as I love the effect for certain projects. Always do test samples!

Work on top of a piece of paper so that you can catch the excess powder when you shake it off your fabric, much as you would if working with glitter. After you have shaken off as much as you can, use an air puffer to blow across the surface to remove more.

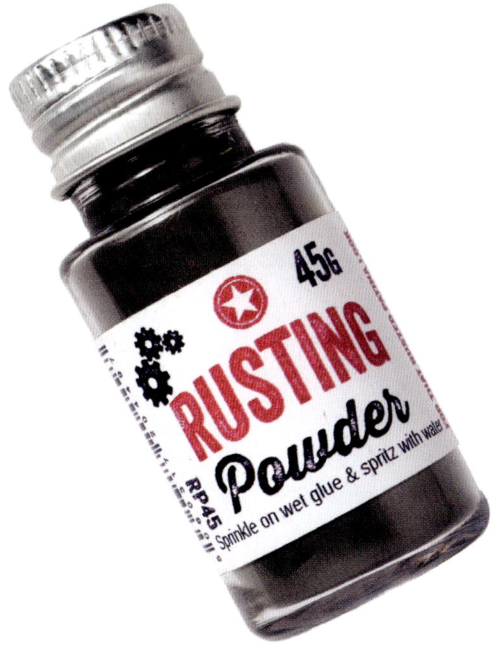

BELOW, TOP: A fine paint brush was used to thinly paint matte medium onto rubber stamps, which were then stamped onto fabric before applying rusting powder.

BELOW, BOTTOM: A fine glue pen was used to write on the fabric before applying rusting powder.

These samples were spritzed with a mix of 75% water and 25% vinegar.

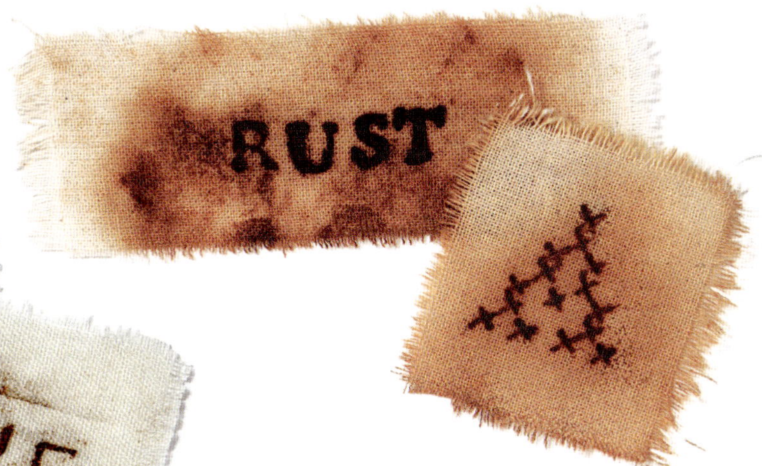

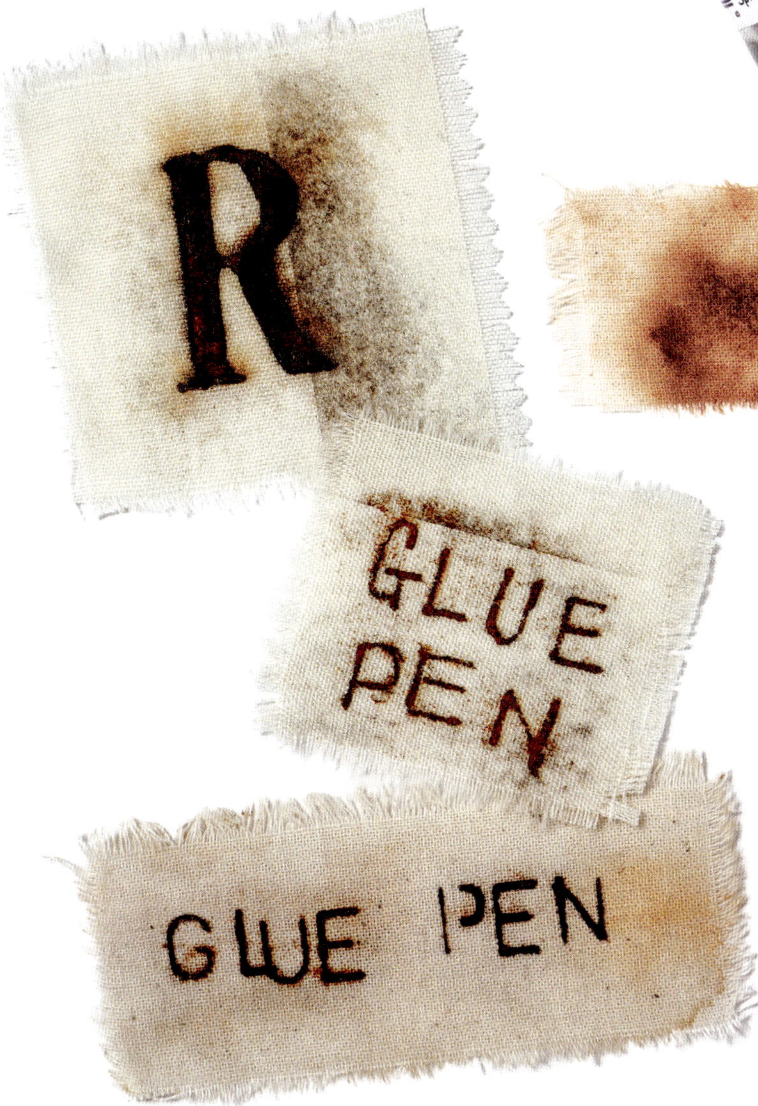

LEFT, TOP: A paint brush was used to thinly paint PVA onto a wooden printer's block, which was then stamped onto fabric before applying rusting powder.

LEFT, MIDDLE: A fine glue pen was used to write on the fabric before applying rusting powder.

LEFT, BOTTOM: A fine glue pen and a stencil were used to write on the fabric.

Each of these samples was spritzed with water.

Written words

I think that words have a habit of finding you – they jump out and ensnare you when you least expect them to. Have you ever read a line of poetry that leaps straight from the page into your heart? Or read a news headline that floors you in your sadness and fury? Taking these words and creating *threads of thought* around them can provide fabulous inspiration for an emotional and heartfelt piece of work.

On a much more mundane level, I never fail to get excited when I go into a café and find sticky notes and messages covering the walls, and imagine my delight when I came across a collection of handwritten shopping lists dated 1956!

BELOW: This collection of shopping lists from the 1950s was a wonderful chance find, providing a little snapshot of homelife at that time. I especially love that '20 Woodbines' is listed in each one!

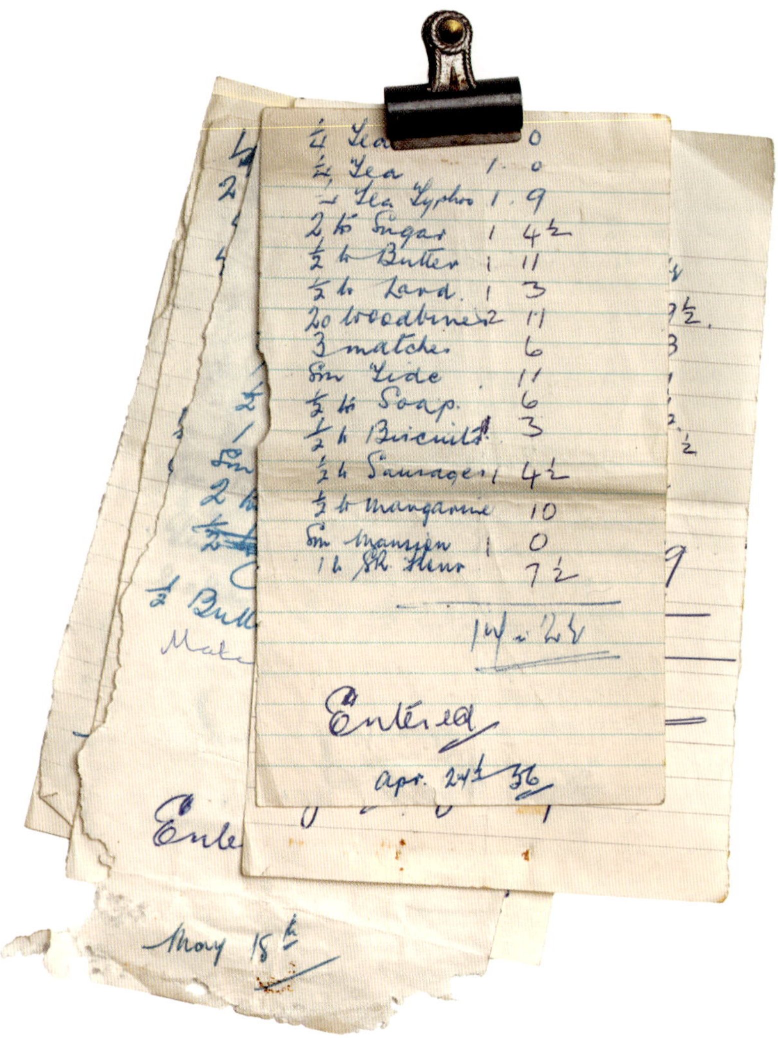

Old needlework books and magazines

'Put all the money you can afford into good materials and handsome accessories.'
Vogue Smart Dressmaking

One of my favourite sources of words, I love glancing through my old needlework books and magazines and often words and phrases catch my eye. I'll write them down along with a note of their origin. I especially enjoy some of the rather rigid instructions for stitching techniques. For example, when stitching the alphabet: 'Every letter must be complete by itself; that is to say, a strand of cotton must not, upon any account, be passed from one letter to another, but each letter should be finished off before the next is commenced.' This is from *Needlework for Student Teachers* by Amy K. Smith (1897).

My favourite quote also comes from this book in the introduction written by 'The Lady Wolverton'. She tells the story of a brigade of old women in her village who spent their time sitting round the fire talking about the old days and complaining about their rheumatism. Her solution was to start a sewing group because 'if their fingers were busy their hearts would rest more'; a sentiment with which I'm sure that everyone involved in a craft would wholeheartedly agree. You'll find these wonderful words stitched onto my *Stitcher's Smock* on page 98 – and yes, I did pass my thread from one letter to another during the stitching!

Witch bottles

Sometimes, while you are engrossed in a story, and least expecting it, you'll read a word or two that spark intrigue and the need to find out more.

Several years ago, I was reading a novel about an antique dealer who came across a 'witch bottle'. I have a fascination for old customs and rituals for protecting the home, so the novel was quickly abandoned as I went on a hunt to find out more. What a wonderfully fascinating rabbit hole of information to get immersed in! If it intrigues you at all, then do your own online search and see where it takes you.

Put very briefly, witch bottles were used around the 17th century to counteract spells cast by witches. At this time, misfortunes such as crops failing, a run of bad luck or illness were often blamed on witchcraft. Witch bottles were made, often by a folk healer or wise person, in glass or stoneware vessels.

Contents of some surviving bottles have been examined and they commonly include urine, nail clippings and human hair – thought to belong to the person who was ill or bewitched. They often contain bent pins and nails – thought to have been added to cause harm to the witch. Other contents have included herbs, red wine and even heart-shaped pieces of cloth! The bottles were buried around the hearth, doorway or windows or put into the fire. Experts believe that the contents were to attract the witch into the bottle, where they would become trapped and stabbed by the pins and nails. If the bottle was burned, then the liquid would boil and cause the bottle to explode. Whatever the means of disposal, the intention was to cause pain or death to the witch, thus causing the spell to be lifted and the person to be cured.

I kept this information in a sketchbook and came across it years later. Fascinated once more, I decided to create some *threads of thought* and see where they would take me. As my pen touched paper the word 'witch' turned to 'wish' and I began to imagine creating a bottle where the intention was to attract good fortune, rather than as an object of protection against bad. I knew immediately that the first item in each bottle would be a cloth heart.

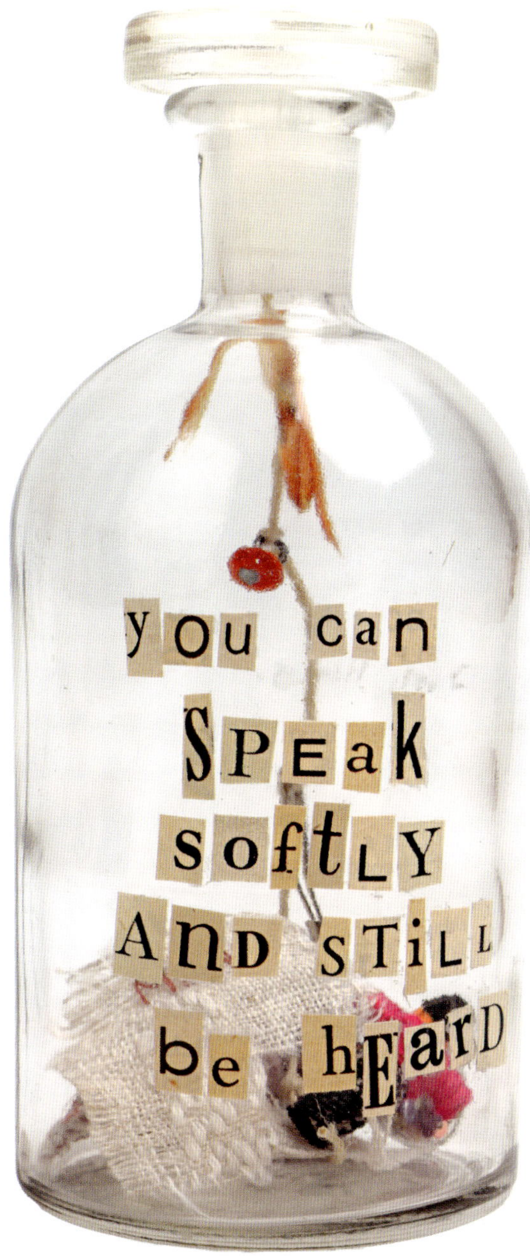

LEFT: *You Can Speak Softly and Still be Heard*. Wish bottle made from a vintage laboratory bottle. I glued letters cut from old newspapers and magazines onto the outside.

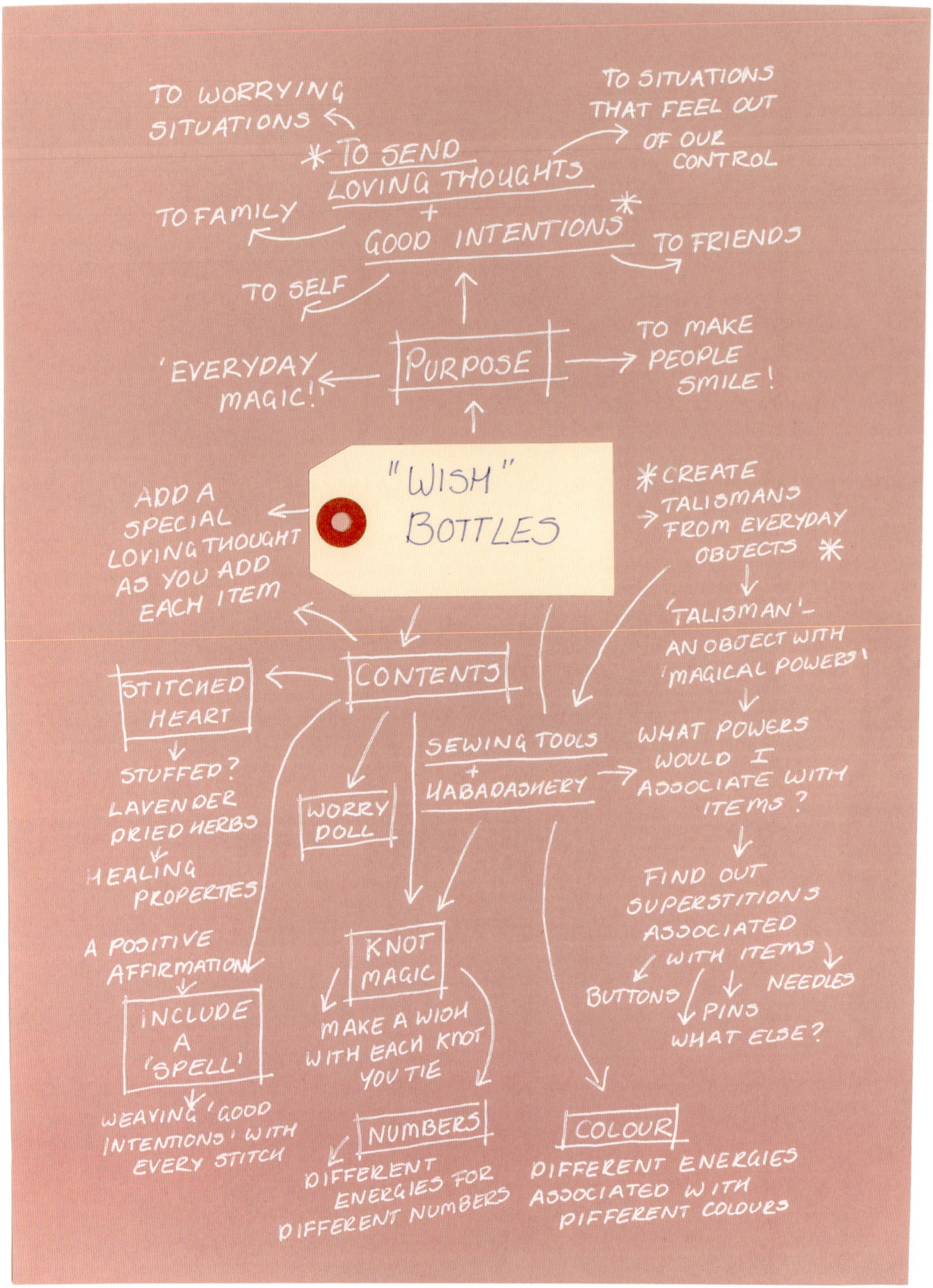

TO WORRYING SITUATIONS
TO SITUATIONS THAT FEEL OUT OF OUR CONTROL
* TO SEND LOVING THOUGHTS + GOOD INTENTIONS *
TO FAMILY
TO FRIENDS
TO SELF
PURPOSE
'EVERYDAY MAGIC!'
TO MAKE PEOPLE SMILE!
"WISH" BOTTLES
ADD A SPECIAL LOVING THOUGHT AS YOU ADD EACH ITEM
* CREATE TALISMANS FROM EVERYDAY OBJECTS *
'TALISMAN' – AN OBJECT WITH 'MAGICAL POWERS'
WHAT POWERS WOULD I ASSOCIATE WITH ITEMS?
FIND OUT SUPERSTITIONS ASSOCIATED WITH ITEMS
BUTTONS
PINS
NEEDLES
WHAT ELSE?
CONTENTS
STITCHED HEART
STUFFED?
LAVENDER DRIED HERBS
HEALING PROPERTIES
A POSITIVE AFFIRMATION
INCLUDE A 'SPELL'
WEAVING 'GOOD INTENTIONS' WITH EVERY STITCH
WORRY DOLL
SEWING TOOLS + HABADASHERY
KNOT MAGIC
MAKE A WISH WITH EACH KNOT YOU TIE
NUMBERS
DIFFERENT ENERGIES FOR DIFFERENT NUMBERS
COLOUR
DIFFERENT ENERGIES ASSOCIATED WITH DIFFERENT COLOURS

Wish bottles

For this project, I drew on my background in complementary therapies. Around 30 years ago I studied and practised aromatherapy, colour therapy and crystal therapy and I was a Bach Flower Remedy practitioner and reiki master. I practised rituals and created ceremonies and, while it's been many years since I worked with others in this way, little practices and beliefs become part of everyday life and I'm a firm believer in 'everyday magic'.

Whatever your religion or beliefs, creating a bottle of love and good intentions for yourself or another person can only be a good and uplifting thing to do. I also love the idea of creating wish bottles to direct positive energy towards situations in the world that feel out of our control.

CREATING WISH BOTTLES

First, ask yourself: What's the purpose of my bottle? Who or what is it for? What qualities do I wish to bring? Creating your own *threads of thought* will bring ideas for what objects you could use as talismans, and areas that you may wish to find out more about. Perhaps explore folklore and magic, find out about the spiritual properties of colour, crystals and numbers and the healing properties of plants and herbs. A wish bottle really is a lovely project to research.

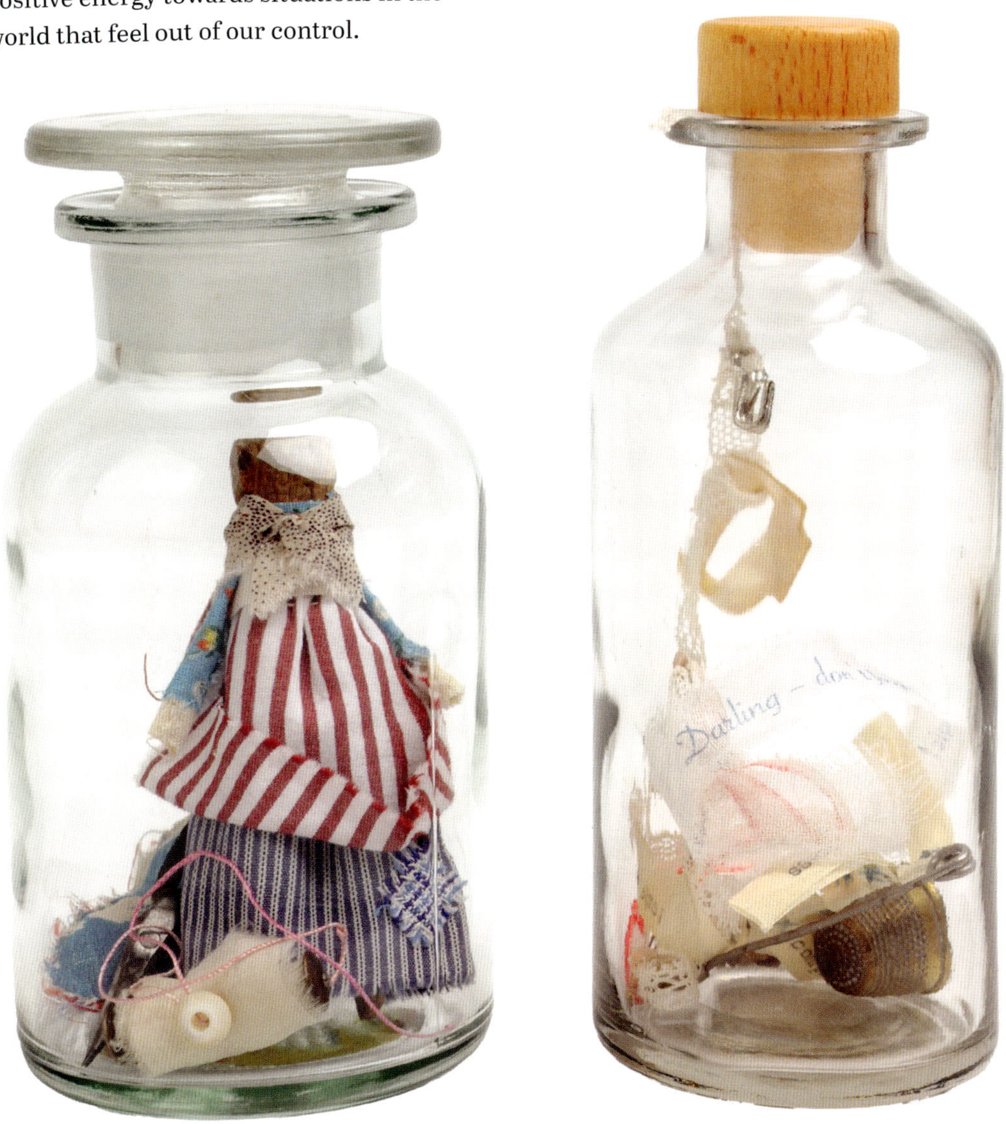

LEFT: *Wish Bottles.* When choosing your bottle take into consideration the size of the neck as it has to be big enough to allow you to place your talismans inside. I used long tweezers for these.

SUGGESTED BOTTLE CONTENTS

Have fun with this!

Cloth heart: Inspired by my witch bottle research, I like to include a cloth heart. I made little stuffed hearts (remember that it will need to be small enough to go through the neck of your bottle) decorated with fabric scraps and tiny stitches.

Doll (inspired by Guatemalan worry dolls): Drawing on happy memories of making peg dolls with my mum and now making them with my grandchildren, I decided to include a peg 'worry doll'. I love the idea of adding happy memories to my bottle. This doll is also inspired by Mandy Pattullo's collection of beautiful peg dolls featured in my book *Cloth Stories*.

My mind went back to my exploration of east-coast fishwives and the qualities that they would bring to my spell jar – resilience, strength, enterprise, independence, loyalty and a strong sense of family.

Spells or affirmations: I included a positive message or affirmation in each bottle. They were either printed on silk or stuck to the outside of my bottle in 'ransom note style' lettering cut from old magazines.

Knot magic: I purposely set an intention (with a word or a wish) as I knotted objects onto a piece of string or lace. I chose objects that would help 'hold things together' such as buttons, buckles, hooks and eyes, safety pins and a bunch of ribbons. After all, we could all do with a bit of help in 'holding it together' every so often. Numbers are considered to have specific energies, so I deliberately chose the number of knots for the energy I wished to bring. The number five is associated with freedom, adventure and adaptability, while the number seven is associated with inner wisdom and a quest for knowledge and truth.

BELOW AND OPPOSITE: You can really have fun creating your talismans for your wish bottles. Mine included silk with a printed affirmation wound around an old sewing machine bobbin, a peg 'worry doll', knot magic with haberdashery items knotted onto string, a darned patch, a heart made from snippets of fabric and tiny stitches and words typed onto silk ribbon attached to a vintage safety pin.

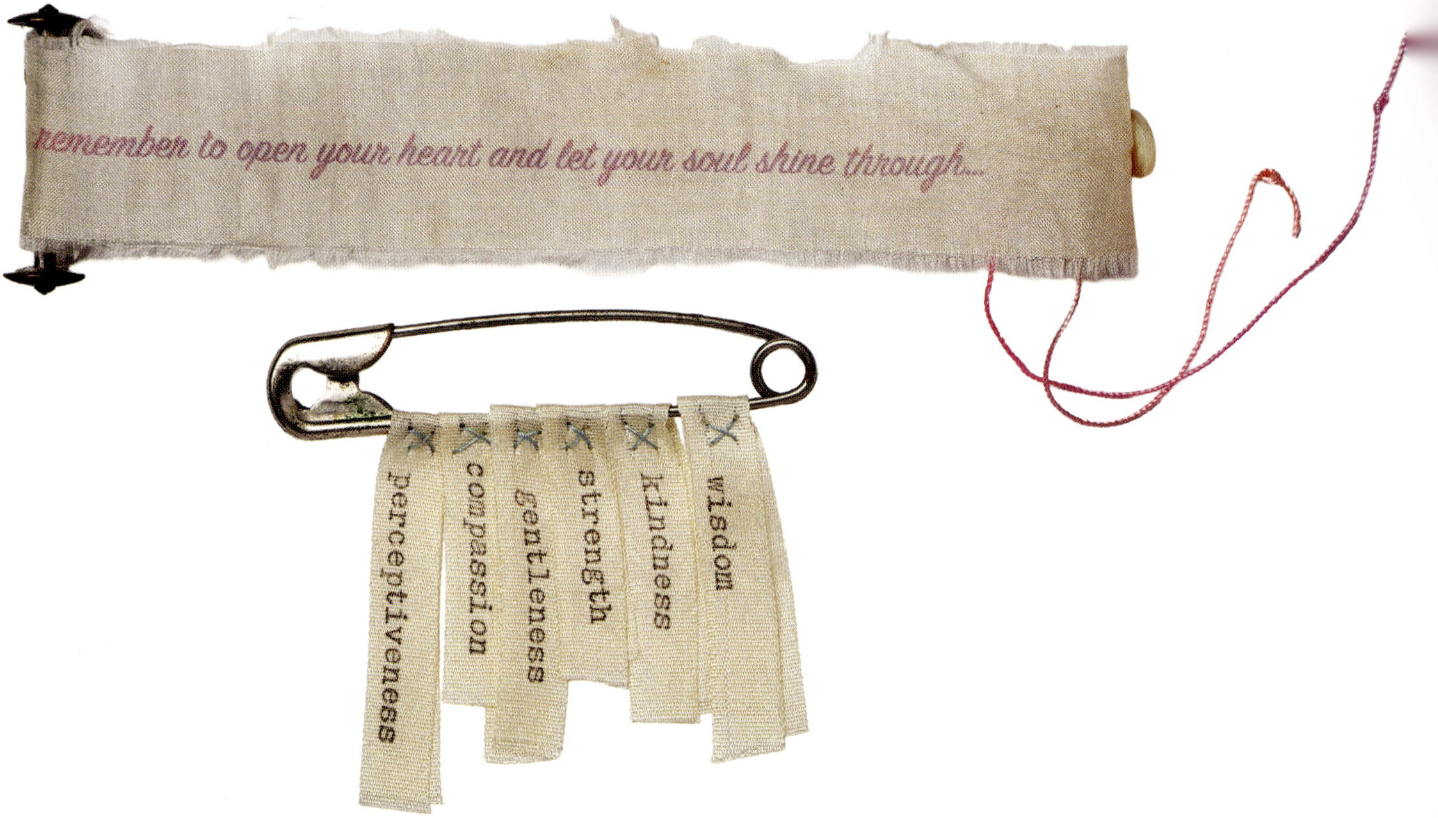

An old shoe or boot button: Apparently, it is bad luck to lose the button from your shoe, so I thought I'd include an extra button for good measure. It's said that the only way to reverse the bad luck is to spit in the left shoe or spit over your left shoulder!

Further contents could be any of the following:

- An old safety pin holding qualities typed on silk ribbon – wisdom, kindness, strength, gentleness, compassion and perceptiveness.
- A rainbow of buttons bringing the energies of each colour.
- A jar of 'sparkles' – for when you have lost yours.
- A jar of sand or earth from a special time or place.
- A thimble for protection.
- A pair of scissors – because sometimes we need to cut ties. I made a wish as I wrapped the thread round the handle.
- A scrap of old fabric with a darn as a reminder that we don't have to be perfect, and are much more interesting as we age.
- A needle and thread because, with those two things, we can mend most things.

Although this may be a fun project to research, plan and make, don't underestimate the healing power of ritualistic acts and intentional thought ... not to mention the everyday magic.

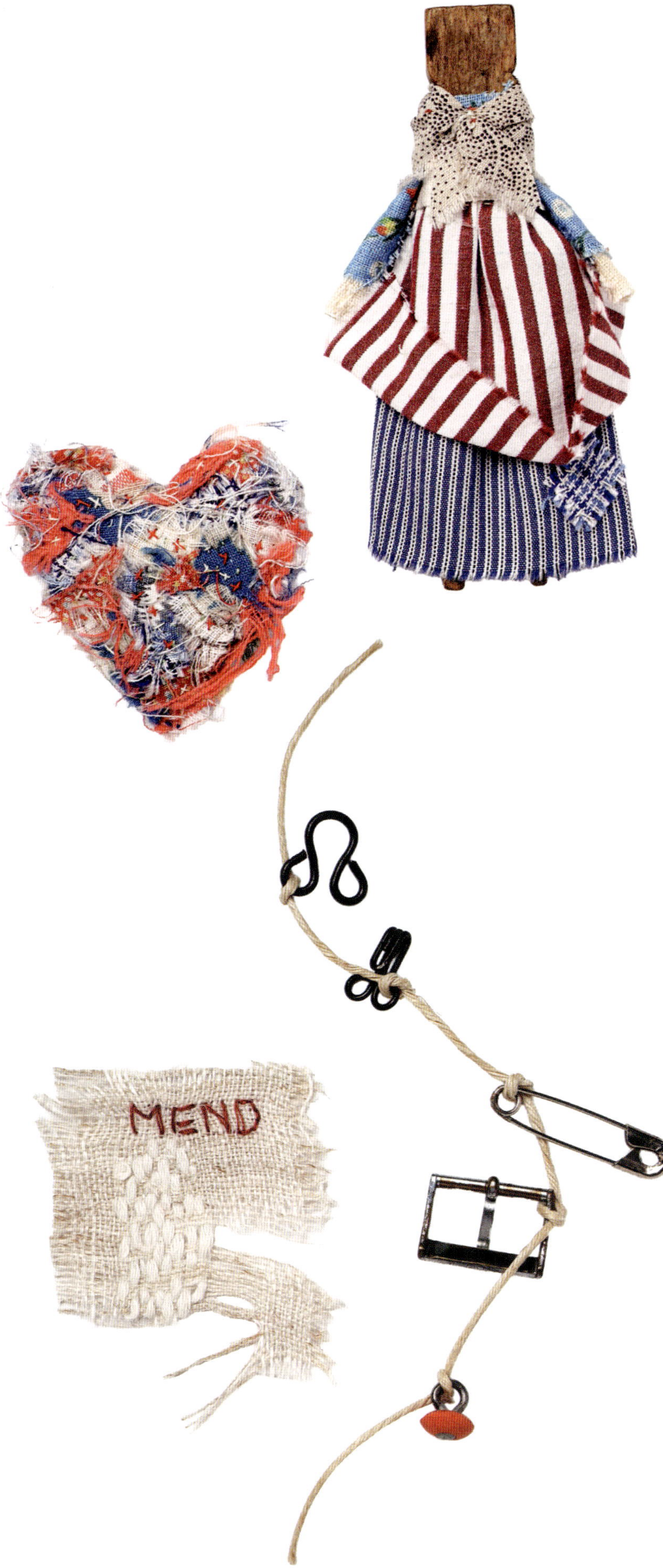

Anne Brooke

Words as prompts

Anne Brooke is a textile artist living in Yorkshire. She brings together stitchers from all over the world with her online community 'hannemadebyanne'. Each year she sets her community the challenge of a small weekly sewing project and in 2025 her challenge was #52Words. Anne has always been inspired by colour and texture, so she decided to explore these further through 52 prompts. She says:

> *When thinking of texture, you immediately use words such as rough, smooth, bumpy, lumpy, and I wondered how these could be interpreted into stitch. I realized that sometimes I would look at a technique or stitch, and a word would come to mind, or I would have a word I loved and had to explore how it could be interpreted.*

Anne decided that this challenge would be one piece, stitched over the 52 weeks within a 48cm (19in) embroidery hoop with techniques and stitches layering and intermingling with each other.

> *Each week my prompt went live with the word, my interpretation, and suggestions of what to do via a video. It's fascinating to see the work that is done after the prompt goes live. Some are like mine, but others take the words and put their own spin on them.*
>
> *It is hard to choose but some of my favourite words have been:*
>
> **Coil:** *Who doesn't love a bullion knot? Quite a few people it turns out, so I have made it my mission to convince them that this is a lovely stitch to add to your repertoire.*
>
> **Wall:** *I have a love of learning and this year I learned to crochet – but in my own way. Building a wall of crochet added a lovely 3D effect to the hoop.*
>
> **Wrap:** *As a Yorkshire lass, I had to add some 'Yorkshire flowers' to the hoop. This is the spider's wheel part of the Yorkshire button before it is stuffed.*
>
> **Limpet:** *I can't help collecting things when going on a walk, so this was inspired by the many limpets I have collected, mainly on the Yorkshire coast.*

BELOW: *#52words2025.* 19in quilting hoop with linen, fabric, threads and embellishments. The techniques used were inspired by each week's word.

OPPOSITE, CLOCKWISE FROM TOP LEFT: Coil, Wall, Limpet and Wrap.

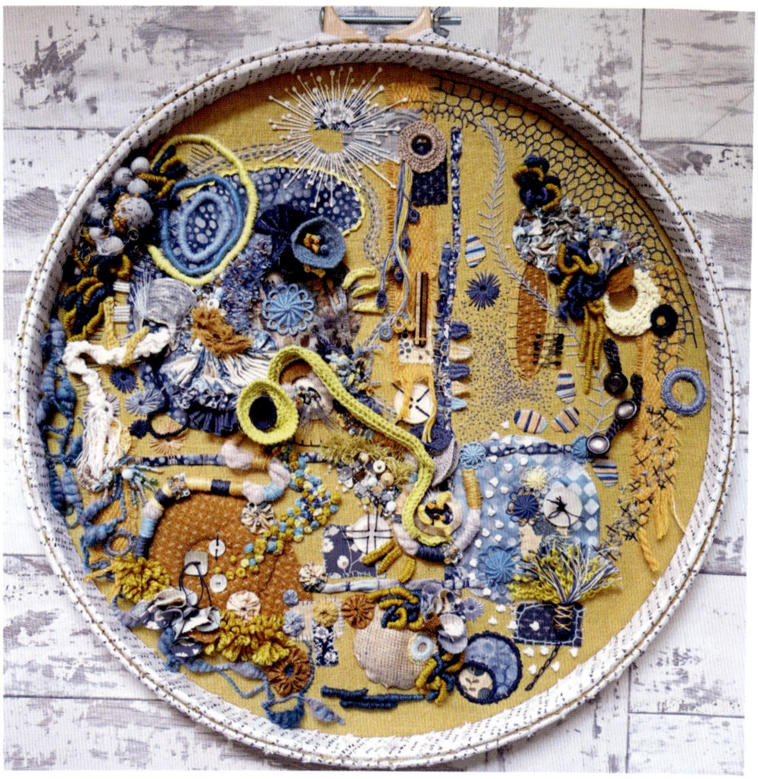

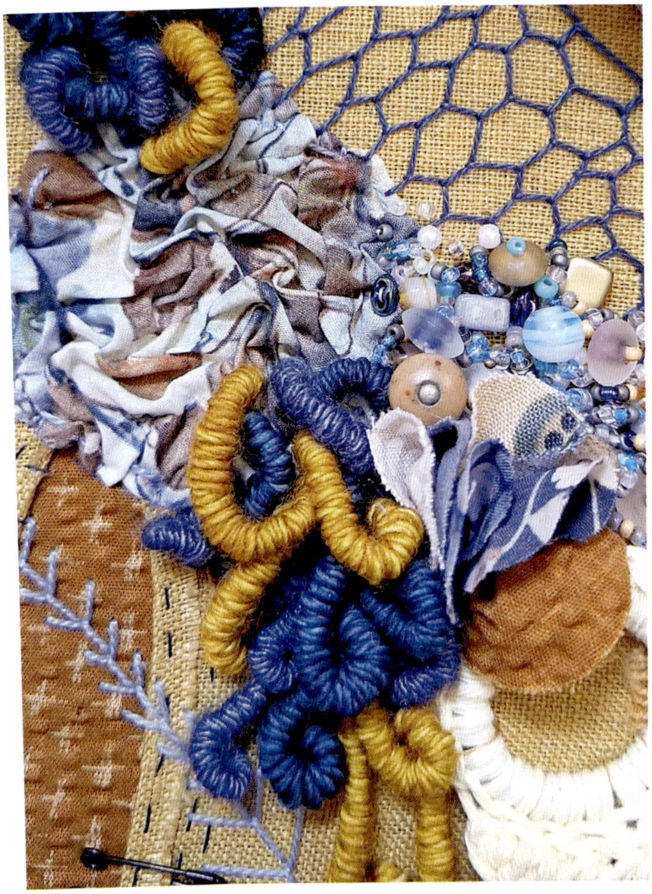
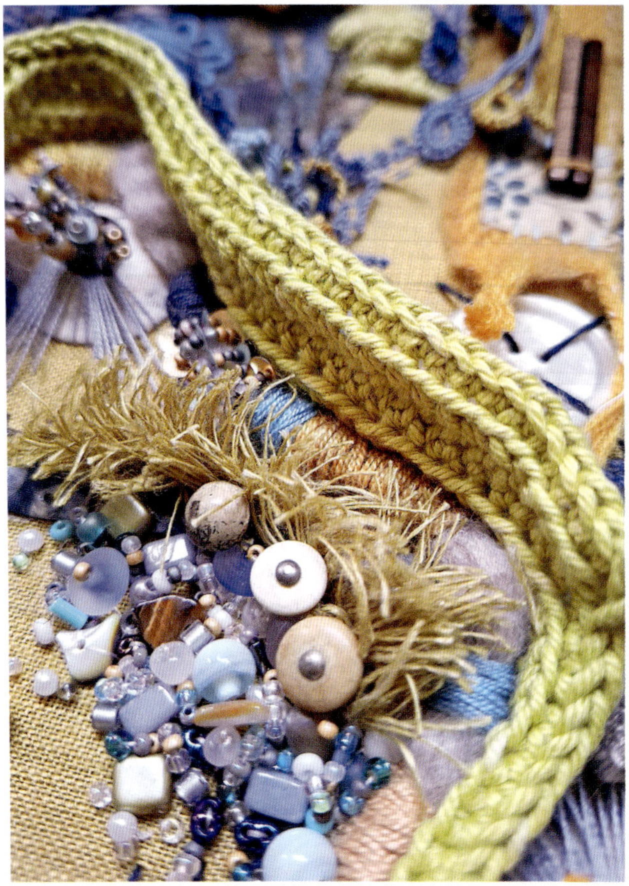
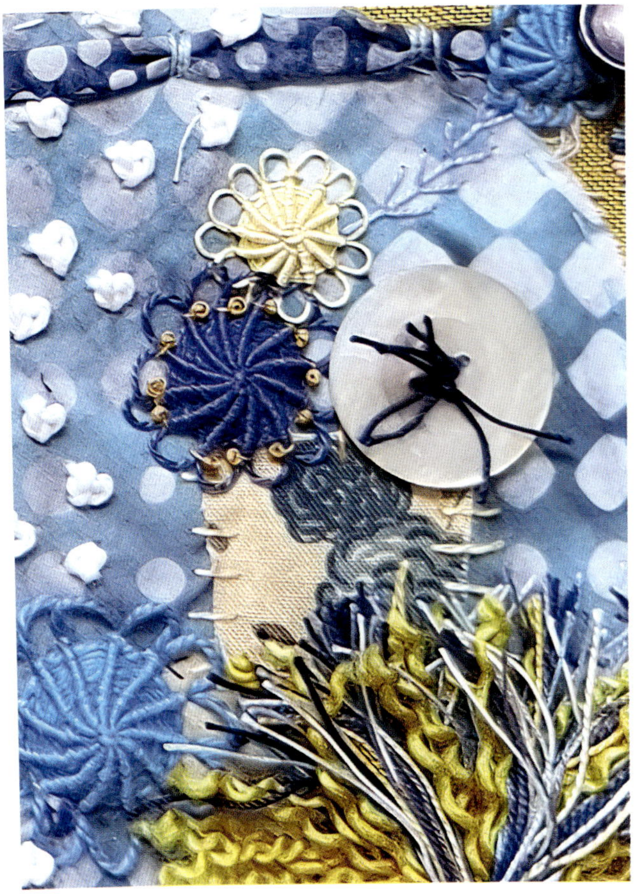
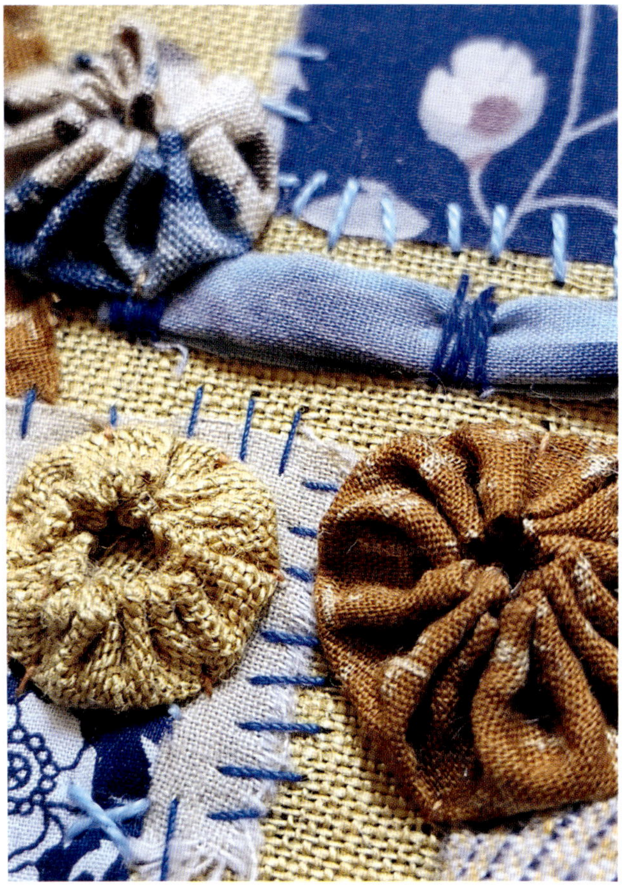

Catherine Hill

Words from memories

Storytelling, words and hand stitching are at the heart of Catherine Hill's work. With each letter slowly hand embroidered using vintage Sylko thread in her favourite colour of Turkey Red, her work reflects her life. Her stitched Keepsakes hold memories of her busy childhood home in Lancashire.

DUFFLE COAT TOGGLES

My duffle coat was a well-worn and cherished hand-me-down made of woollen cloth and wooden toggles. I could tackle any weather that winter had to offer, wrapped up tight in my duffle coat. These precious wooden toggles were found in my mum's button tin.

Hand-embroidered words: 'Snow is falling ... school finishes early ... bus stops at the bottom of the hill and we've a long walk back home in the dark ... wellies, duffle coat, scarf ... forgot the gloves today and my hands are frozen ... snow is deep and getting deeper ... strong wind and driving thick snow ... our school bags get heavier with every step ... home at last ... warm air on my face ... smell baking – flour on mum's apron ... it's pie for tea ... my favourite.'

BELOW AND OPPOSITE: *Duffle Coat Toggles*, 5 × 141cm (2 × 55½in), unravelled. *Dad's Pencils*, 6 × 84cm (2½ × 33in), unravelled. *Door Key*, 8 × 57cm (3 × 22½in), unravelled. Vintage Sylko thread, naturally dyed cotton cloth made from a deconstructed old pillowcase. Hand embroidered text in couching and back stitch with handmade cord from vintage thread.

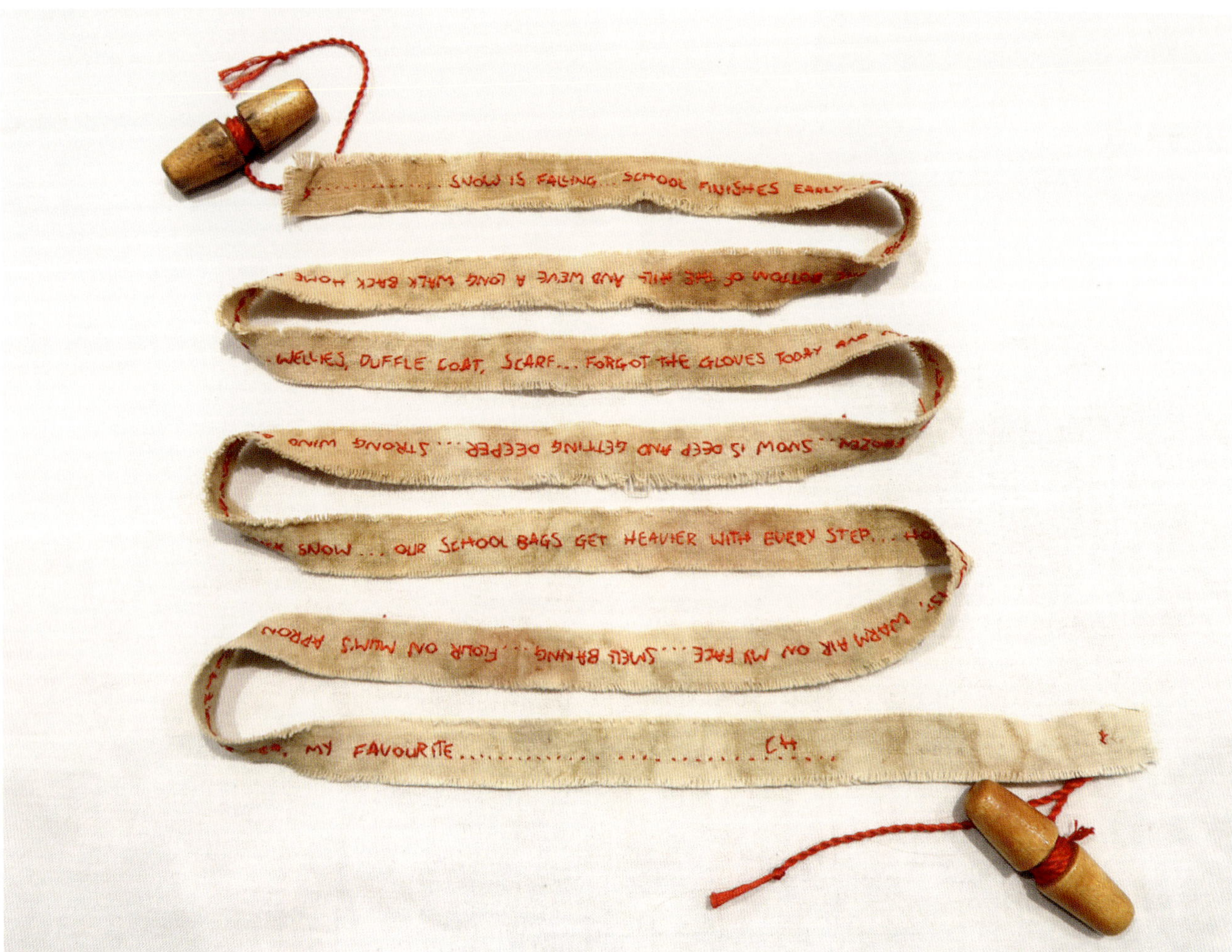

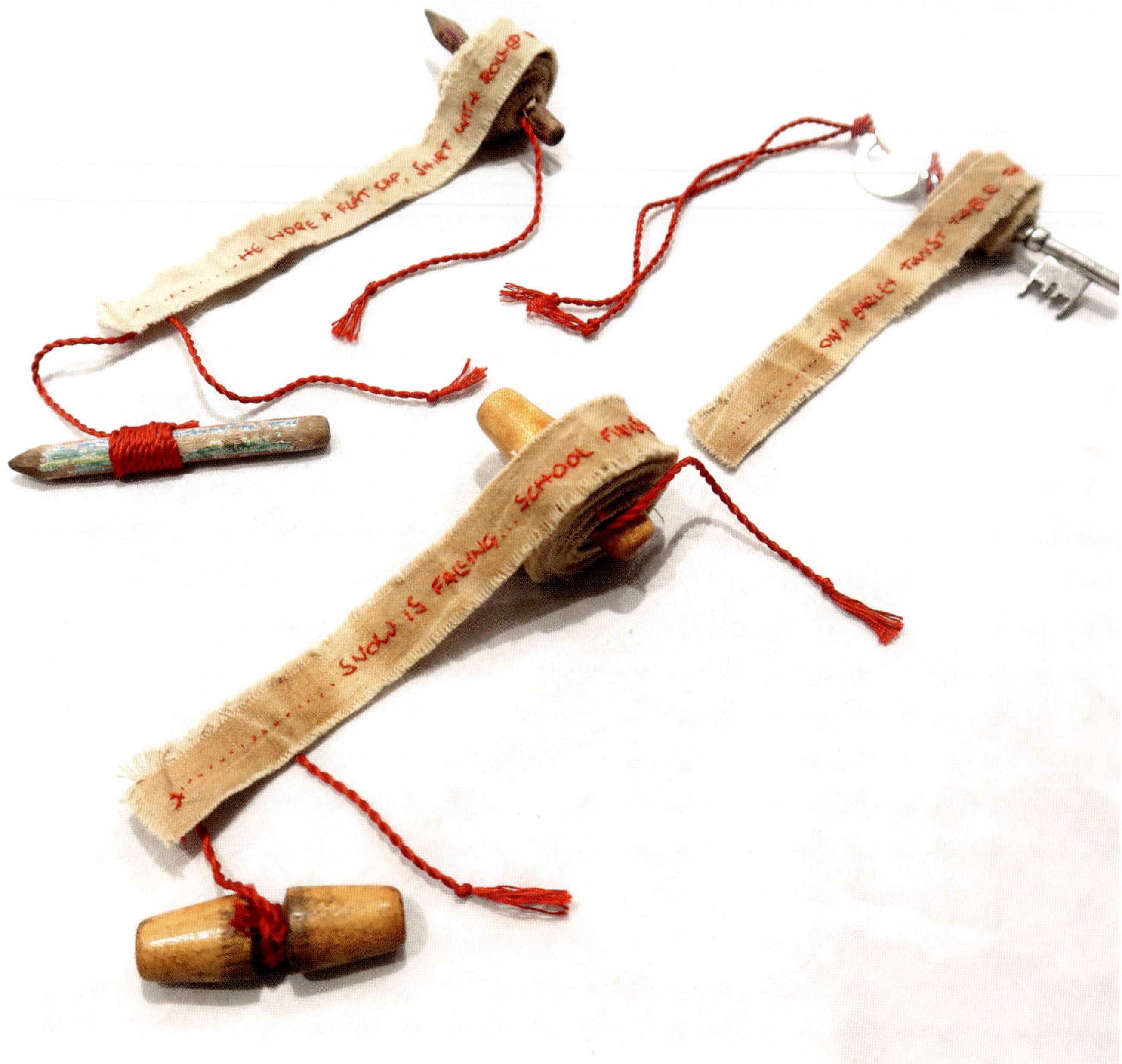

DAD'S PENCILS

Whether he was working on stone flags or timber, Dad always had a sharpened pencil tucked behind his ear and ready to use. These treasured pencils were discovered on my dad's workbench in the cellar.

Hand-embroidered words: 'He wore a flat cap, shirt with rolled up sleeves and always had crisp turn-ups on his trousers filled with grit. Of an evening he'd put his dusty cap down with his keys, a pencil he'd sharpened with a Stanley knife and a torn scrap of cereal box he used for writing on.'

DOOR KEY

I walked past them every day before I left the house and there was a comfort in seeing them there – Mum's keys. If they were on the hall table, it meant she was home. This key once opened my childhood home.

Hand-embroidered words: 'On a barley twist table that bakes in the sun, at the foot of the stairs in the hall, on a fob on a chain near a shiny black phone, lives a bundle of keys to our home.'

Treasured words

Some projects become a labour of love. In my first book, *Cloth Stories*, I shared a patchwork project (with instructions for this wonky log cabin-style of stitching) that was inspired by my granny's well-used sayings. I wanted to preserve her words, spoken in Doric, the local dialect of north-east Scotland that I first heard in my childhood and have been repeated increasingly by my mum in recent years.

I felt compelled to develop the idea further and work on a wonky patchwork quilt that would not only celebrate the women that came before me, but also a way of life. I've stitched more of my granny's sayings on the central patch of each block, but around the sides I've stitched some of my mum's words – little excerpts from her stories of childhood.

I'm incredibly lucky that my mum is a natural storyteller and that in her mid-seventies she started writing them down. Her collection of memories became a book, much of it written in the Doric, and this is now a much-treasured possession. Starting in the early 1930s, she tells tales of her family and how her dad Wullie Smith was *gaen up in the world fae cottar tae crofter* or, in other words, going up in the world from farm labourer to owner of a tiny smallholding.

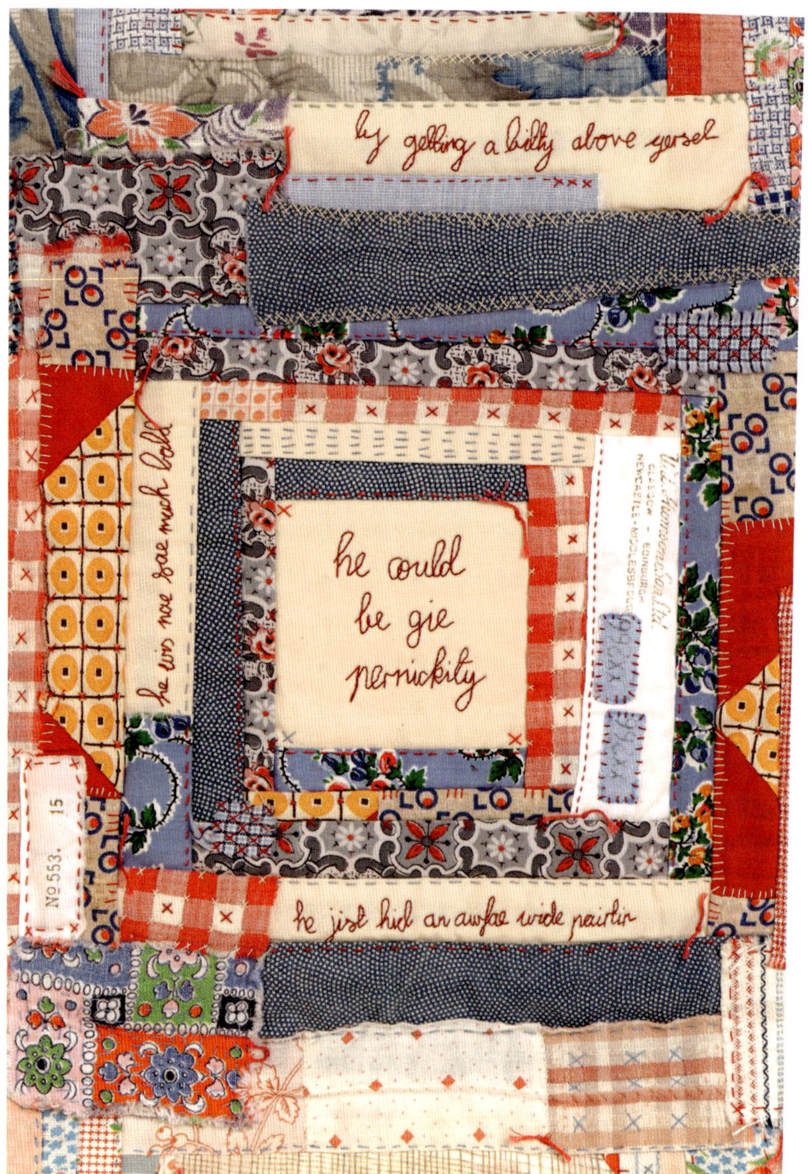

RIGHT: *Mum's Quilt* (detail). *He could be gie pernickity*, meaning 'he could be awfully fussy about detail!'

As my mum's memory declines, I can't describe how important these 'couthy wee tales' have become to me and how the act of stitching this piece has been, in the words of Louise Bourgeois, truly a 'process of emotional repair'.

The stitched words are tiny fragments of these stories, a sentence taken from here and there, one of my favourites being *ma fit on the treadle jist wouldnae work wi ma brain, so ah hid tae stick tae shewin awthin by haun,* which translates to 'my foot on the treadle just wouldn't work with my brain, so I had to stick to sewing everything by hand.' Perhaps this goes some way to explaining why I am reluctant to use a sewing machine!

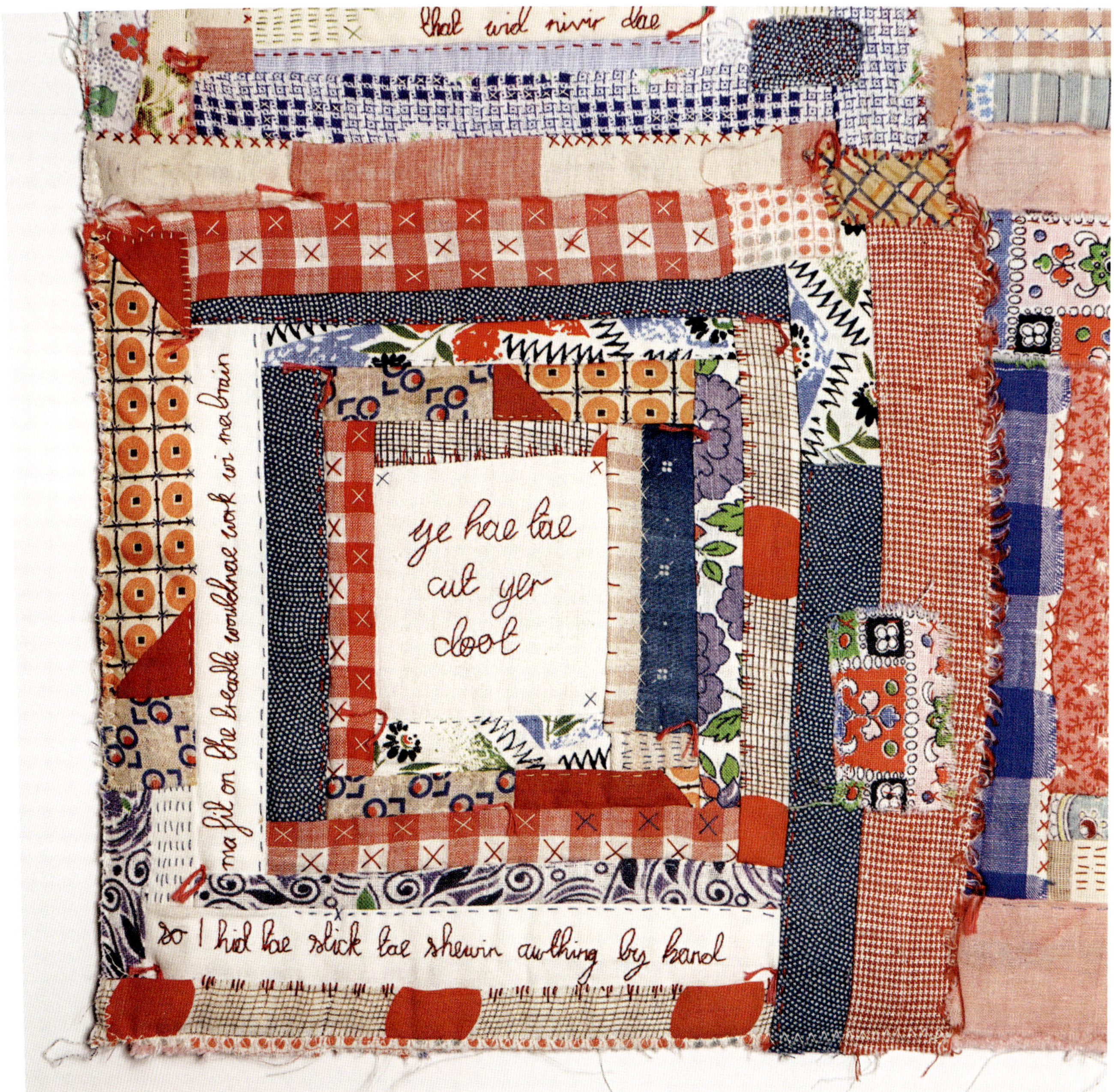

BELOW: *Mum's Quilt* (detail). *Ye hae tae cut yer cloot*, meaning 'you have to cut your cloth' – in other words rein in your spending to suit your budget.

A labour of love

Each block was worked separately on a foundation of worn brushed cotton sheeting. I gathered a large selection of materials such as 1930s and 1940s dress fabric scraps, pieces of old aprons and shirts including buttonhole bands and collars, scraps of my first school sewing project and cloth unpicked from old quilts. I wrote my chosen words on sticky notes, arranged them on paper and worked out everything else as I went along.

I wrote my words in pencil on rectangles of cotton and used fusible web to attach them to my foundation fabric blocks. Working on one patch at a time, I stitched each phrase in back stitch and then added fabric strips in a loosely based log cabin design. I followed my own style of working where fabrics are ripped and layered, and edges are left raw. I worked intuitively, building each block with colour and pattern before adding decorative stitching. Although I worked on the blocks individually, I deliberately repeated fabrics across the whole quilt, ensuring that the overall look was balanced.

I worked on the quilt sporadically, setting it down for periods of time while I worked on other things. The blocks travelled with me to workshops around the country and I took great pleasure in sharing their stories. I'm slow at stitching, but I don't shy away from adding layer upon layer of decoration – I simply take my time and let it take as long as it takes.

My next stage was to stitch all the blocks onto a backing, for which I used a piece of old woollen blanket. It was important for me to repurpose materials because this is what my family would have done in the past. Nothing would have been bought new and not even the tiniest of scraps would have been wasted.

After all 12 blocks had been stitched in place, I added further joining strips and patches to blend them together. I then chose a piece of old eiderdown fabric to back my quilt and used a sashiko thread to tie the layers together.

This piece isn't completed, as I've not yet finished the edges. I know that its future home is draped over the back of my special chair, but I don't feel ready for it to take up residence there yet. I don't feel ready to finish just now, so I have a feeling that the edging will be added one small piece at a time. When a project is so emotionally charged, I find that it sets its own pace. Maybe it will become a winter project, worked late afternoons in front of the fire as the light fades, or maybe it will be stitched in the garden on sunny summer evenings, or maybe something else. I don't know the answers yet, but I know it'll tell me when the time is right.

OPPOSITE: *Mum's Quilt*, 65 × 90cm (25½ × 35½in). Words and phrases stitched in back stitch on old quilt backings. Patchwork made from vintage fabrics including quilt pieces, pieces of clothing, feed sack cottons, old shirt collars and tablecloths. All hand stitched together and embellished with further hand stitch. Stitched onto an old woollen blanket and backed with fabric from an old eiderdown.

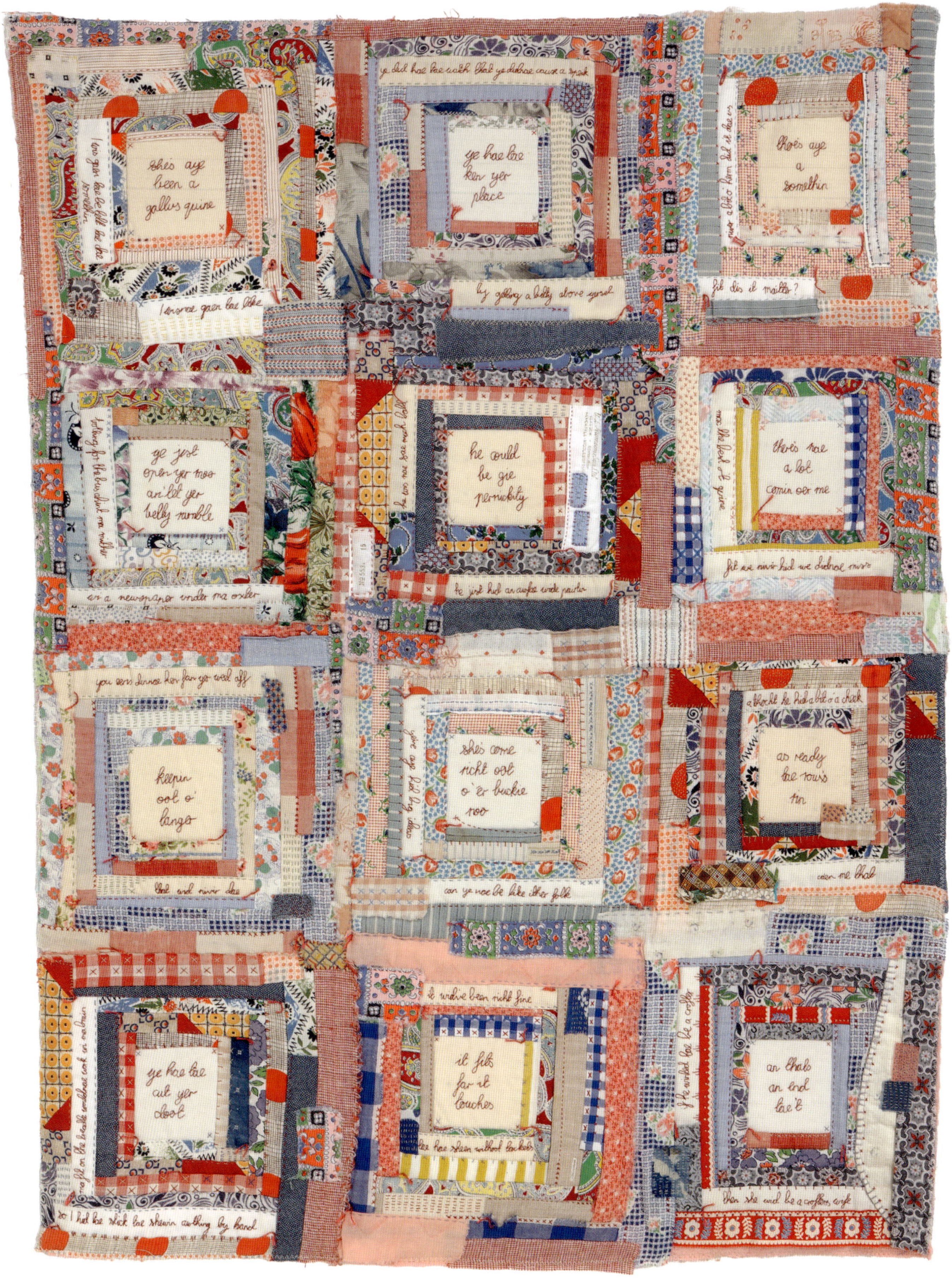
she's aye been a gallus quine
ye hae tae ken yer place
she's aye a somethin
by getting a belly above yersel
fit dis it matter?
he could be gie pernickity
there's nae a lot comin ower me
as a newspaper under ma oxter
he just hid an awfa wide pairtin
keepin oot o' langs
she's come richt oot o' 'er buckie roo
as ready tae rows tin
can ye nae be like ither folk
ye hae tae cut yer cloot
it fits far it touches
an that's an end tae't
it wid've been richt fine
then she wid be a crofter's wife
so I hid tae stick tae shewin aathing by hand

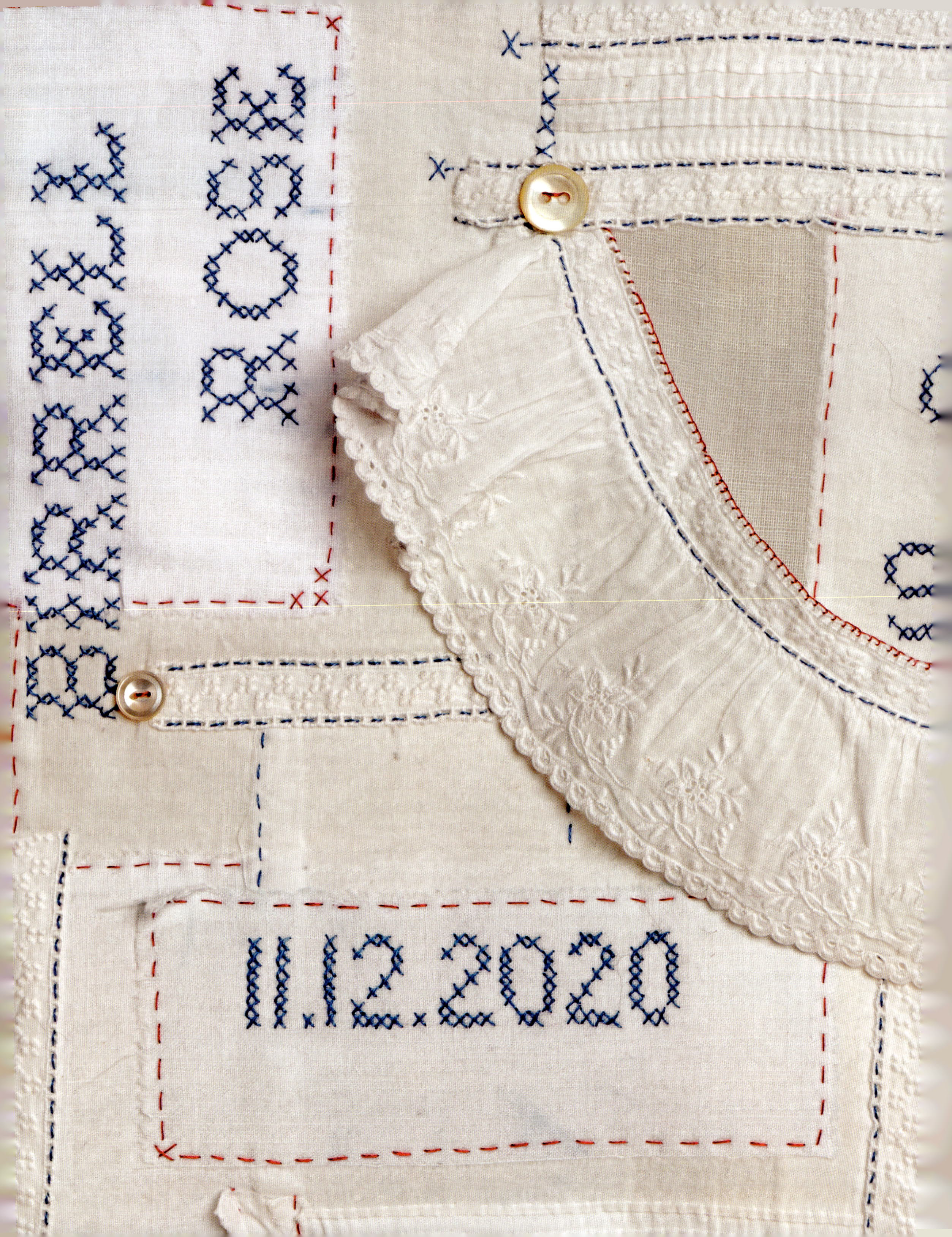
BIRRELL
ROSE
11.12.2020

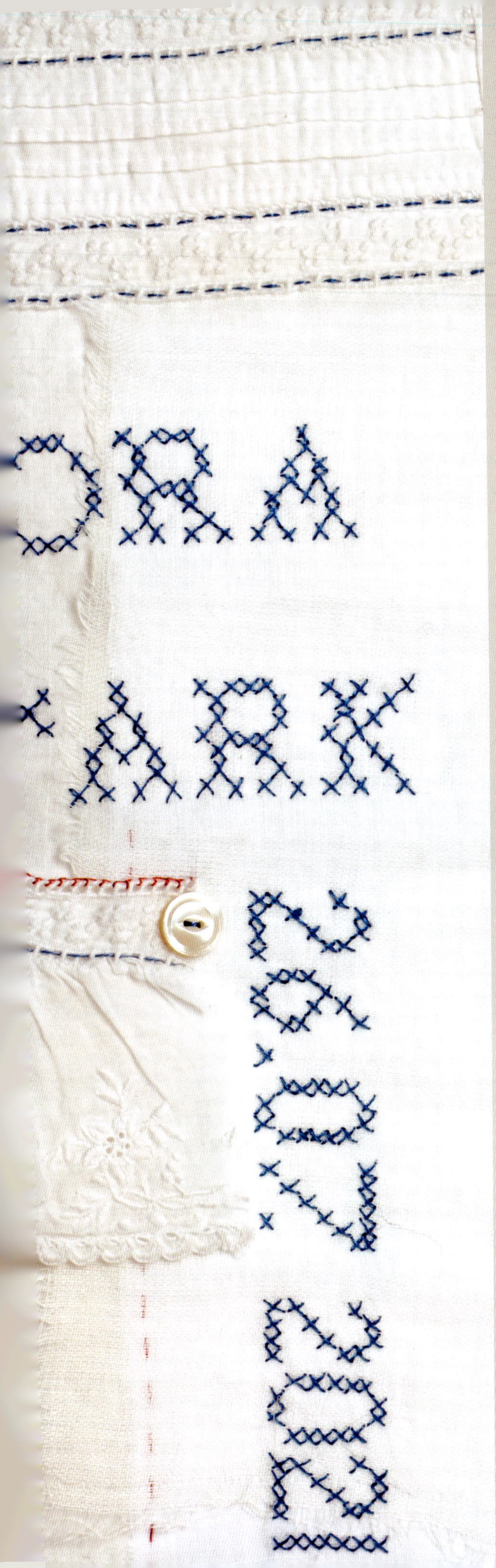

Clothing and stuff

For the last chapter, I'm turning my attention to the wardrobe and its contents. To be honest, my attention is never very far from thinking about clothes – they're my guilty pleasure and I've always loved them.

I remember the excitement, and often disappointment, of getting new clothes as a child; how I coveted the 1970s Afghan coat belonging to my brother's girlfriend, and the feeling of anticipation as my mum and I went on a shopping trip to look for 'something similar'. The excitement was short-lived as I returned home with a purple monstrosity with fur-trimmed hood and lined with a thin layer of foam, the synthetic fabric causing 'sparks to fly' as I walked down the street!

For me, clothes are imbued with story; the stories of buying or making them, the aspirations, anticipations and, of course, the everyday happenings and special events that took place when wearing them.

Found garments

Vintage garments and garment pieces feature highly in my gathering of meaningful materials, and I use them often as a backdrop to tell people's stories. I not only embellish and then wear them, but I also take them apart and stitch them back together again. Whatever I do, I am led by the garment – its shape, its construction and by the story I am ultimately hoping to tell.

Although I have picked up some beautiful French pieces of workwear at antiques fairs, I mainly tend to buy online. I follow dealers and specialists on Instagram, where there's a certain amount of luck involved as found garments have become popular, and special pieces are snapped up instantly. I've listed some of my favourite vintage UK sellers at the back of the book (see page 126).

Charity shops or thrift stores can also be a good source for clothing to either embellish or repurpose. I'm often on the hunt for men's striped shirts, made from good quality cotton.

RIGHT: An old French workwear garment with a collage of vintage and antique scraps attached using Bondaweb and ready for stitching. The large tablecloth 'patch' covers a huge rip on the back of the garment.

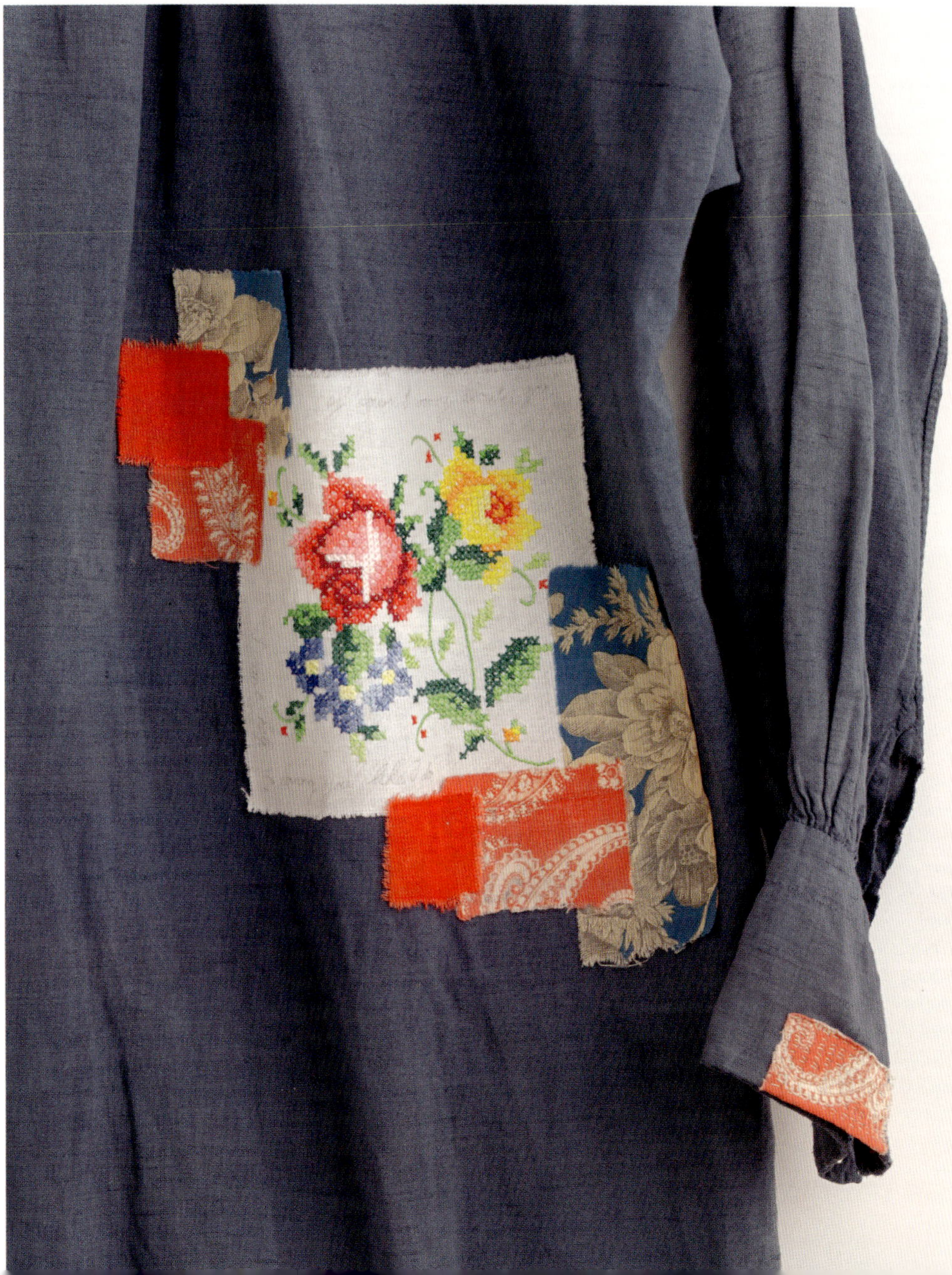

Wearable stories

I find that these garments are permanently 'works in progress'. Weeks or months after I think I've finished stitching and started wearing, I'll be looking in the mirror and my garment will whisper an idea for another little addition that would finish it off just perfectly ... and so it goes on.

Adding personal stitching will transform any piece of clothing, old or new. It can be as simple as replacing the plastic buttons on a shop-bought coat with mismatched mother-of-pearl ones, or adding a short line of stitching in a contrasting colour along part of a lapel or collar.

I start my making process as I would any other project – by gathering a collection of materials starting, of course, with a piece of clothing to use as the background to my story. Personally, I would only consider working with natural fibres and I love old French workwear items.

On a practical note

For a wearable story garment, you need to consider the finished piece's durability and washability. Ask yourself right from the start: How much wear will this get? Do I want it to be machine washable or am I happy to hand-wash? Your answers will affect not only your choice of garment, but also your treatment of it. Something for everyday use that is to be thrown in the washing machine will need to be far more robust than something for occasional wear.

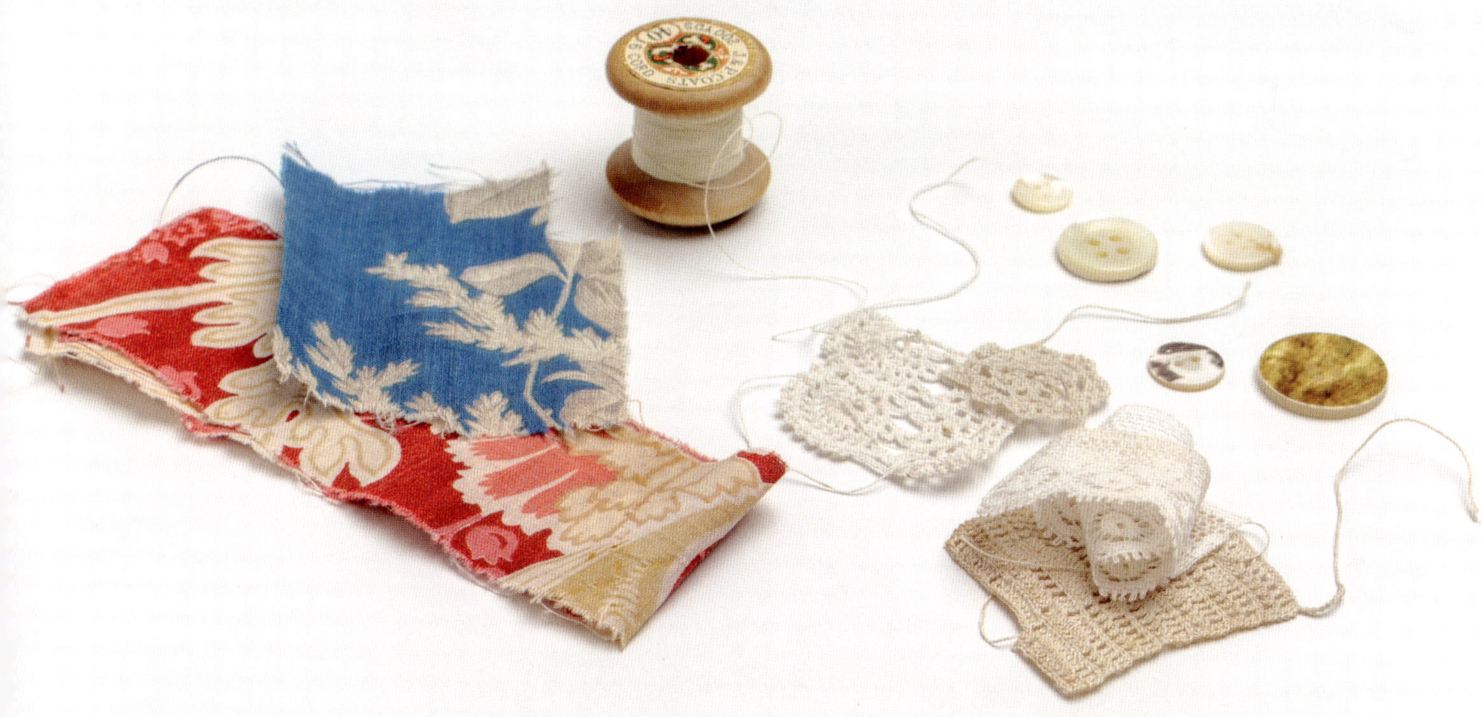

BELOW: I've gathered a selection of fabrics, mother of pearl buttons and scraps of hand crocheted lace to use on my garment. I love to use vintage threads where possible.

My making process

Having chosen my garment, I gather a collection of fabrics, pieces of lace, scraps of embroidered table linens and perhaps a few of my favourite mother-of-pearl or old linen buttons. I spread my garment out and lay my gatherings on top, which allows me to look at the overall picture and remove anything that looks out of place. I'll then 'audition' a selection of threads.

In this piece, I chose to work with antique fabric scraps, even though they are fragile and won't stand up to repeated wear and washing, because I loved how they looked against the blue workwear tunic. I attached them with fusible web and stitched repeated rows of running stitch over them to strengthen them in places, but I'm aware that they will wear and tear through use. My plan is to simply patch over them when they do, adding to the appearance and story of the piece.

ADDING MORE STORY

When you are working with old materials and garments, every piece of fabric and every button that you use will carry its own hidden story. However, I also like to add another storyline by including words. Sometimes the words will be the inspiration behind the piece itself, but if I have nothing specific in mind, I turn to my collections to see what jumps out at me. I've spoken about my collection of Ada's letters previously, and she was my muse for the details of the 'story shirt' pictured here. I have lifted little phrases from the pages of her letters and sewn them in back stitch around the edges of various patches.

'I would have loved to have shared her fire ... and her company' feels particularly poignant, as Ada was referring to how she would have loved to have shared Christmas Day 1942 with her mother, instead of being in her billet as a Land Girl.

BELOW: I've added small patches of fabrics and decorative stitching to highlight the lines of the collar and neckline.

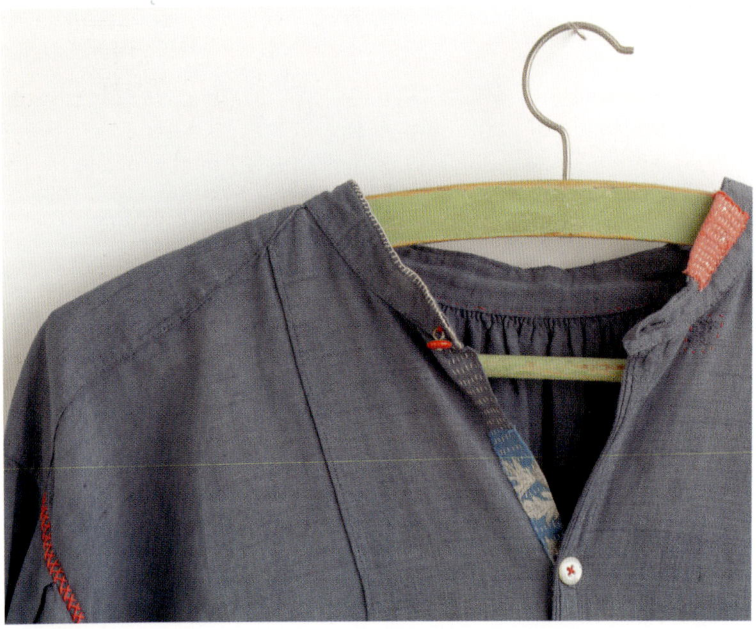

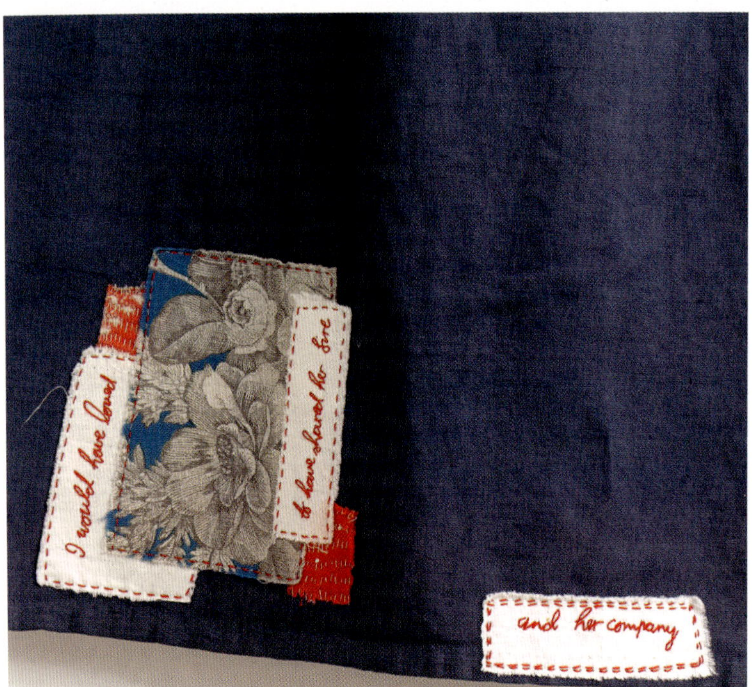

LEFT: Rather than stitching 'blocks' of text, I like to add interest by stitching it in small sections following the lines of my patches. 'I would have loved to have shared her fire ... and her company.'

STARTING TO STITCH

I start by examining my garment and noticing its features. I look for any damage – tears or holes that need patching or worn areas that may need covering or darning. I love to find original darns and will often highlight them by stitching round them in a contrasting colour.

I then add decorative stitching to highlight interesting areas in the construction, such as the neckline, shoulder and sleeve seams, and around the cuffs and hem. This can look good in a bold stitch such as herringbone or blanket stitch. I like to stitch small sections rather than, for example, all round the collar.

There can be some beautiful construction features in old workwear garments such as gussets under the arms and in the side seams and gathers at the back of the neck – all designed to give additional fabric allowing for ease of movement as the wearer carried out their everyday physical tasks. I like to draw attention to these details with stitch.

PATCHING

As I am stitching, my mind turns to the placement of decorative patches. I approach this as if I am making tiny cloth collages. I'll start by placing any patches needed to cover areas of damage, and then add others wherever I wish. I pin my fabric and lace pieces onto my garment and then try it on to see how they look. It's also important to see how it hangs on the body – you don't want to add an intricate detail somewhere and then find that it is hidden in a fold. Once I have the placement of pieces worked out, I trace any text onto my patches in pencil.

The means of attaching your collaged fabric patches can vary. You may wish to turn the edges to prevent them from fraying and hand stitch them in place. I prefer to work with raw edges, but I will sometimes machine stitch them in place before adding decorative hand stitching. If the fabrics I am using are particularly fragile, or if they are covering a large hole or tear in the garment, I will often use fusible web to attach them, thus adding an extra layer of stability.

I then add my decorative hand stitching, bearing in mind how robust it will have to be depending on its placement and the use of the garment.

Be prepared when working with old garments and particularly those that have been well washed and worn, that the fabric may rip (sometimes quite spectacularly) through use. I resolve this by adding more patches and embrace the serendipitous effect that results from the necessary random placements.

BELOW: I stitched my decorative patches onto my garment by machine, before embellishing them by hand. 'Gee it is going to be grand.'

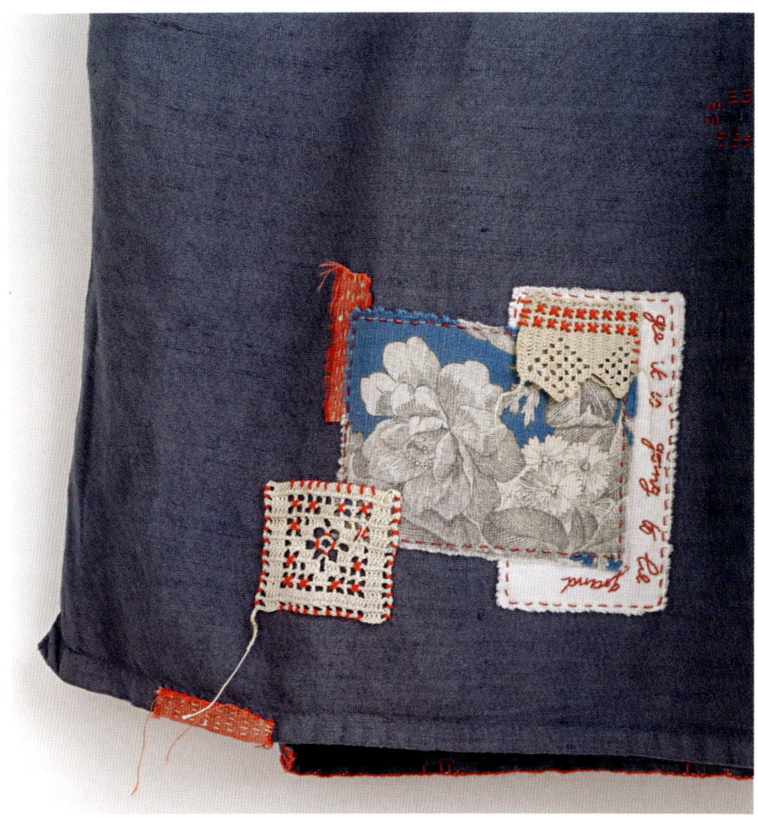

A stitcher's story smock

I rather love the idea of creating themed wearable garments, so, inspired by ideas from my 'sewing box studies' (see pages 59–63), I decided to start with a 'stitcher's story'. My chosen garment, by Rosehip design, is made from an old embroidered tablecloth. It was originally white, but I decided to dye it with a dye pod in the washing machine. I took the colour of the embroidered flowers into consideration when choosing the dye colour.

I approached this piece slightly differently to the process outlined on the previous page, as there were some story elements that I particularly wanted to add, so I made these my starting point. I had a picture in my mind of a seamstress with her scissors always to hand. I imagined them hanging from her waist on a chain, so this became my first motif. I also especially wanted to feature the wonderful quote that I mentioned earlier: 'If their fingers were busy, their hearts would rest more.'

I traced my scissor outline and words onto a sheet of sticky, water-soluble embroidery stabilizer and then experimented with different placements on the smock. Once I was happy, I took a photograph – looking at an image on your screen helps you to consider the overall composition, as anything that looks out of place or dominates becomes more obvious on the screen. Starting with the scissors, I then stitched each element before washing away the stabilizer. I've stitched with two strands of stranded cotton or used perle cotton no 8 throughout.

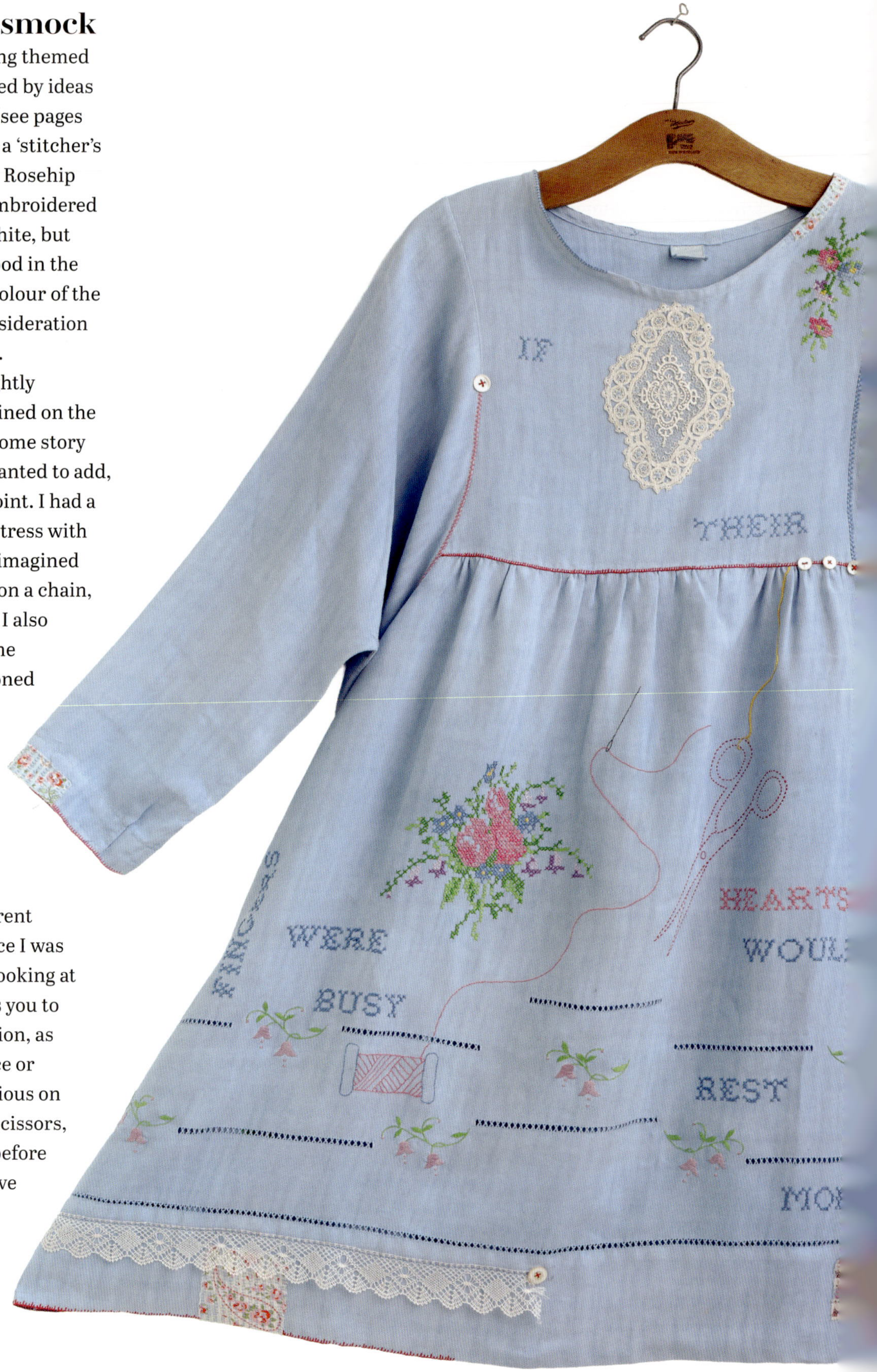

The next addition was the big cross stitch floral design. I couldn't resist stitching a design that would have adorned thousands of homes across America. It's from a vintage book by Anne Orr, an American designer who created nearly 100 books of needlework designs between 1910 and 1945. I drew my chosen floral design onto graph paper, working out the thread colours in coloured pencil, and then enlarged it slightly on my printer. I then printed this onto another sheet of sticky embroidery stabilizer, positioned this on my smock and worked my stitching using an embroidery hoop.

After these three elements were stitched, I put the smock on my mannequin to work out the placement of other bits, starting with the beautiful lace panel. It was only then that I began to highlight the lines and details of the garment itself, and made decisions about what other features I wanted to add. This project will be ongoing – I've not even started on the back yet and, as I sit here looking at it on the mannequin, it is whispering more suggestions.

Consult your sewing box *threads of thought* for inspiration for your own stitcher's story, or ask yourself: Who else could I make a garment for?

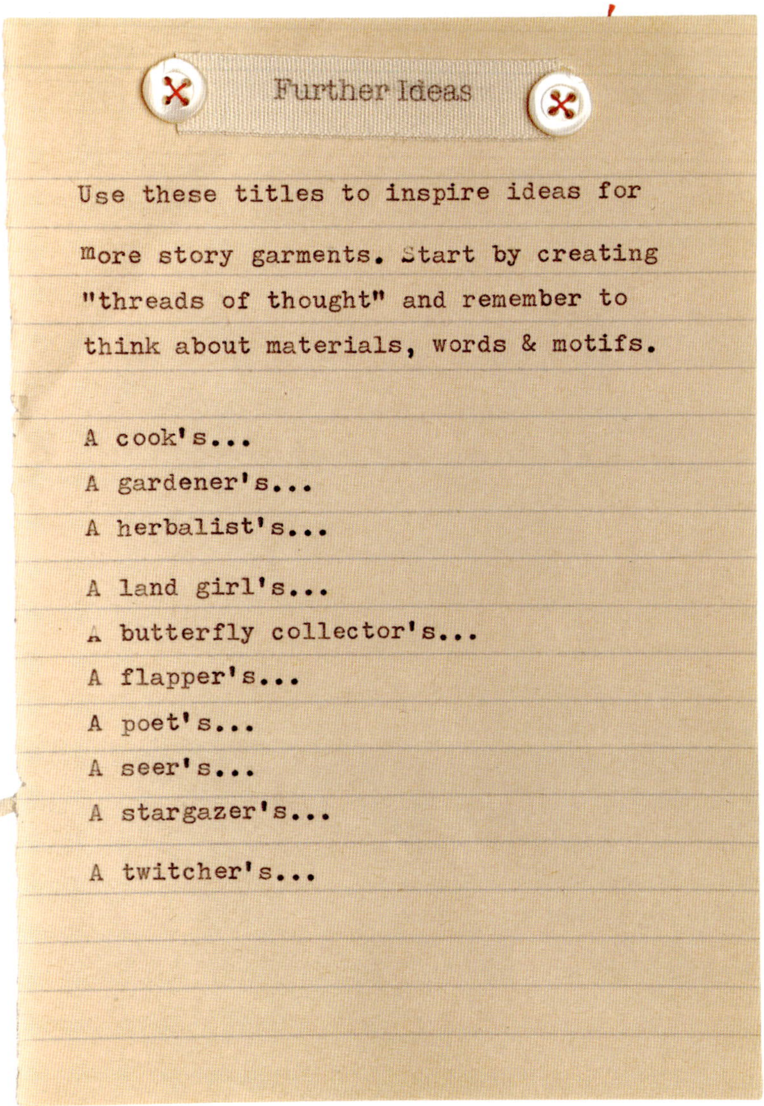

OPPOSITE: *A Stitcher's Story Smock*. Top made from old tablecloths with vintage cotton patches and lace fragments. Further embellished with cross stitch designs and lettering, with outlines of scissors, needles and thread in back stitch and running stitch.

Decorative story garments

There are fewer restrictions when using garments decoratively as opposed to creating wearable pieces. I always seem to be drawn to the old and the shabby, which is perfect for decorative use.

If the finished piece doesn't need to be washable, there is more scope for embellishment with papers, ephemera and a variety of mixed media. Old garments really can be the perfect canvas for illustrating and telling stories of people and life.

Thoughts and prayers

I've brought together meaningful materials, words and motifs from three entirely different sources to create this simple piece.

The child's foundation garment came from one of my textile dealer friends who knew I would love it, as it had obviously had a hard life. I imagine it having been worn every day by a small girl and possibly several elder siblings before her. From what I have been told, these garments were worn as part vest, part corset, wrapped round the child's body like swaddling. They were believed to make the child feel more secure, while also helping their posture. This made me think of the role of motherhood and the strong desire to create security for our children ... and to try to shape them, however misguided this impulse may be!

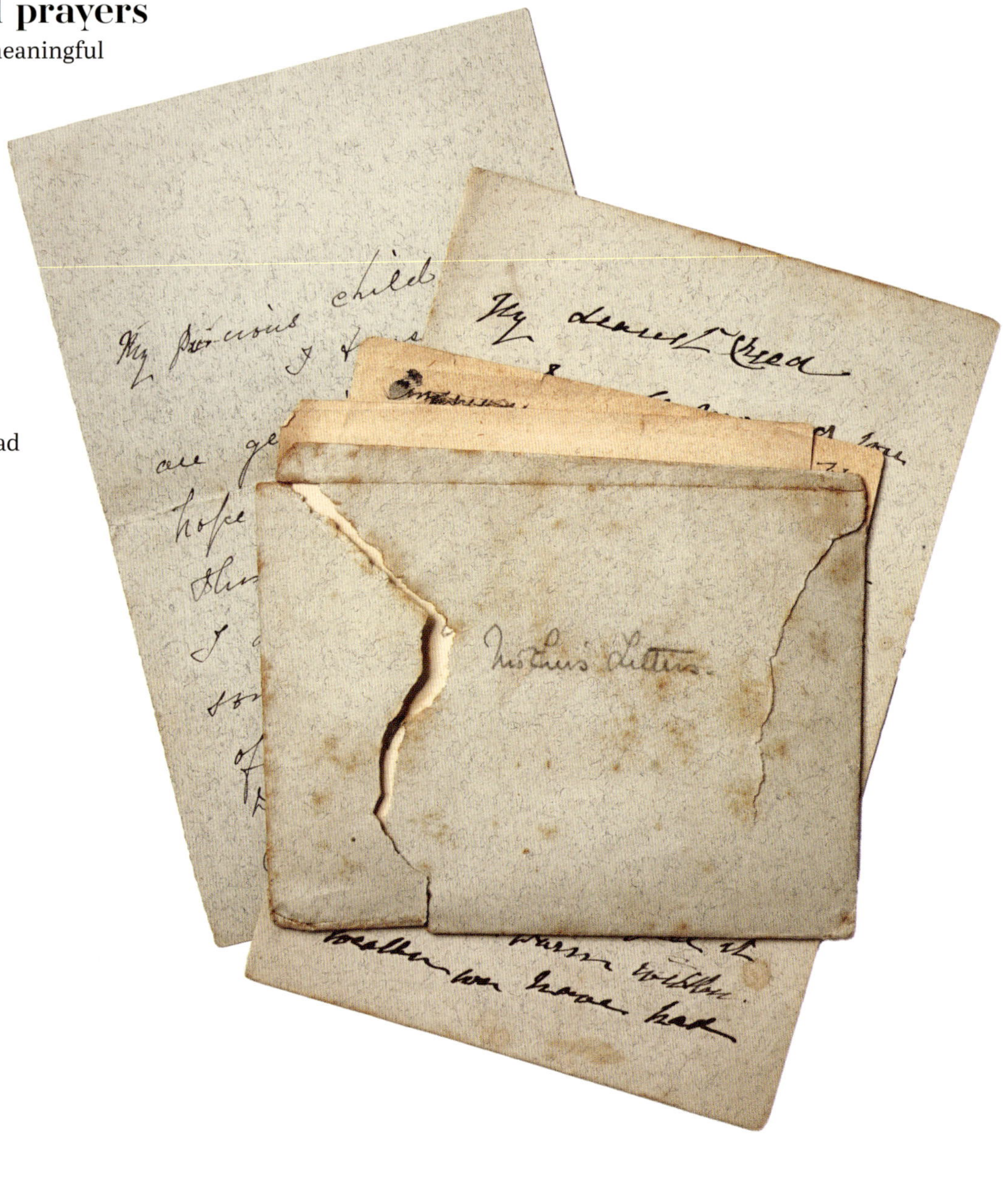

RIGHT: A bundle of pure emotion! This small collection of undated letters was in my possession for months before I could finally bring myself to disturb and read them.

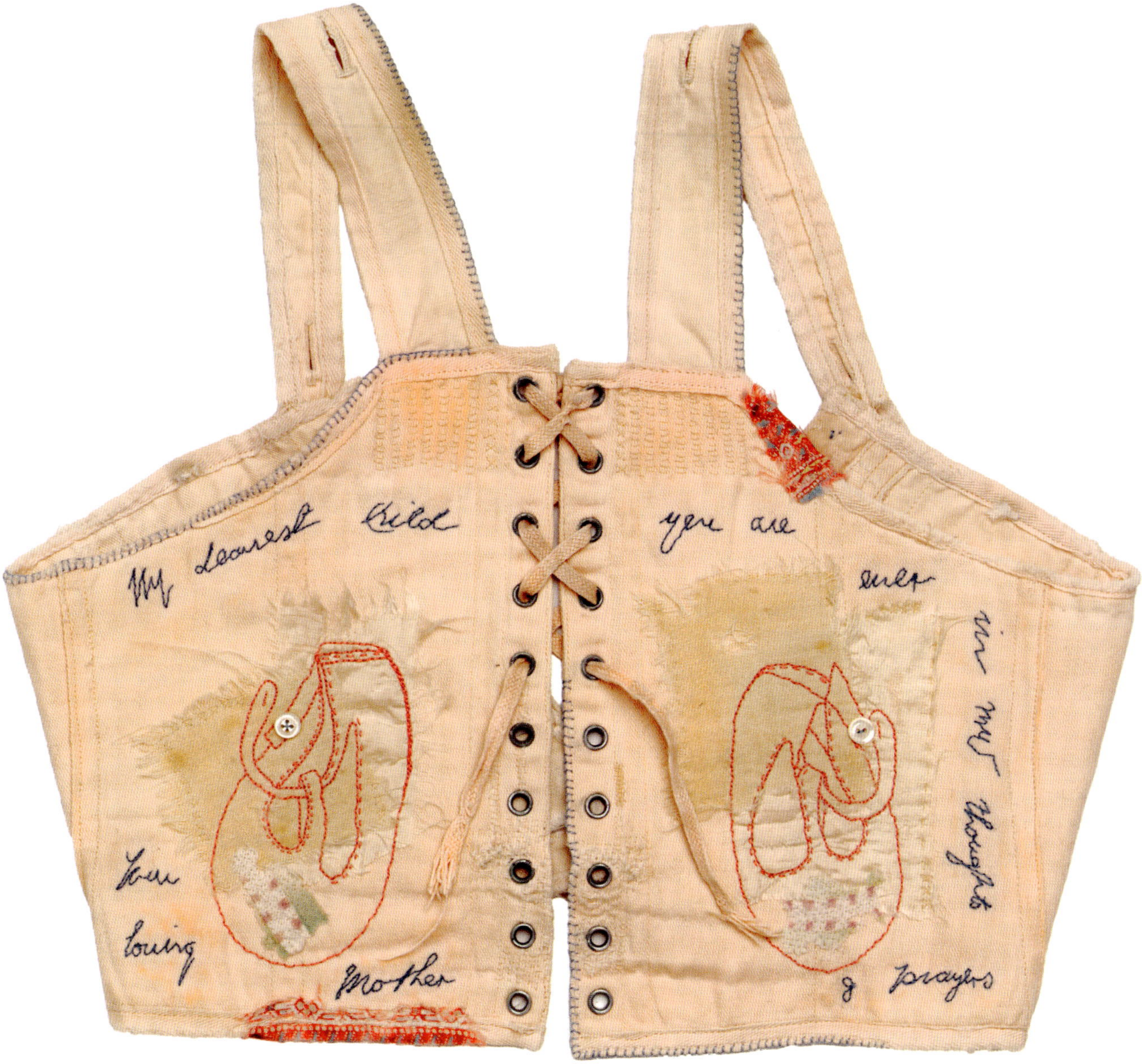

As soon as I set eyes on it, I knew that I had the perfect words waiting in the wings – words from a little bundle of letters, folded and stored in an old torn envelope marked 'Mother's Letters'. They felt so full of emotion that it was months before I could take them out of the packet and try to read the shaky, spidery handwriting. I can decipher very little of what they say, but they each open with 'my dear child', 'my very clever child' or 'my precious child' and are signed 'your loving mother'.

The motif is a small pair of shoes. Found in a junk shop and battered almost flat, they look like they had been discarded and forgotten long ago, but I do wonder what the child (or children) who wore them went on to do. Each item holds the stories of lives that I can only begin to imagine, but through stitching they become entangled in my own thoughts around how wildly complex and yet completely simple it is to love as a mother.

ABOVE: *Thoughts and Prayers*. Child's foundation garment with antique fabric fragments and hand stitching in old silk threads.

Sam Miller

Sam is a London-based, mixed-media artist. Her work is imbued with story, but she doesn't intend for the story to be 'fixed'. She explains:

> *What matters most to me is that the work leaves space for the viewer. Each person will bring their own associations, their own histories, their own echoes to it. For some it might stir nostalgia, for others a sense of fragility, for others still a recognition of beauty enduring, despite time's passing. This piece titled* I Feel All This Echo *is embroidered onto an Edwardian child's fine wool dress, and that choice of garment already carries a kind of weight. A child's dress is so intimate, so fragile, and yet it holds an emptiness too: we'll never know who wore it, never know her story. That's part of the point. The piece is full of absence as much as presence, and it asks you to step into that space with your own imagination.*
>
> *Onto this delicate surface I've embroidered images drawn from the past, photographs of older men and women. Perhaps they were the parents of the child, or perhaps we're glimpsing the child herself projected into the future, grown and married. There's no single answer, and I like it that way.*
>
> *Butterflies flutter through the piece. They've always fascinated me as symbols: in Greek, psyche means both 'soul' and 'butterfly', and the Romans believed butterflies represented the souls of the dead. They capture so beautifully the fleeting, fragile nature of time and memory. Like echoes, they don't stay still, they shimmer and move on. The pearls appear in the flowers, stitched carefully into their forms. I like the pearls for their own history. Each one is a small record of time, layered and built up slowly in response to a grain of grit. There's something poetic about that: pearls literally embody the process of transformation, irritation turned into beauty, the slow patience of nature. To me, they mirror how memory accumulates and how we, too, are shaped by what life leaves behind.*
>
> *At its core, the piece is about time – how it passes, how it leaves traces. Clothing makes that especially poignant because garments hold the shape of bodies, they carry intimacy. That's why the title* I Feel All This Echo *feels right. It's not about one story, but about resonance itself: the way the past murmurs through us, fluttering like a butterfly, shimmering like a pearl, whispering through the folds of a forgotten dress.*

BELOW AND OPPOSITE: *I Feel All This Echo*. Edwardian child's woollen dress embellished with found objects and hand stitching.

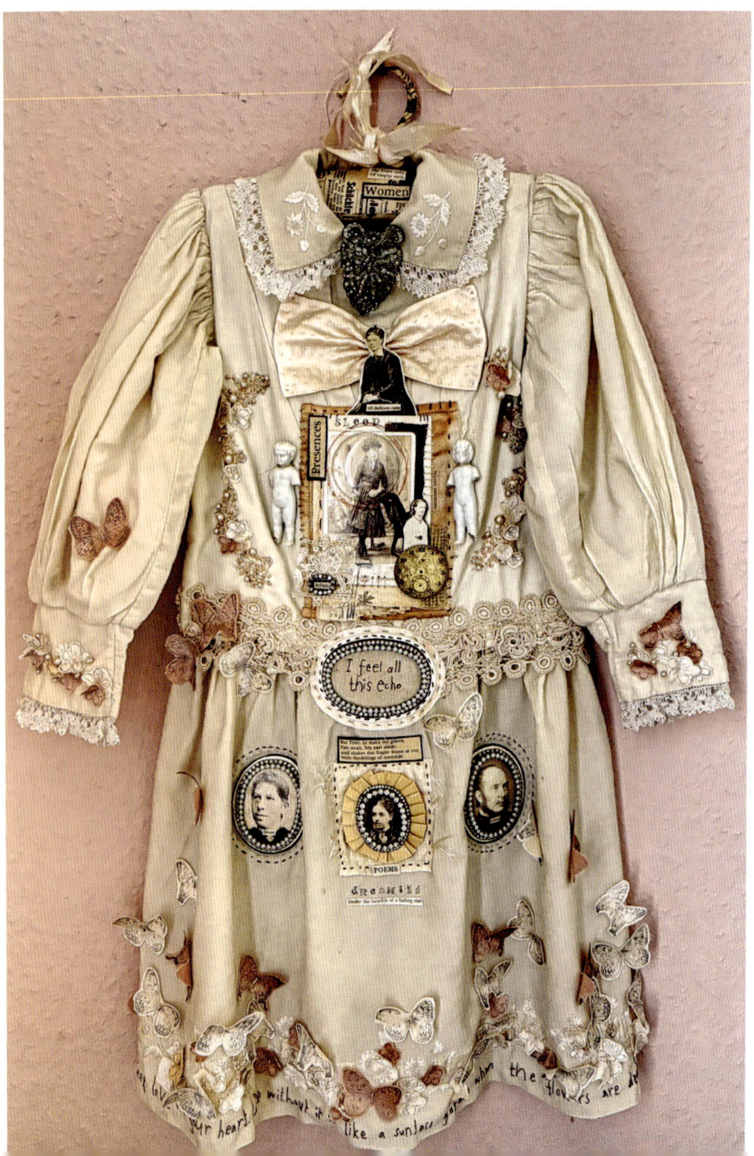

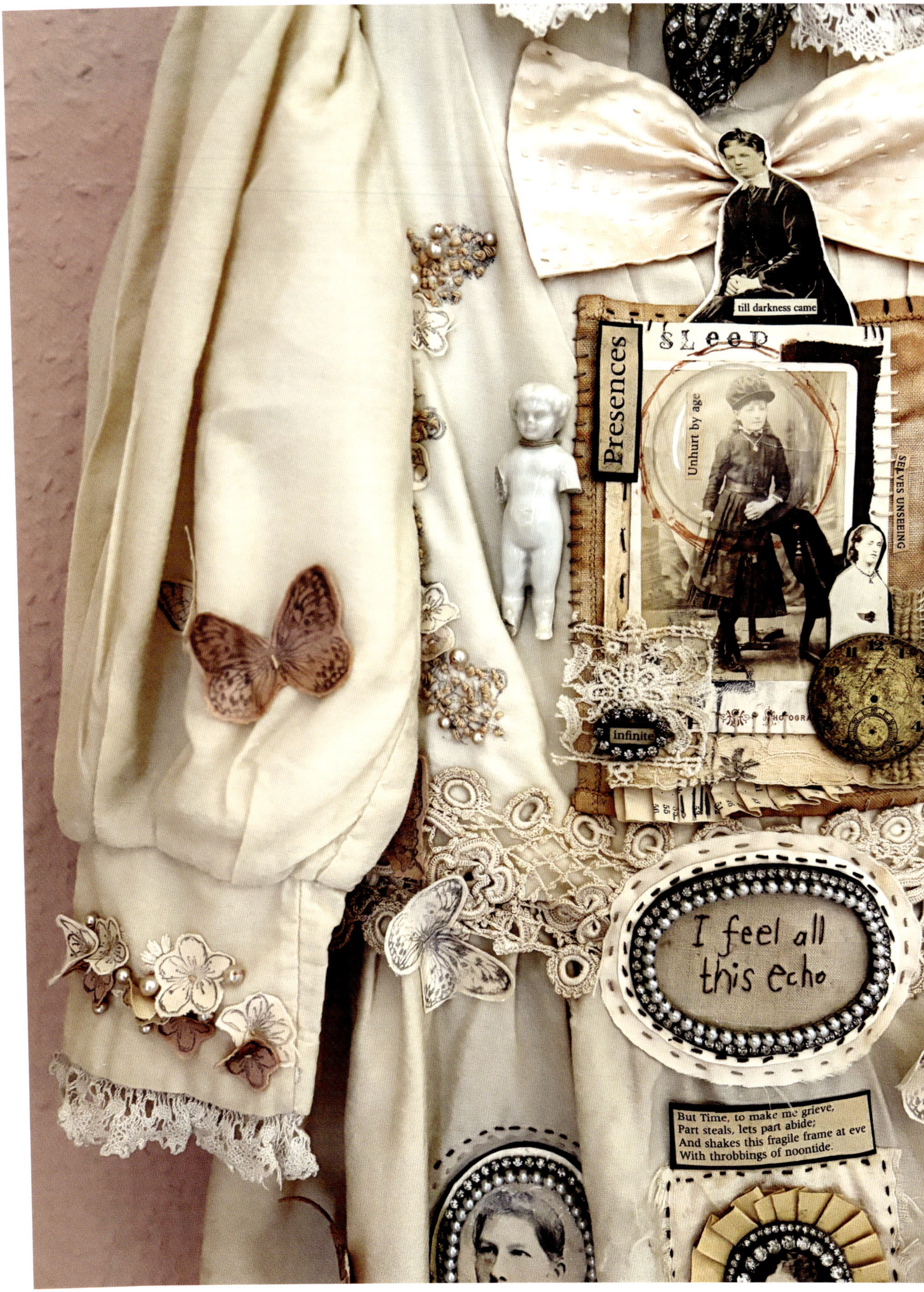
till darkness came
Presences
SLeep
Unhurt by age
SELVES UNSEEING
infinite
I feel all this echo
But Time, to make me grieve,
Part steals, lets part abide;
And shakes this fragile frame at eve
With throbbings of noontide.

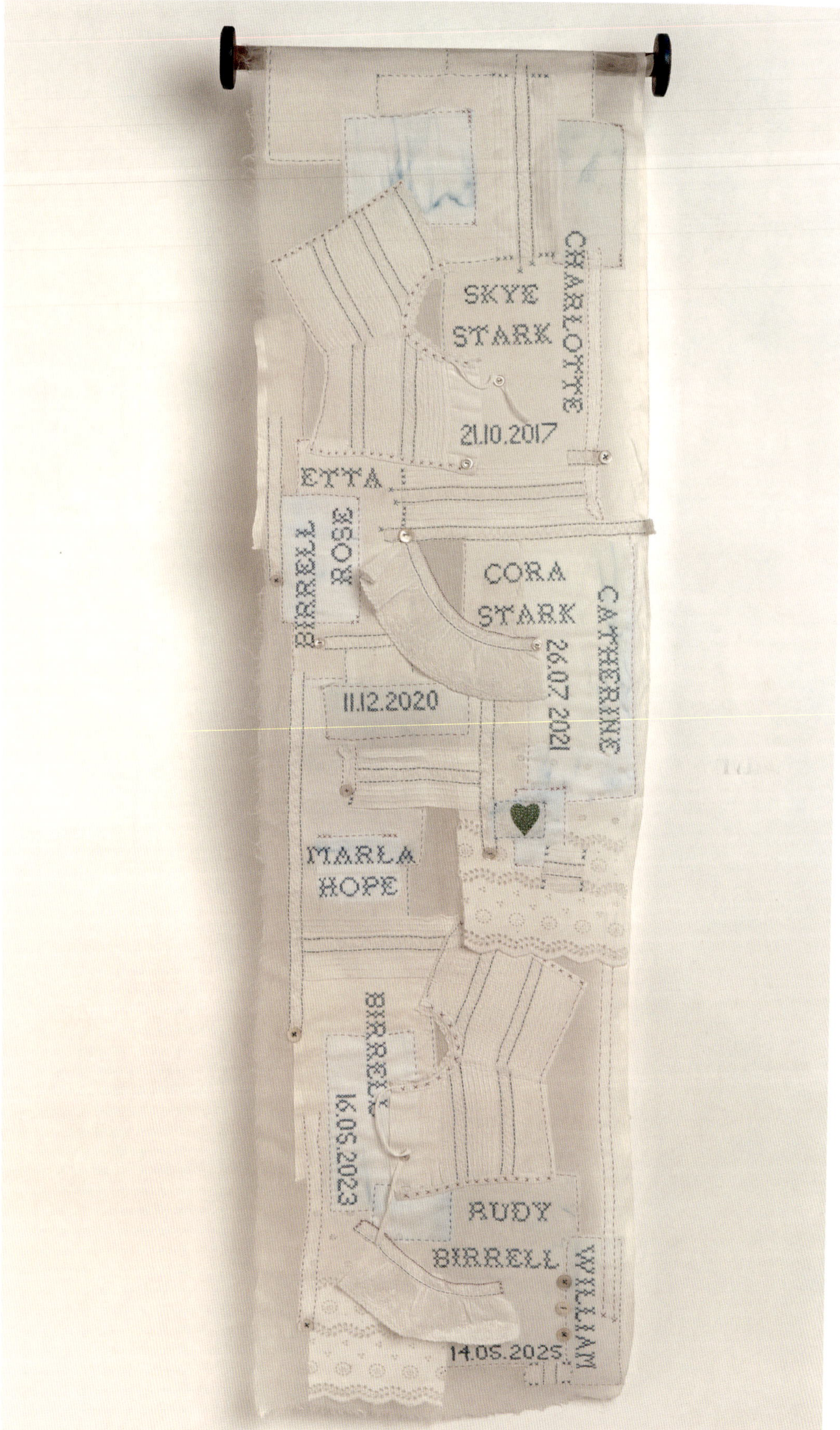
SKYE
STARK
CHARLOTTE
21.10.2017
ETTA
ROSE
BIRRELL
CORA
STARK
CATHERINE
26.07.2021
11.12.2020
MARLA
HOPE
BIRRELL
16.05.2023
RUDY
BIRRELL
WILLIAM
14.05.2025

Unpicked stories: deconstructed garments

There's something very satisfying about taking garments apart. Taking time to unpick seams stitch by stitch, thoughtfully cutting around bodices and yokes and making tiny, precise snips with scissors before ripping, listening to the sound of the fabric as it tears a line separating one piece from another.

I begin my process by laundering, and then thoroughly examining the garment as I iron it. Next, I'll start dismantling, especially treasuring hand-stitched seams and elements such as cuffs, collars, yokes, bodices, pockets, buttonholes and button bands as well as the fabric itself. I may compose my pieces from two or three garments, bringing the different elements together to create a new story.

Counting my blessings

My husband and I are blessed with having five wonderful grandchildren and this piece is inspired by them. It's made from two antique baby christening gowns with their intricately detailed bodices and long, flowing skirts. The stitched names and dates of birth are inspired by the lettering found in antique samplers, which would have been painstakingly stitched by girls during needlework lessons.

I've used christening gowns in this way in previous work, but I happily allow one idea to lead to another if it takes me in new directions. Having been gifted a bundle of beautiful gowns, I decided to use them to create a personal project for this book.

Cotton gowns, often made from broderie anglaise and decorated with lace and floral embroidery, were popular in the early 20th century and they can be quite easily found from antique textile dealers at varying prices. Like many others, I can be conflicted in the decision to cut up a beautiful item such as this and I make my decisions based on each individual piece and the circumstances under which it has come into my hands. I'm generally drawn to garments that are already damaged, but if a dress is pristine and you can't bear to take it apart, then you could still be inspired by this project. You could leave the dress whole and simply embellish it with the stitched names and birthdates. This would look beautiful, displayed hanging on a wooden coat hanger.

OPPOSITE:
Counting my Blessings, 35 × 110cm (13¾ × 43½in). Two cotton christening robes, deconstructed and patched onto a silk organza background and hung from an old wooden weaving bobbin. Hand stitched throughout in vintage silk thread.

MY MAKING PROCESS

1. I worked with two different dresses, giving a slight contrast in the white of the fabrics and additional detail. One dress had beautiful pin tucks and lace trim, and the other had a broderie anglaise skirt with stitched floral detail. I also used some leftover scraps from a previous project, dyed a very delicate blue in places.

2. I started by deconstructing my dresses, the first decision being how I would cut the precious bodice and then tear pieces from the skirts. I echoed the shape of the hanging with long, narrow fabric pieces. I unpicked lace that had been inserted in the pin tucks and kept some of the gathered hemline intact.

3. I drew each grandchild's name and date of birth onto graph paper using a traditional cross stitch chart. I then traced each word onto vellum and cut them out individually to help with placement. The long and narrow shape of my piece is inspired by the shape of the original dress.

4. I worked out the size of my background fabric by mocking it up in paper and playing around with dimensions until it looked in proportion. I then played with various layouts of materials and text until I was happy with the result. I took a series of photographs to remind me of placement.

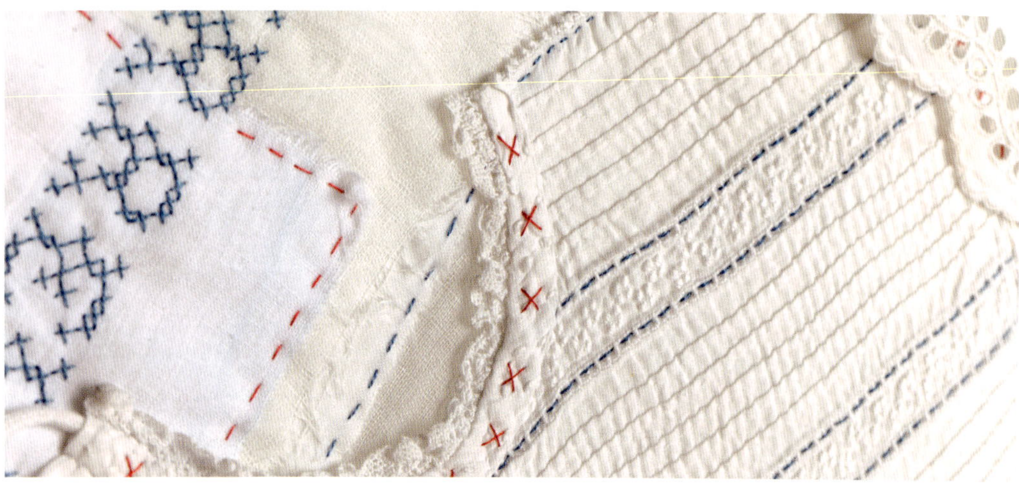

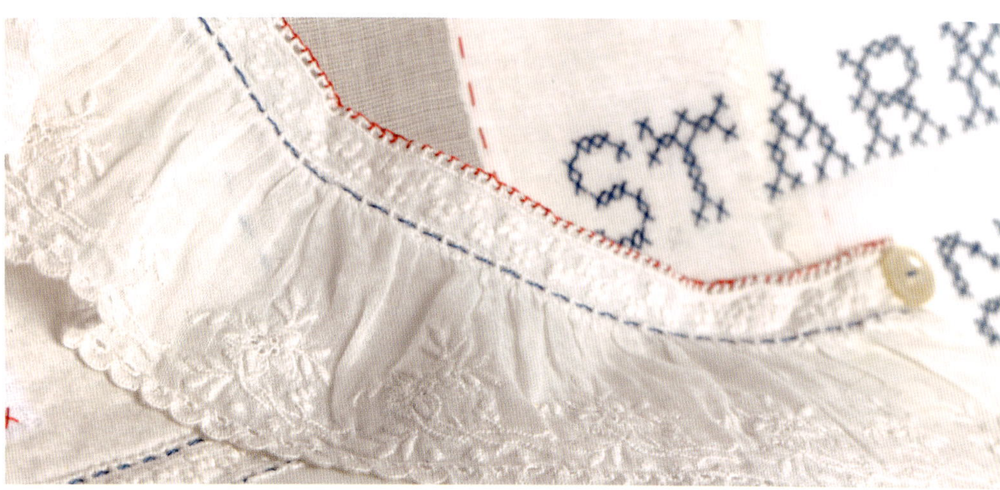

RIGHT: *Counting my Blessings* (details).

5. I chose to use a very fine cotton voile for my background. I wanted the finished piece to be delicate, almost fragile in nature, reflecting the fragility of life and the sheer miracle of each of these tiny humans arriving safely into our world.

6. I attached the base layer of fabric patches with fusible web, but subsequent layers were pinned in place.

7. I stitched the names and dates using embroidery stabilizer (as outlined on page 74), and then added decorative stitching around the patches, highlighting edges and features.

8. The addition of some mother-of-pearl buttons completed the piece.

I went on to create this second piece, *Etta Rose*, from vintage handkerchiefs using the same methods.

BELOW: *Etta Rose*, 26 × 26cm (10 × 10in). Made from torn scraps of vintage handkerchiefs collaged onto a handkerchief background. I've used stitching to highlight details of the various handkerchiefs and water-soluble embroidery paper to cross stitch my granddaughter's name and birthdate.

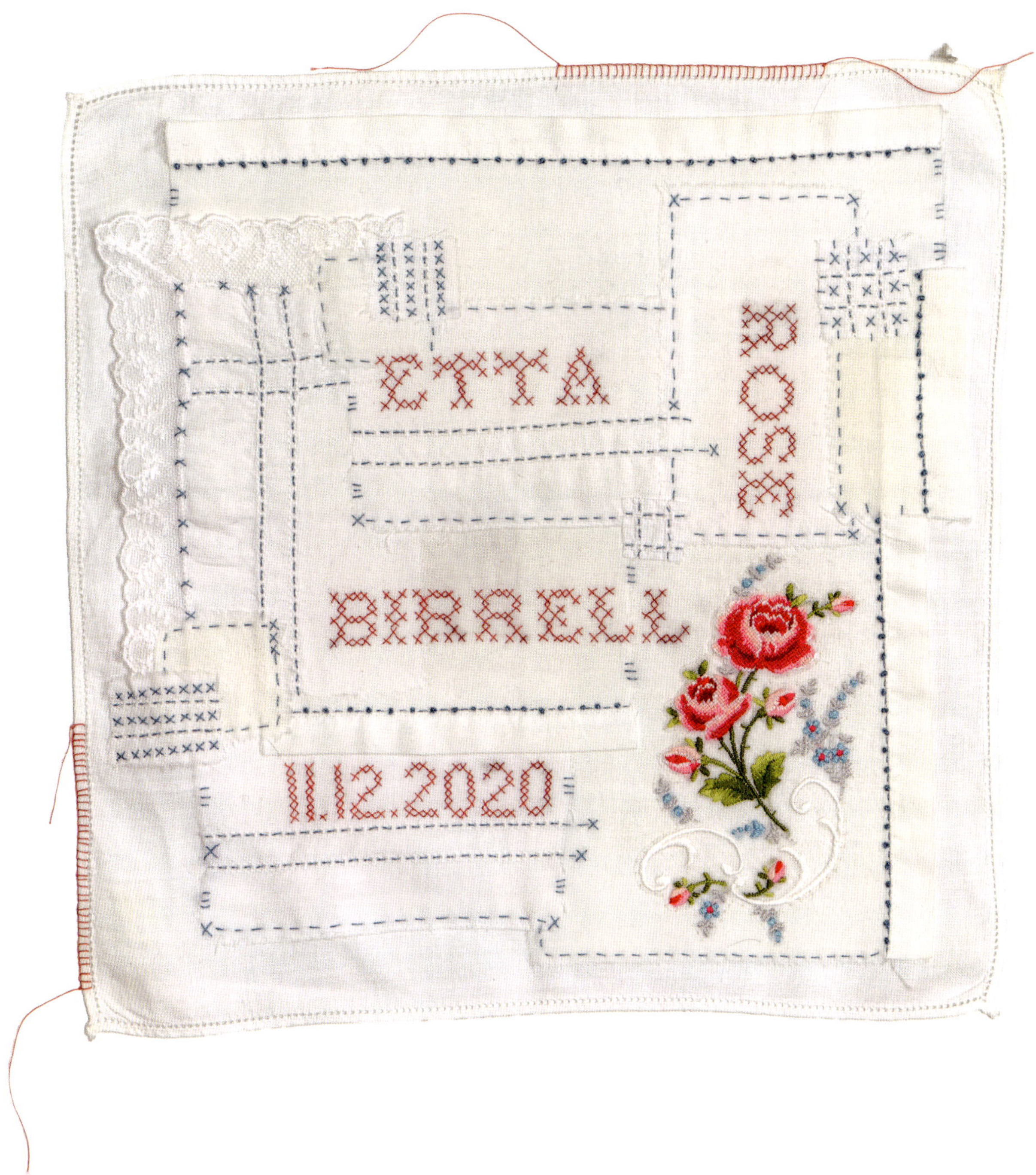

Cloth jewellery

No exploration of the closet would be complete without looking at accessories.

'Shabadashery' collar

Made from an old detachable collar, scraps of your favourite fabrics, fragments of lace and odd bits of haberdashery – what a glorious list of ingredients!

You will need:

- A vintage detachable collar, or you can cut one off a shirt. Use one that's not overly stiff or you can remove some of the starch by washing
- Chain: I used antique brass-plated chain 4 x 6mm (⅛ x ¼in)
- 8mm (¼in) jump rings
- Small clasps: I used 10mm (⅜in) trigger clasps
- Jewellery pliers, for opening and closing the jump rings
- Scraps of fabric, lace and a collection of buttons and other haberdashery items
- Something to make a centrepiece
- A small piece of felt

Collars are thick to stitch, so I used a sewing machine, but you could stitch everything by hand if you prefer.

BELOW:
Shabadashery collar made from an old detachable shirt collar, scraps of table linen and vintage cottons.

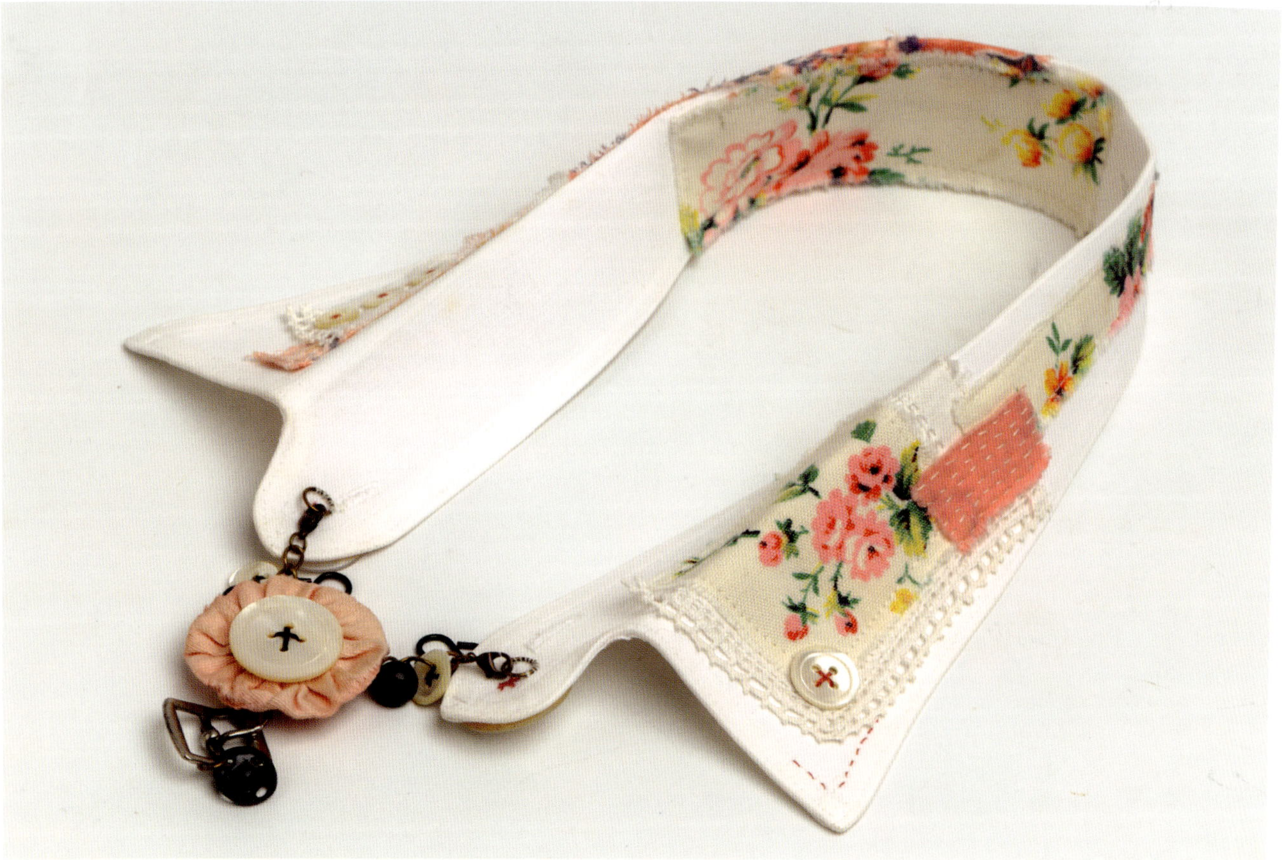

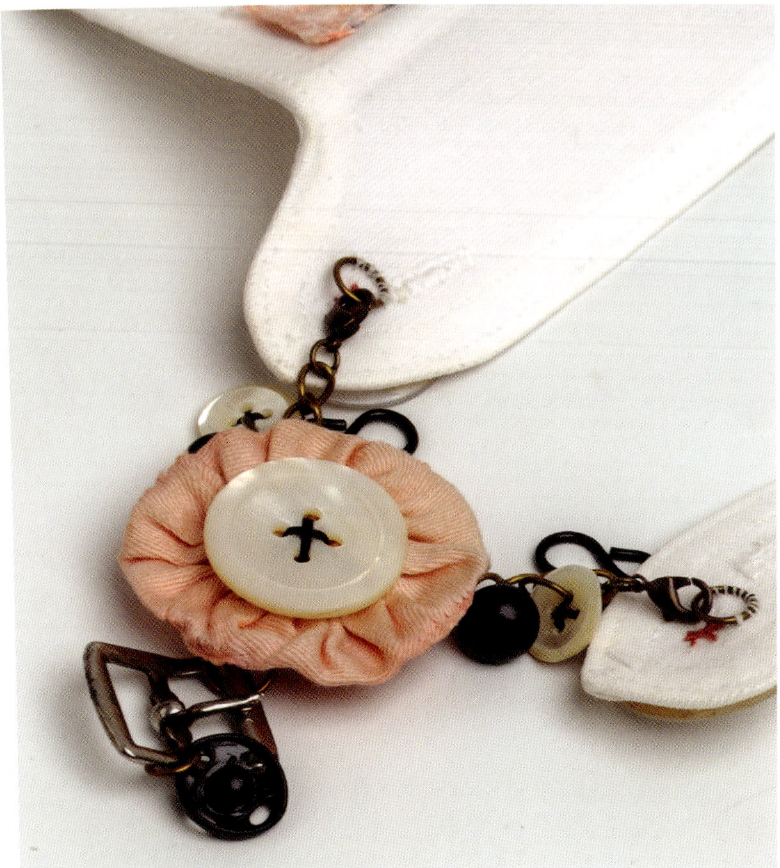

LEFT: Detail of centrepiece made from a 'Suffolk puff' or 'yoyo', mother of pearl buttons, small shoe buckle, old press studs and boot buttons.

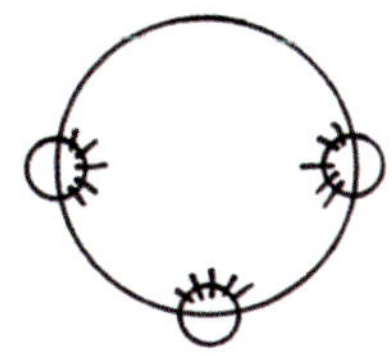

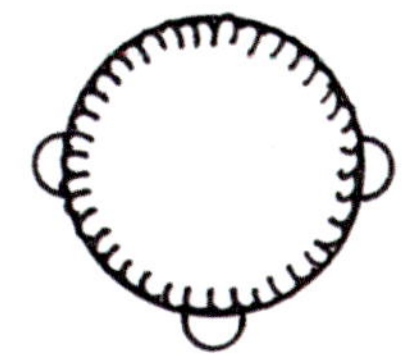

TO CREATE A CENTREPIECE

You could use any of the following:

- A Suffolk puff – mine is from an old quilt but you could make your own.
- A large button with a metal shank on the back – the jump rings and chain can be attached to this. I've used one of my covered buttons with a photo of my granny on it (see page 111).
- A lace rosette made by cutting a lace strip about 16cm (6¼in) long and stitching the two ends together with a narrow seam. Run a gathering stitch around the top and then gather.

You'll need to support the Suffolk puff or rosette on a base to give you something to attach the jump rings to. Cut two circles of felt slightly smaller than your centrepiece. Stitch three jump rings onto one of the pieces of felt with a small part of the ring extending over the edge (diagram 1). Depending on the thickness of your felt, you may wish to add a layer of interfacing or fusible web (such as Bondaweb) for additional stability. Place the other circle over the top and overstitch the edges with a small blanket stitch (diagram 2). You now have attaching points for your chain and for something to dangle from the bottom. Stitch onto the back of your centrepiece with a button.

Then cut two 3cm (1¼in) lengths of chain and attach to your centrepiece with jump rings (there are numerous online tutorials if you are unsure how to do this). Attach your haberdashery trinkets to the chain with jump rings. Finish with a trigger clasp on the end of each chain.

RIGHT: I've left the writing with the brand and size visible on the inside of the collar. It's down to personal choice how much of the collar you leave uncovered. I like to leave the shape of the original collar intact.

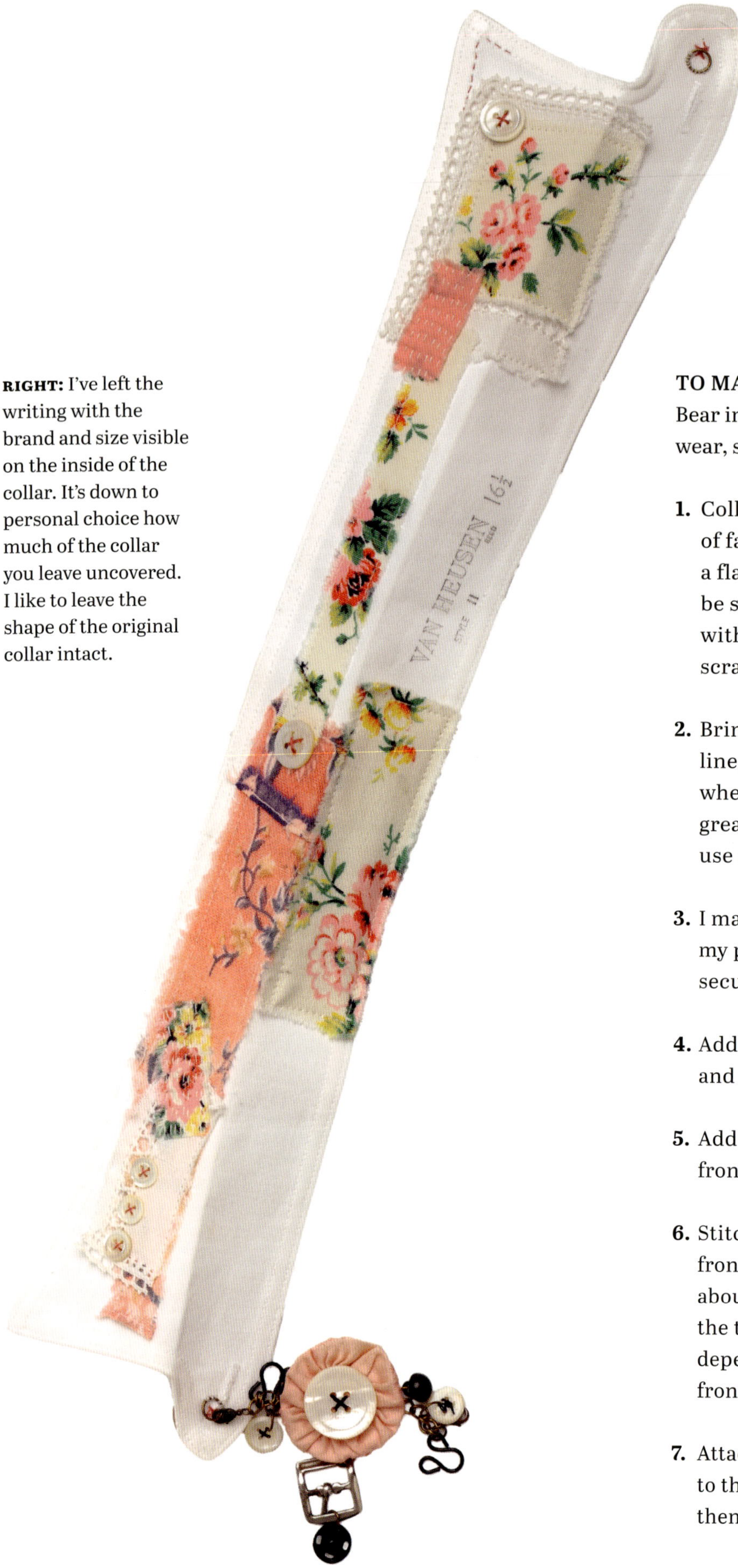

TO MAKE THE COLLAR

Bear in mind that collars get dirty with wear, so washability is essential.

1. Collage together a simple arrangement of fabrics. Although you are working on a flat surface, remember that it won't be seen like this. I like to add interest with the edges of tablecloths and scraps of lace.

2. Bring some of the patches over the fold line, even though they won't be seen when it's being worn. The collars look great if they are displayed when not in use and the inside is visible then.

3. I machine stitch round the edges of all my patches to make sure that they are securely attached.

4. Add decorative hand stitching, buttons and so on.

5. Add two large buttons to the collar fronts.

6. Stitch a jump ring on the inside of each front. Position them in the middle, about 1.5cm (½in) from the edge to hide the trigger clasp, though this may vary depending on the shape of your collar front.

7. Attach the clasps on your centrepiece to the jump rings on the collar, and then simply detach for laundering.

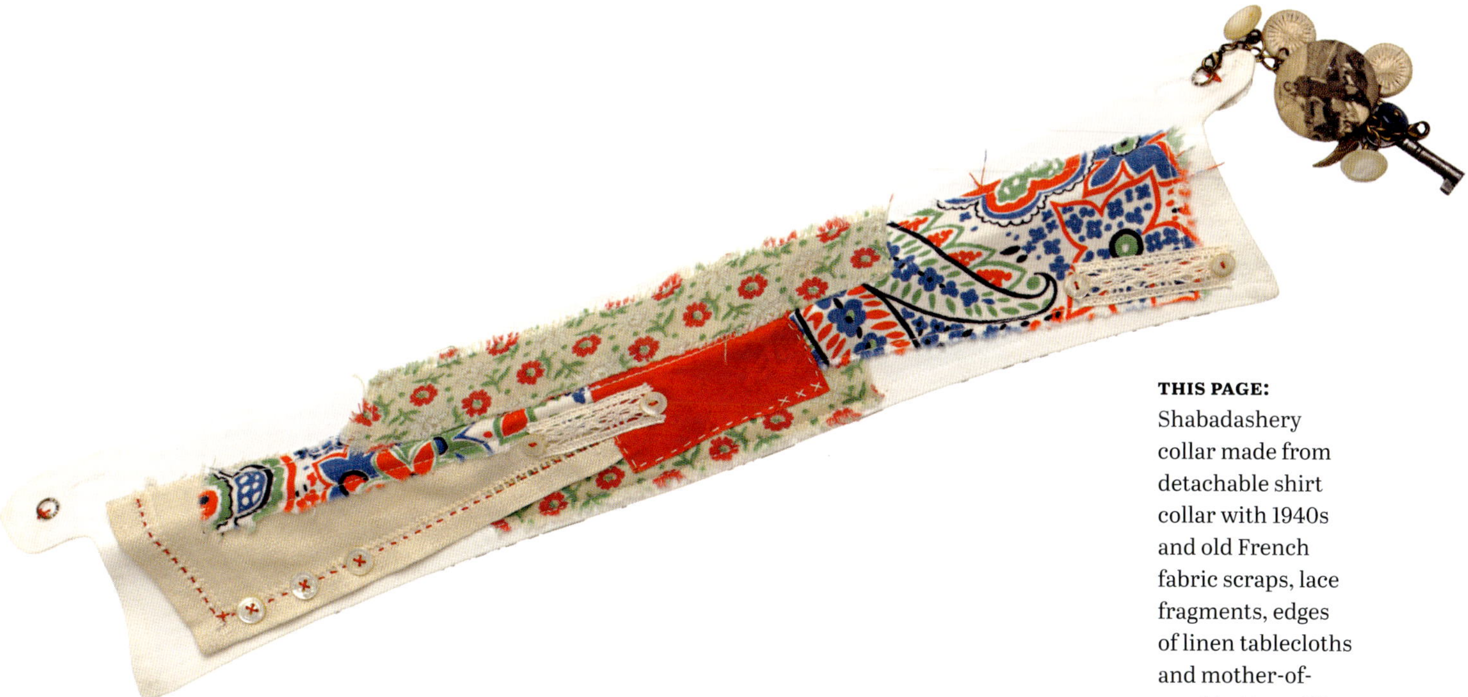

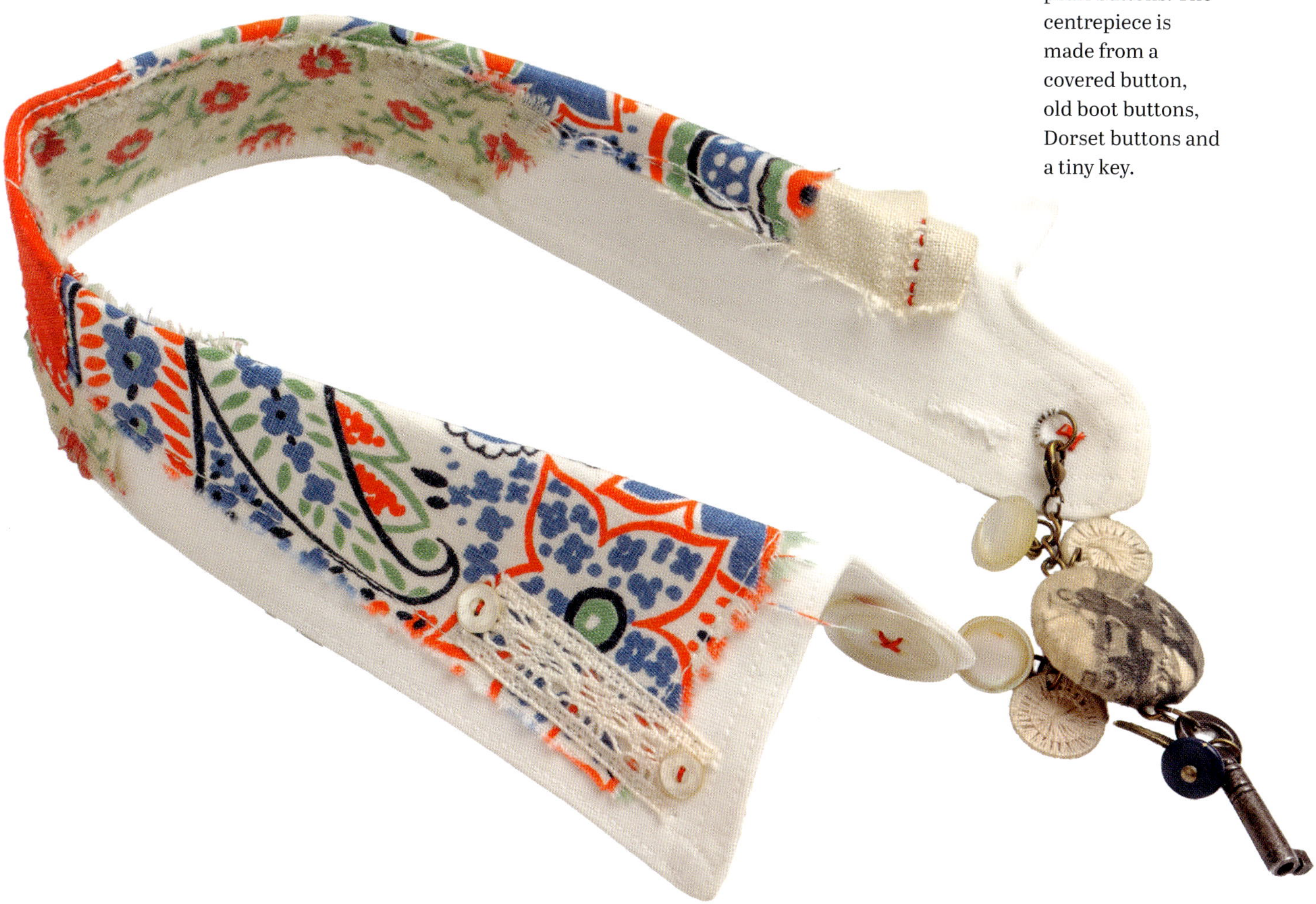

THIS PAGE: Shabadashery collar made from detachable shirt collar with 1940s and old French fabric scraps, lace fragments, edges of linen tablecloths and mother-of-pearl buttons. The centrepiece is made from a covered button, old boot buttons, Dorset buttons and a tiny key.

Cristina Rebeccani Coretti

OPPOSITE: *Loasa Tricolor*, 8 × 5 cm (3 × 2in). Antique linen embroidered oval inspired by a sketch by Colonel Francis Hall, Ecuador, circa 1820. *Antique linen hanging pocket*, 5 × 6cm (2 × 2½in). A tiny hanging pocket to hold dreams and secrets. Hand embroidered and dipped in coffee. *Delicate*, 6 × 8cm (2½ × 3in). Antique linen hanging pocket with mother-of-pearl buttons, antique lace and Miyuki beads.

Cristina's exquisite jewellery pieces, embroidered on canvases of antique linen using her soft muted palette of threads, convey quite perfectly the faded pages of an antique herbarium. Cristina explains:

Born and raised near Lake Maggiore in northern Italy, I have always been curious about flowers and plants. Armed with a little field guide, a precious gift from my father, I spent hours in the meadows near my home, observing and classifying wildflowers, always drawn, even then, to the tiniest flowers, fascinated by their intricate details. It was only many years later, when my two sons had left home, that I found time to explore the idea of combining my continued interest in botany with embroidery, the latter a self-taught skill I acquired gradually as an adult, although my mother was an excellent embroiderer.

Inspired by the plants I encounter on my woodland walks and by the illustrations in my ever-increasing collection of old botanical books and herbarium pages, I avoid traditional stitching techniques and instead use stitches like pencil marks or brushstrokes.

Believing strongly that jewellery is an essential form of self-expression, revealing of the personality of the wearer, it was only natural that I would find a way to incorporate my embroidery in a form of entirely individual wearable art.

The tiny pockets, made with antique linens, lace, beads, pearls and buttons, often contain a handwritten message or meaningful quote. Oval pendants of linen become a portable page from an antique herbarium. Some are strikingly large, others hardly larger than a robin's egg. Contemporary in their economy of design, my use of antique fabrics, lace, beads and threads is also expressive of the nostalgia that often overwhelms me for a time in which I have never lived.

Working on my pendants, large or small, or on my pockets, I lose myself completely. Each piece involves an absorbing, intricate process and the hours pass uncounted as I focus on getting each detail just the way I want it. I draw, embroider, sew, dye, paint, add quirky detail and explore technical solutions, finding the entire creative process incredibly satisfying.

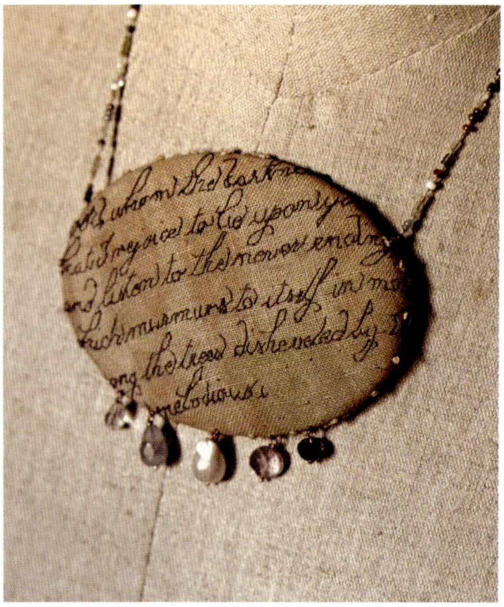

RIGHT: *Baudelaire's Words*, 8 × 5cm (3 × 2in). Antique linen embroidered oval with quartz, amethyst and freshwater pearl. Charles Baudelaire's words are embroidered in their old-fashioned calligraphy.

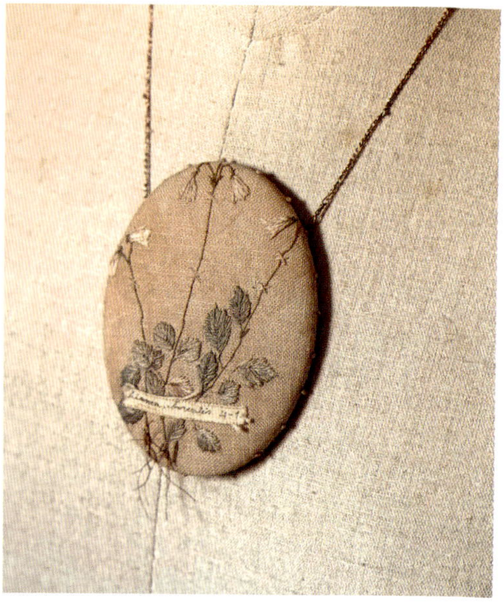

FAR RIGHT: *Linnaea borealis (Caprifoliaceae)*, 5 × 8cm (2 × 3in). Antique linen embroidered oval. Crocheted chain, intertwined with tiny Miyuki Japanese beads.

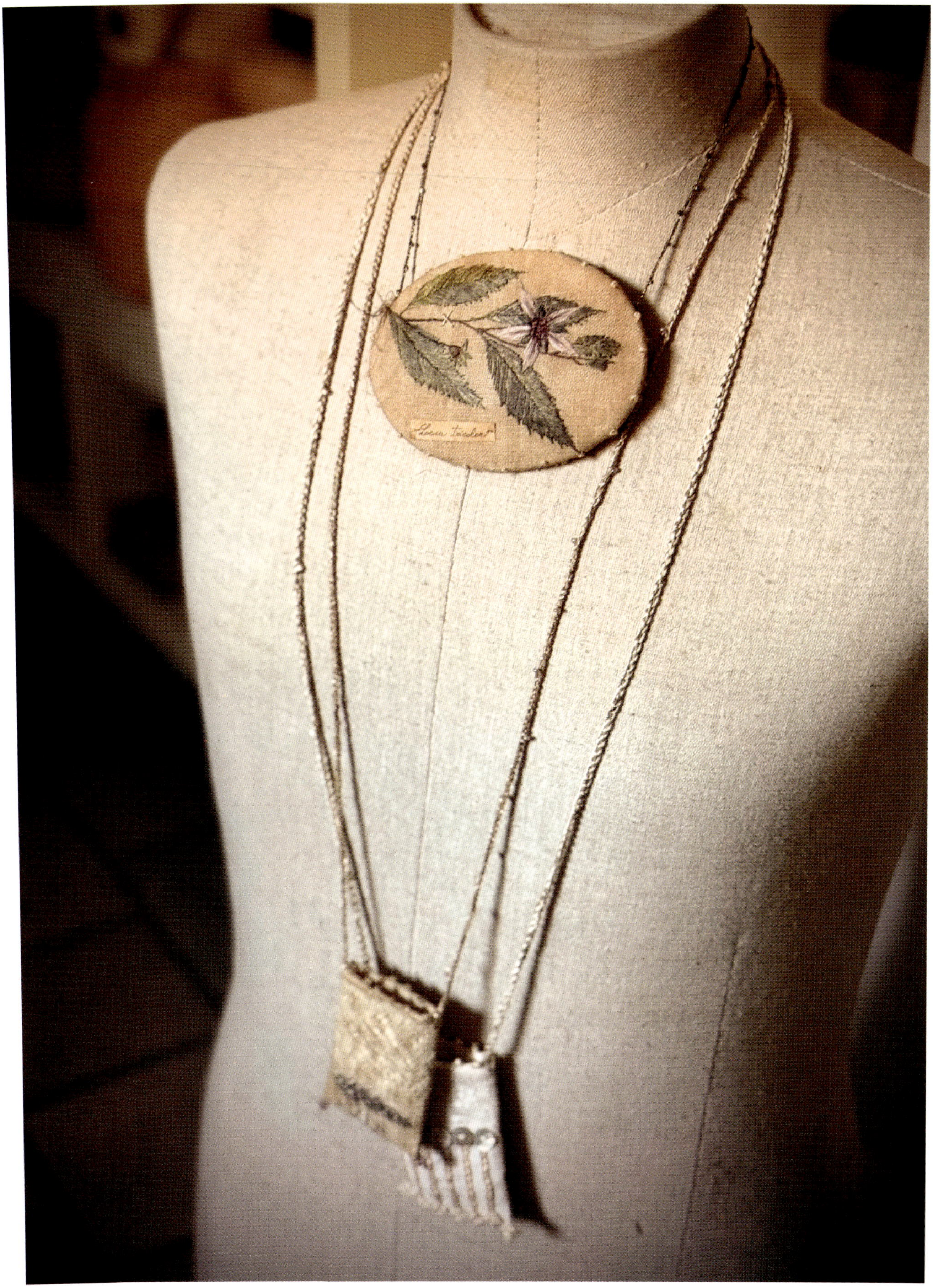

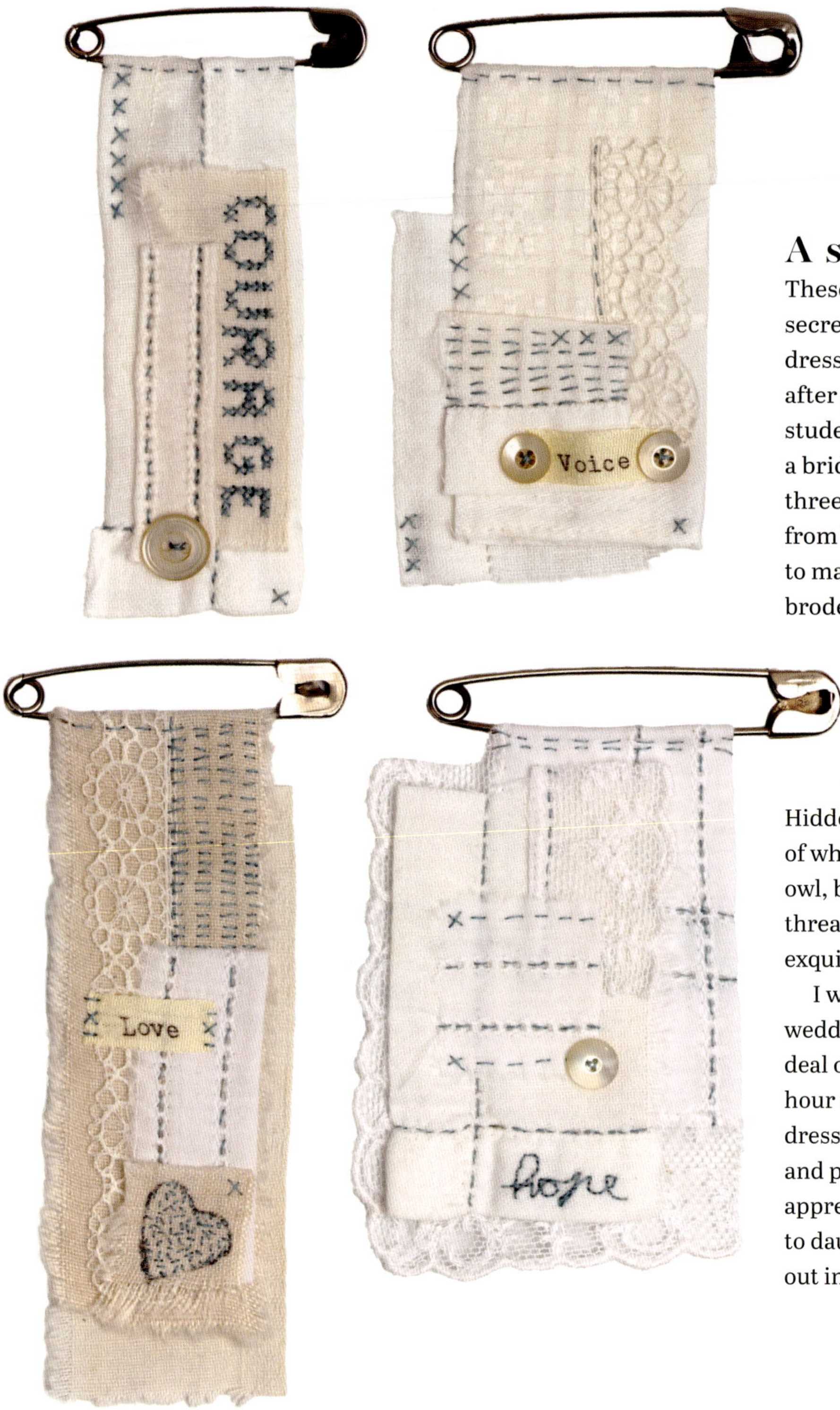

A secret message

These little charms are inspired by a secret message hidden in my wedding dress. I married in 1982, immediately after graduating from college. As a textile student I had no wish to buy a dress from a bridal shop so, armed with a picture of a three-quarter length, ballerina style dress from *Vogue* magazine, I asked my mum to make me one. This she did, from white broderie anglaise, with layer upon layer of underskirts and a pink ribbon tied around the waist.

On my wedding day, just as I was about to put on my dress, my mum showed me a little secret. Hidden in layers of underskirt was a flap of white fabric. On this was the image of an owl, beautifully hand embroidered in white thread, the white on white making the exquisite detail barely visible.

I was deeply touched. At a time when weddings didn't really warrant a great deal of fuss, my mum had spent hour upon hour stitching this little message into my dress (owls are seen as symbols of wisdom and protection). All these years later, I can appreciate even more this gift from mother to daughter as she cut her ties and sent me out into the world.

THIS PAGE: *Hidden Charms*. Made from vintage handkerchief scraps, linen and lace fragments and tiny mother-of-pearl buttons, hand stitched in silk thread. Hanging from vintage safety pins.

OPPOSITE: Old apothecary boxes make perfect display cases. I love the idea of gifting someone with a prescription such as: 'Joy – to be taken daily!'

HIDDEN CHARMS

Taking inspiration from this secret message, I decided to create a collection of 'hidden charms', each representing a 'superpower' to be passed to another in times of need. I imagine them worn hidden from view, but they could be displayed or worn however you like.

I honoured my mum's secret message by using white materials; however, I wanted the stitching to be visible. Inspired by Etta's sampler on page 107, I decided to use old handkerchiefs. I did some research and discovered that during the Victorian era, there was a whole romantic language of non-verbal communication conducted with the use of a handkerchief!

You will need:

- A collection of cotton handkerchiefs. I used the scraps left over from my sampler.
- Additional white or cream fabric scraps and fragments of lace, silk ribbon and tiny buttons.
- Safety pins for fastening. I used some old, beautifully shaped pins, but you could use pins designed for use in brooch making.

Then:

1. Decide on a 'superpower' for each charm. I chose Hope, Kindness, Joy, Love, Courage and Voice.
2. Experiment with different ways to create your text. I stitched Joy and Hope in a back stitch, the word Courage in a tiny cross stitch, and typed the remaining words onto silk ribbon.
3. Tear or cut small scraps from the handkerchiefs and layer them together with your other materials. Make the most of details such as corners and edges, lace and drawn thread designs. Add a tiny button or two if you wish. Keep your arrangements simple and create interesting outlines.
4. Add your stitching using one gentle contrasting colour – treat it as a stitched meditation, focussing on the word. Stitch with your heart rather than your head, and allow your thoughts to be woven through the fabric with your needle and thread.
5. Make a row of running stitch to secure the fabric round the safety pin. The beauty of these pieces lies in their simplicity.

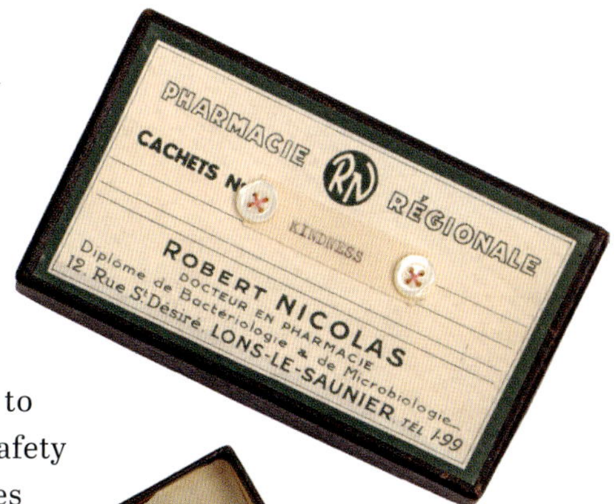

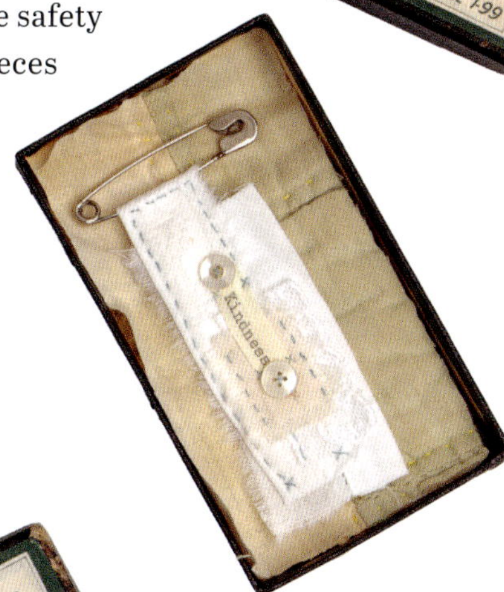

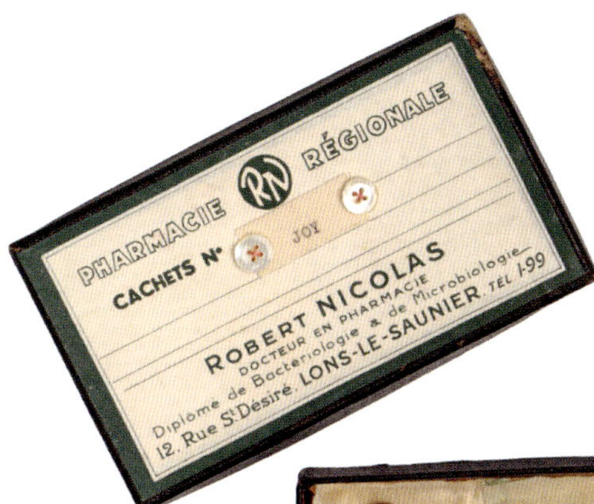

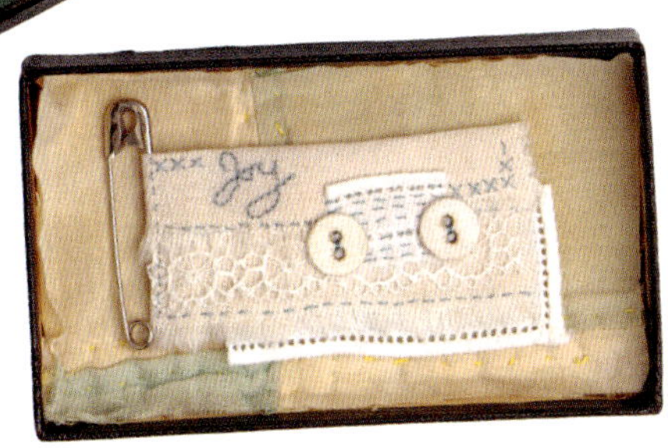

Lynn Barron

UK artist Lynn Barron's bags are constructed mostly with hand stitching and the words are screen printed onto antique fabrics. They speak directly to my heart, as does her beautiful description of her working process.

WHISPERS IN THE STITCH

Each handmade bag begins not with thread, but with a whisper – a murmur from the past carried in the weave of worn French fabric. These textiles, faded and frayed, are not merely remnants; they are relics of lives once lived, of hands long vanished.

The fabric may have once been part of a bodice sewn by an anonymous dressmaker in 18th-century Provence, her fingers calloused from years of work, her artistry unrecorded but deeply felt. She may have laboured in the shadow of Versailles, crafting gowns for women whose names history preserved, while her own slipped into silence. Yet her needlework – delicate pleats, hidden gussets, clever reinforcements – endure in the folds of these salvaged materials.

To craft a personal bag from such cloth is to enter into dialogue with time. The maker today does not simply sew;

RIGHT AND OPPOSITE:
Hand stitched bags, 25 × 28cm (10 × 11in). The words are screen printed by hand onto antique French linen and then hand stitched together onto antique style brass frames with leather straps. The bags are lined with antique French ticking.

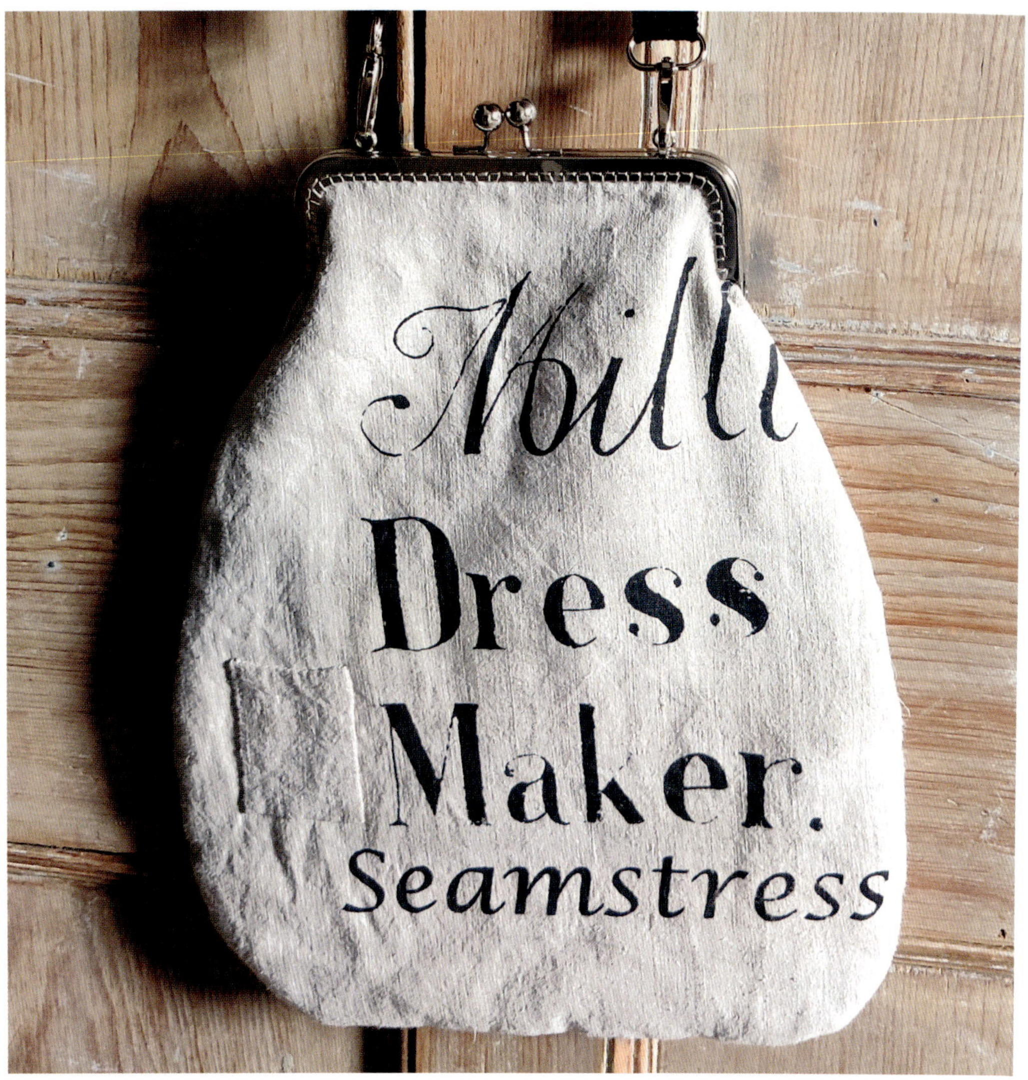

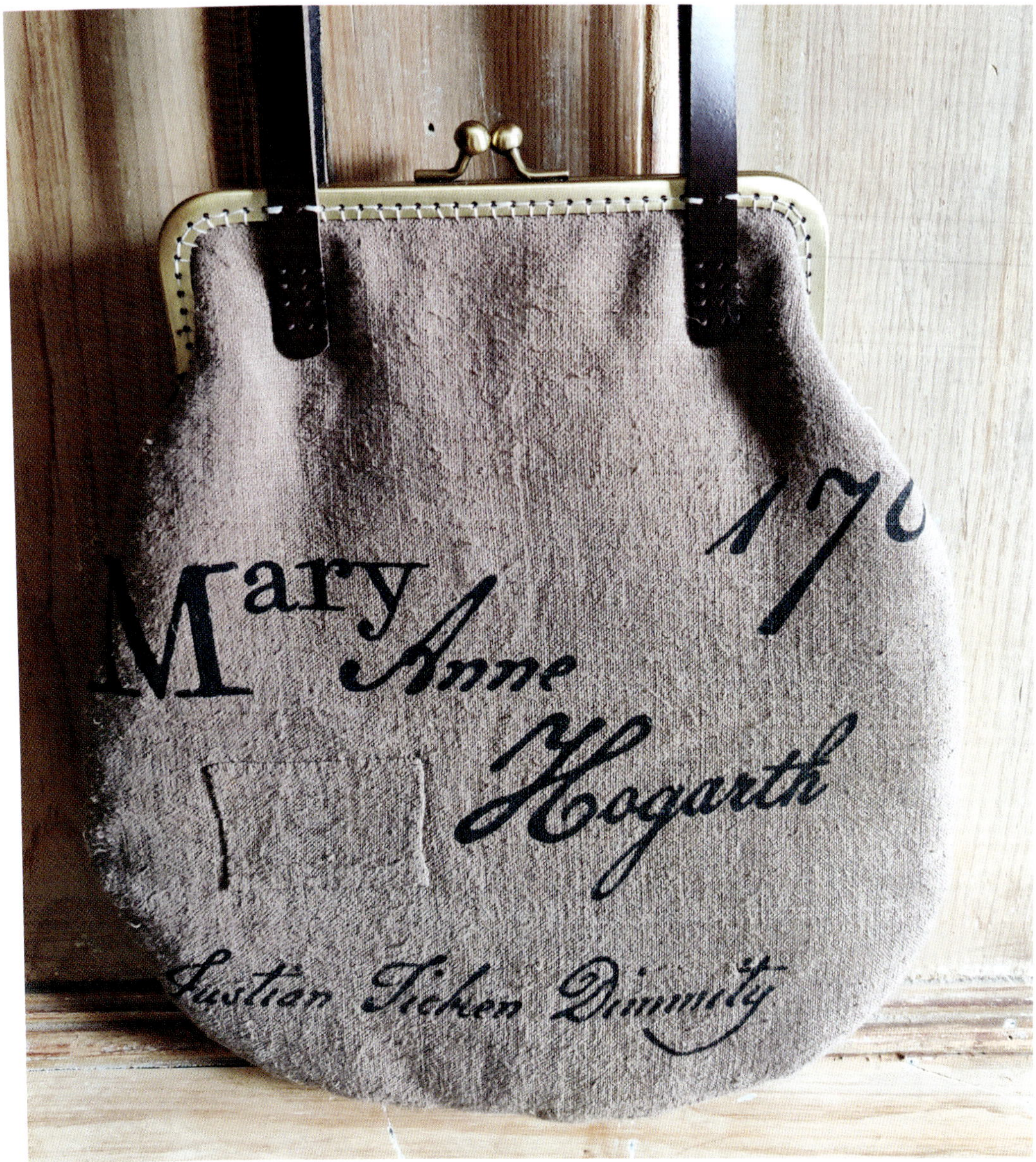

they commune. They listen to the rustle of the fabric, to the ghost of the original seamstress, and they respond with reverence. Every cut is cautious, every stitch deliberate. The bag is not designed – it is discovered, coaxed gently from the textile.

Buttons may be repurposed from a forgotten chemise. A lining might be fashioned from a curtain that once hung in a sun-drenched chateau. These choices are not aesthetic alone – they are emotional. They honour the invisible labour of women who stitched beauty into utility, who expressed themselves in thread when words were denied.

The finished bag is more than an accessory. It is a vessel of memory. It is intimate, personal, meant to be held close, worn daily, cherished deeply. It invites its owner to participate in a lineage of quiet artistry, to carry history. In a world of mass production, these bags stand as quiet acts of resistance. They say: I remember. They say: I see the hands that came before me. They say: Beauty is not new – it is eternal if we choose to preserve it.

Pockets

Worn by women and girls from every walk of life between the mid-17th and the late-19th centuries, pockets are to me a perfect motif for telling women's stories. Do your own research on this subject and you'll see that they come in different shapes and sizes, though many are roughly 'pear' shaped. They were worn tied round the body and hidden under skirts, petticoats or aprons, and held a woman's secrets, independence and whatever tools or trinkets she deemed necessary to get her through her day.

I'm interested in the humble pockets owned by ordinary working women, and I love that many women invested their precious time in transforming their pockets from a basic item into a thing of beauty with embroidered designs – another example of women using needle and thread to transform the functional into something beautiful just because it makes the world a better place.

I think that creating decorative pockets can be a wonderful canvas for storytelling, whether the stories are fictional or personal. I made *A Housekeeper's Pocket* from an old glass cloth, vintage binding tape, 1940s fabric scraps and with words taken from a shopping list dated 1956. Although the back and front of pockets were often stitched together with the wrong sides together and then bound with tape, I stitched mine with right sides together and turned them.

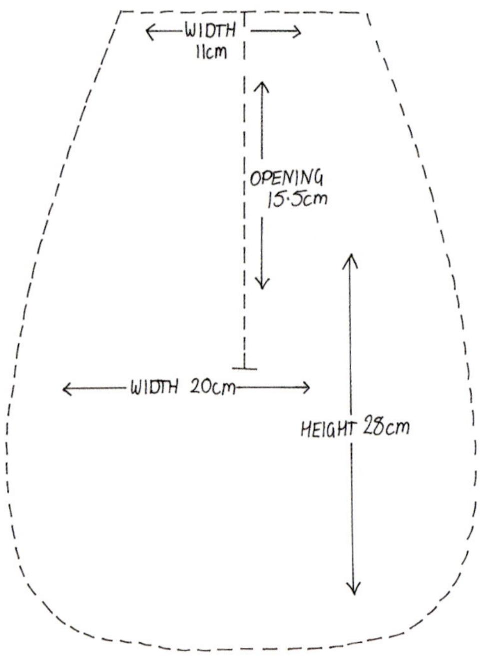

ABOVE: Design your own pocket shape on a piece of A4 paper. I used the above measurements but added 1.5cm seam allowance to allow for turning. You could however simply stitch the front and back together by encasing edges in bias binding.

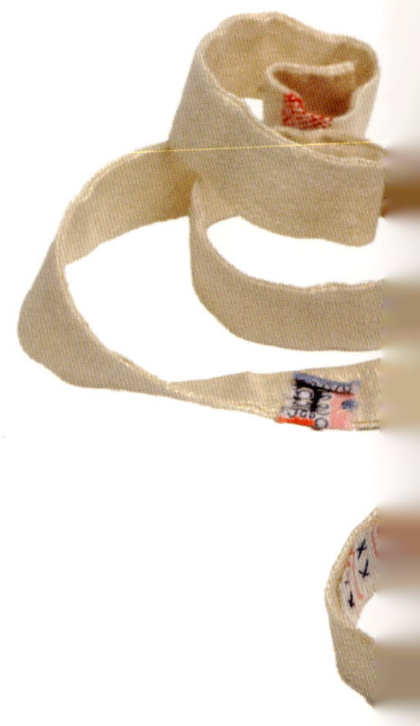

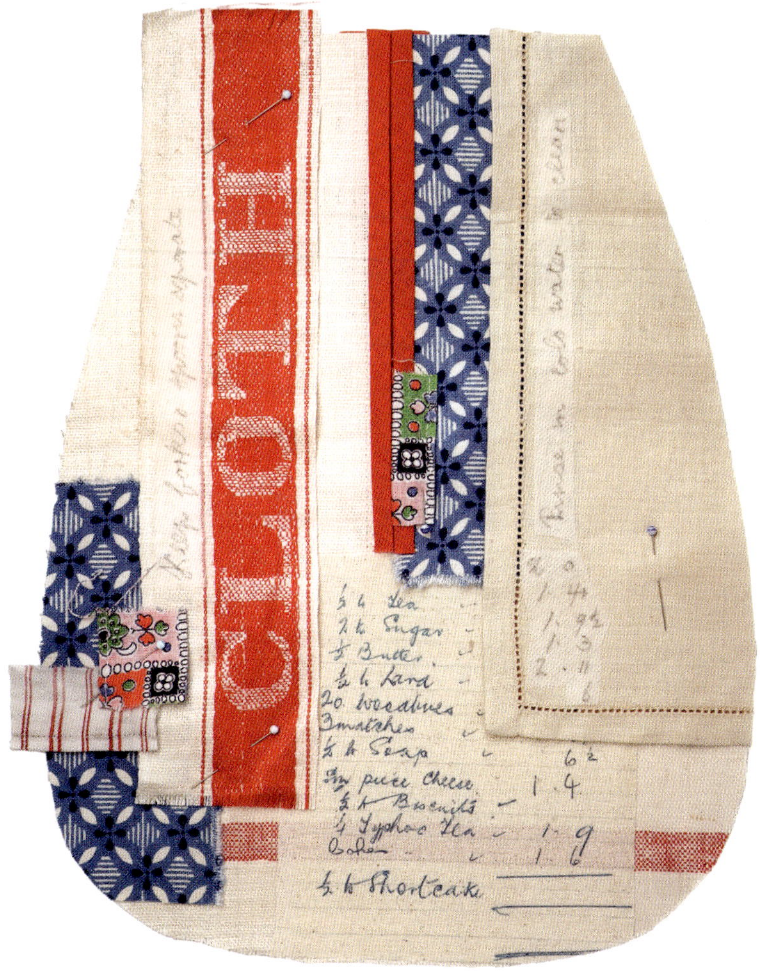

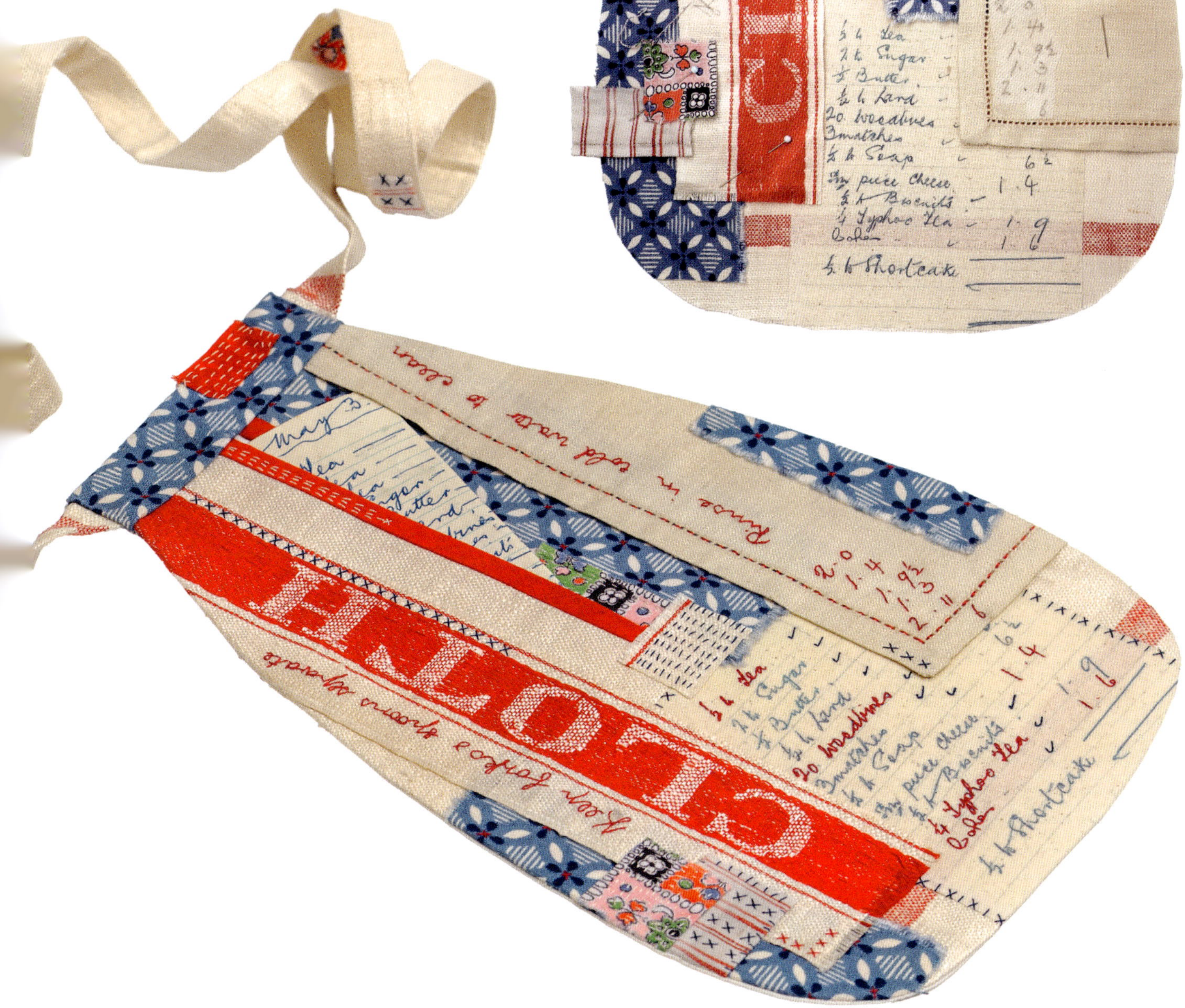

RIGHT AND BELOW: *A Housekeeper's Pocket*, 20 × 28cm (8 × 11in). A shopping list from the 1950s is inkjet printed onto calico and further words come from an old school domestic science jotter, stitched in back stitch. The pocket and strings are made from an old 'glass cloth' and embellished with cotton patches and hand stitching.

Rust-printing fabrics

You will need a collection of rusty objects, rubber gloves, a tray and a water spray bottle.

1. Soak two pieces of fabric in water – I use a lightweight calico. Wring them out slightly and spread one out over the bottom of a tray. I use a plastic cat litter tray and keep it specifically for this purpose.

2. Wearing rubber gloves, place your rusty item on top of the fabric.

3. Place the other piece of fabric over the top. The success of the print depends on the fabric having close contact with the object, so pat the fabric down so that the fabric clings to it. Unless the object is completely flat, it is this top print that is usually more successful.

4. Spritz it with water.

5. Leave the print to develop, checking that the fabric remains damp. I left the samples shown for two days, spritzing with water again on the second day.

6. Wearing rubber gloves, carefully peel back the top fabric to check the print and, when it has developed enough, rinse the fabric thoroughly and let it dry. I cover it with baking parchment to protect my iron when pressing.

You can also try the following:

- Make rusted thread by wrapping wet cotton thread round a rusted object and leaving to stain. Rinse well, taking care not to tangle it.

- Spritz the fabric with a mix of water and white vinegar using around 75% water to 25% vinegar. I don't use vinegar for rusting threads.

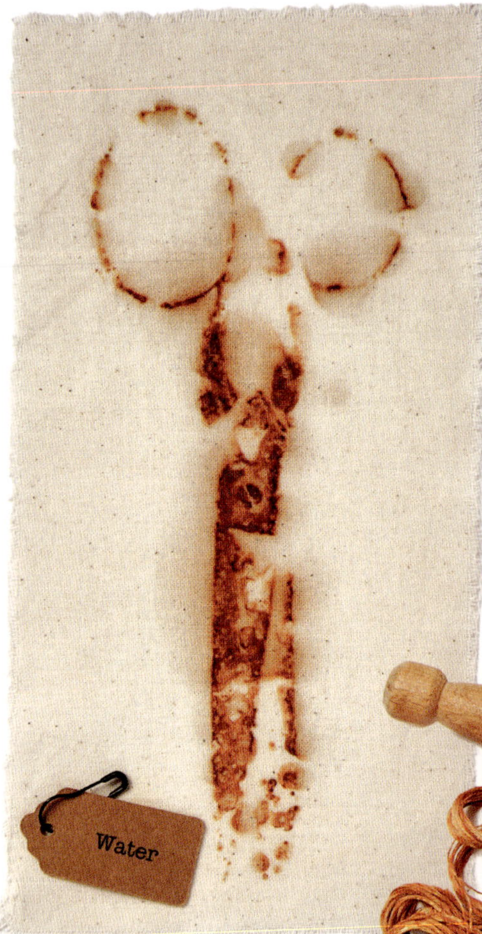

LEFT: Rust print of scissors that were spritzed with water and left to develop for two days.

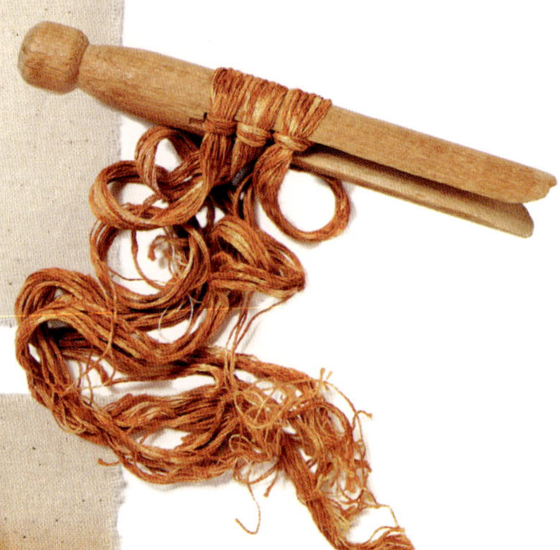

ABOVE: Lengths of ecru stranded cotton were soaked in water and then wound round a large rusty bolt and left to develop for four days, spritzing with water each day. They were then rinsed thoroughly, taking care not to tangle. Note: this process weakens the thread.

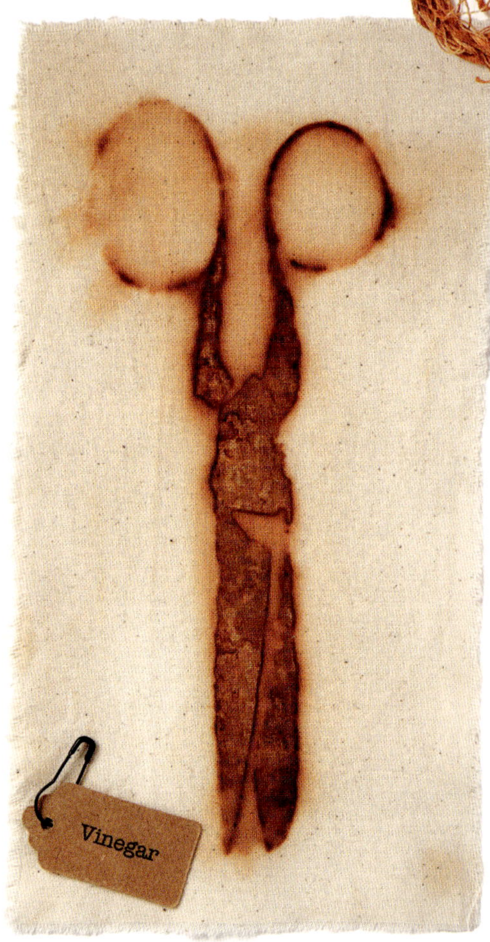

LEFT: Rust print of scissors that were spritzed with 75% water/25% vinegar mix and left to develop for two days.

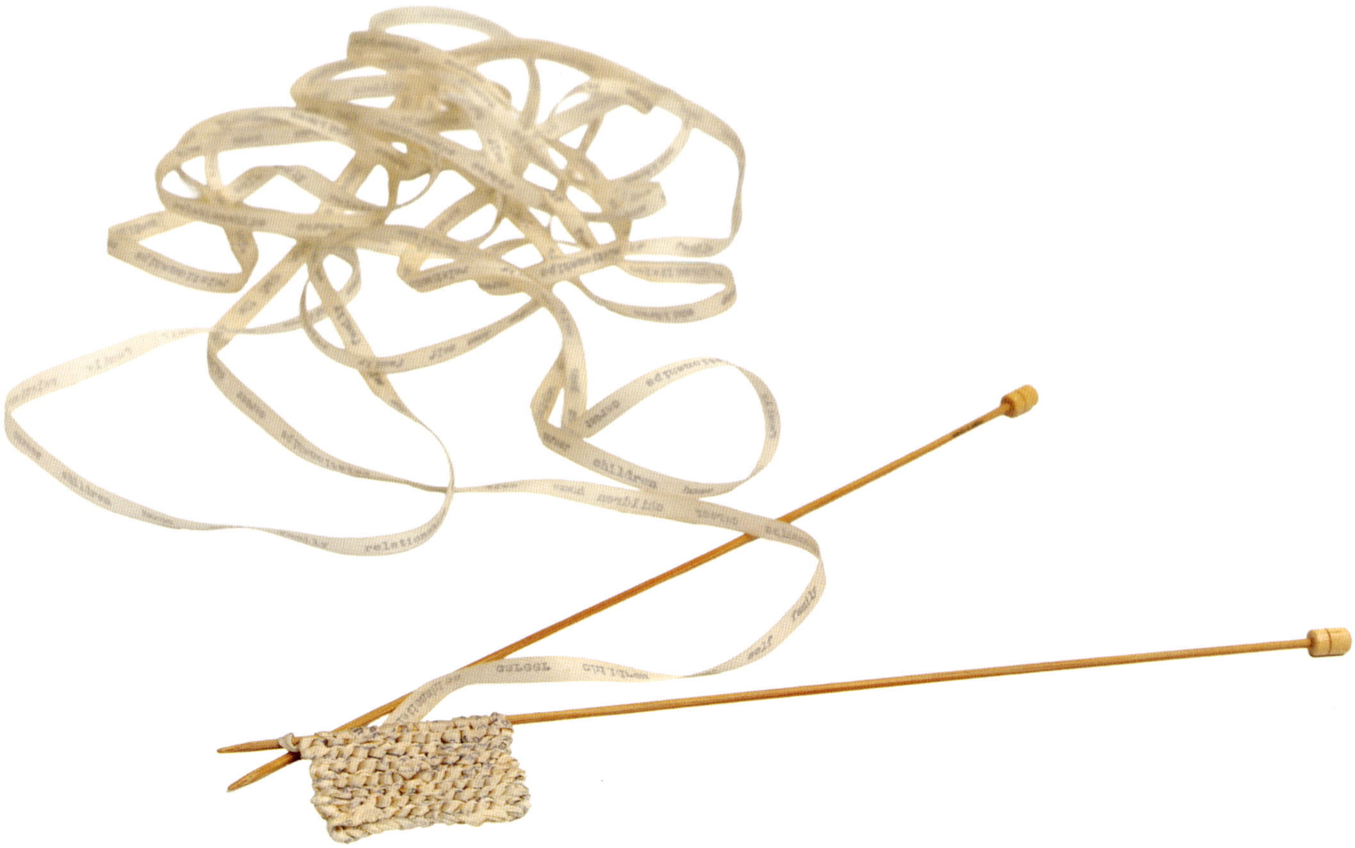

Old work, new perspectives: Women's lives

While planning a series of pockets, I remembered a very old piece of work that was literally lying at the bottom of a drawer. Created as part of a college project, 'Women's Lives' was a series of panels displayed in drawers that explored my own experiences of being a wife and mother. Why drawers? Because things are carelessly thrown into them, and it can be years until we go through them and see what has been accumulated when we've been looking the other way.

These panels were originally constructed using patches of rust-printed fabrics, pieced together and embellished with stitch. The fabrics were imprinted with rusted objects such as pins, safety pins, paper clips, staples and hooks and eyes – each item used to 'hold things together'. There was also a pair of scissors in acknowledgement of there being a time, however painful, when we have to cut loose the people we love and let them venture out on their own. This might sound familiar – I revisited these motifs when I was making my wish bottles (see pages 79–83).

A tangle of ribbon spilled from the drawer with the words 'family, home, relationship, career, children and self' typed along its length. Part of the ribbon was knitted, representing my role, as I saw it, of bringing these different elements together and creating some sort of order from the chaotic tangle.

The additional responsibilities of healer, diplomat, mediator and peacemaker were printed with rusting powder and grouped around a piece of darning. Even now, however misguided, I see it as my role to try to mend whatever is broken with the people I love. This piece was an emotional reflection of huge changes taking place in my life at the time.

ABOVE: *Women's Lives*. I stained a length of silk ribbon with coffee and then dipped it in watered down matte medium before typing my words along its length before knitting. The matte medium gave the soft silk some 'body' to allow it to sit in a tangle.

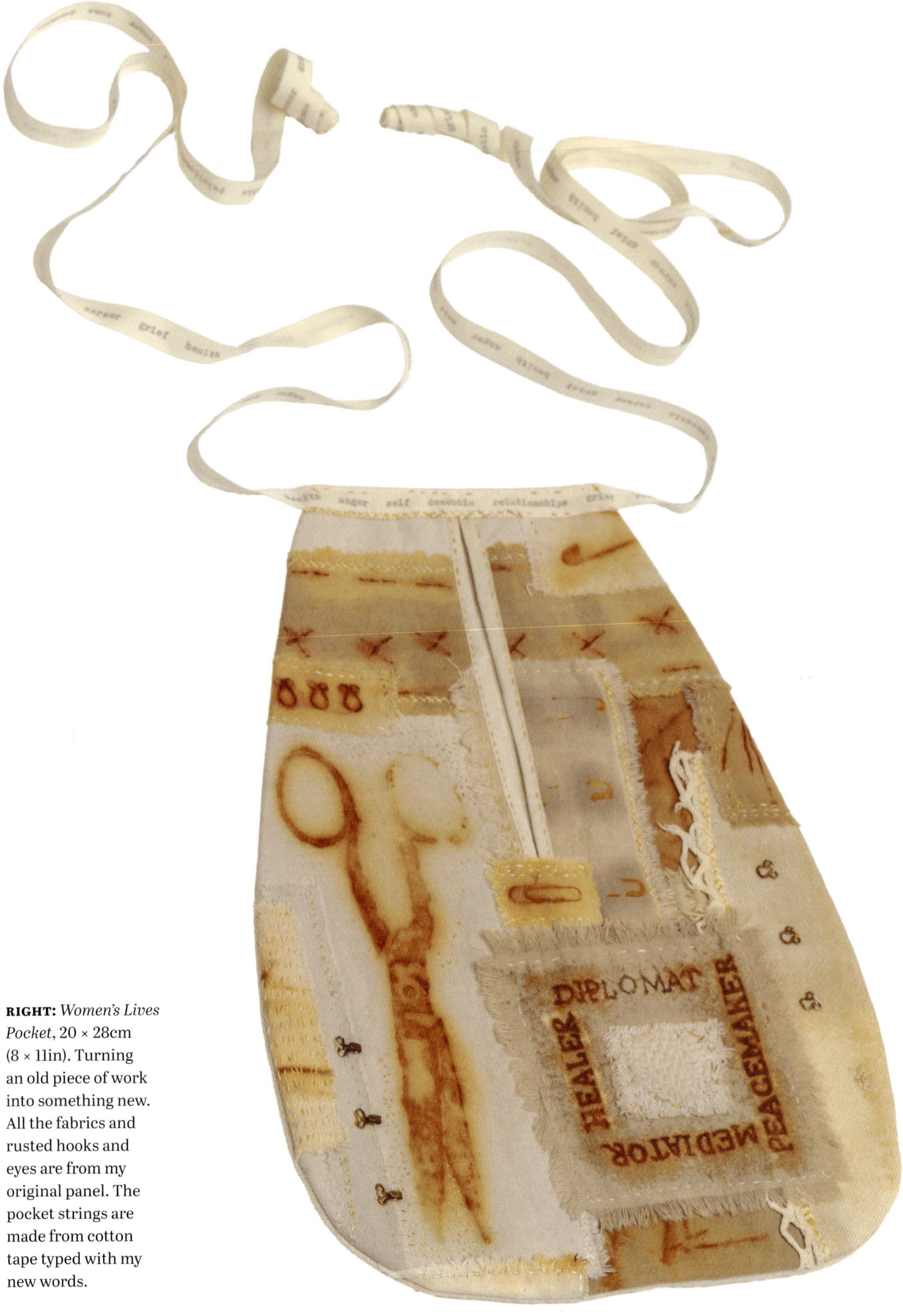

RIGHT: *Women's Lives Pocket*, 20 × 28cm (8 × 11in). Turning an old piece of work into something new. All the fabrics and rusted hooks and eyes are from my original panel. The pocket strings are made from cotton tape typed with my new words.

Revisited

For my new piece, I wanted to create a pocket, exploring the same theme, but 16 years on when I am at a completely different stage of life. Why a pocket? Because they were kept hidden from view, their contents personal, precious and private.

I planned to create new rust-printed fabrics, but instead I found myself rather impulsively taking my scissors to the original panel. I removed it from the drawer and set about unpicking hours of hand embroidery stitch by stitch. I then assembled my pocket from the salvaged patches, embellishing them with stitches made in rusted thread.

I planned to make the ties from cotton tape with words typed along its length, echoing the knitting in the original drawer. I left this until I had finished the construction of the pocket so that I could think about the words. No thinking was needed, however, as they poured from pencil to paper.

Sixteen years later, most of the original words remained the same: relationships, family, home, career, self – but interspersed between them were new words: dementia, grief and anger.

When I permit myself time to create intuitively, allowing the process to flow rather than trying to manage it, I continually find myself taken aback by, but eternally grateful for, the sheer potency of the creative process.

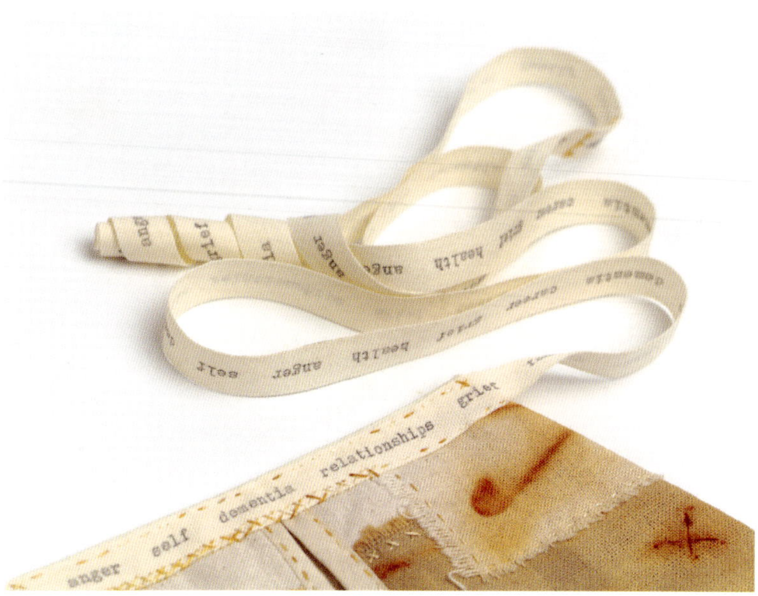

TOP RIGHT: *Women's Lives Pocket* (detail). The words 'family, home, relationship, career, self, anger, dementia and grief' are typed along the length of the pocket strings.

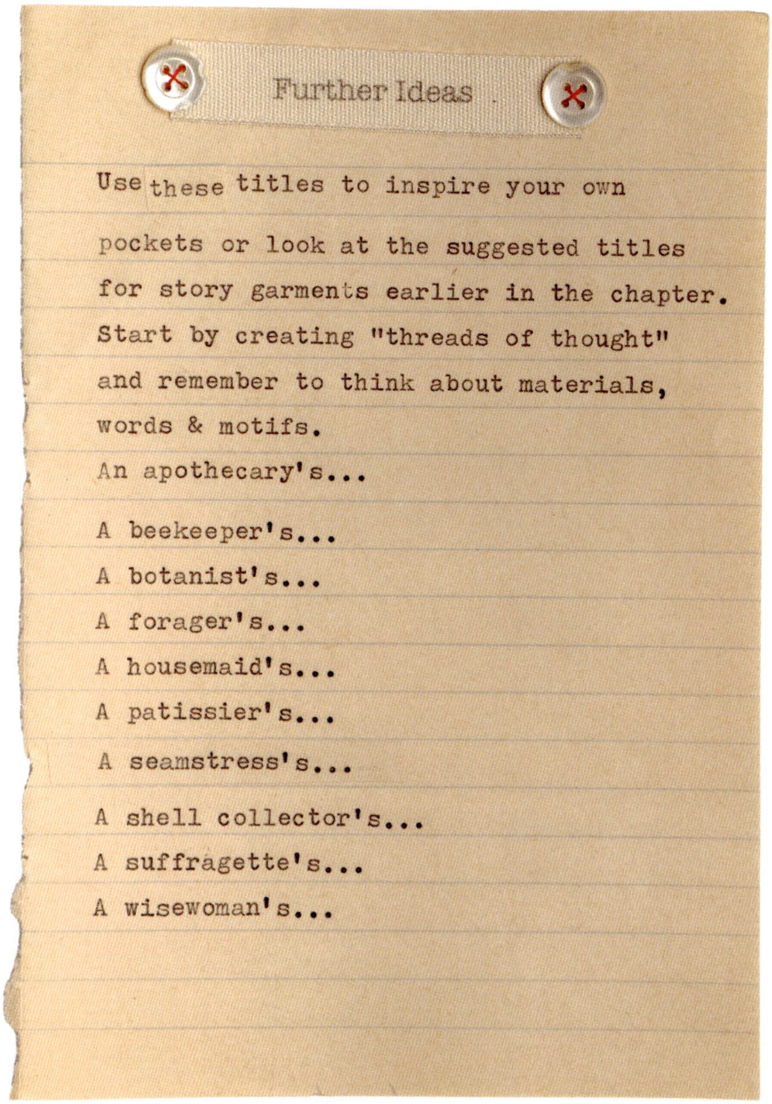

Further Ideas

Use these titles to inspire your own pockets or look at the suggested titles for story garments earlier in the chapter. Start by creating "threads of thought" and remember to think about materials, words & motifs.

An apothecary's...

A beekeeper's...

A botanist's...

A forager's...

A housemaid's...

A patissier's...

A seamstress's...

A shell collector's...

A suffragette's...

A wisewoman's...

Conclusion: Or you could…

I could keep on going! The possibilities for creating personal story-based art from all of this 'everyday stuff of life' are endless and I hope that something I have said will inspire you to create work of your own. I also hope that I've demonstrated that I seldom have all the answers when I start a piece of work (and how boring that would be!). However, the act of gathering materials and making a start is the key to unlocking a rather glorious process of taking one little step and trusting that, in doing so, the next one will be revealed. Ideas never come when I'm sitting around waiting for them.

So, if you don't quite know where to start, pull out some fabrics, lay them in front of you, gather some words and maybe a motif or two and …

BELOW: *If Their Fingers Were Busy*, 31 × 32cm (12 × 12½in). Cloth collage on a woollen blanket foundation. Made from a piece of old quilt, scraps of vintage dress cottons, a tape measure and a paper pattern. The words, typed on cotton tape, are from my favourite saying: 'If their fingers were busy, their hearts would rest more.'

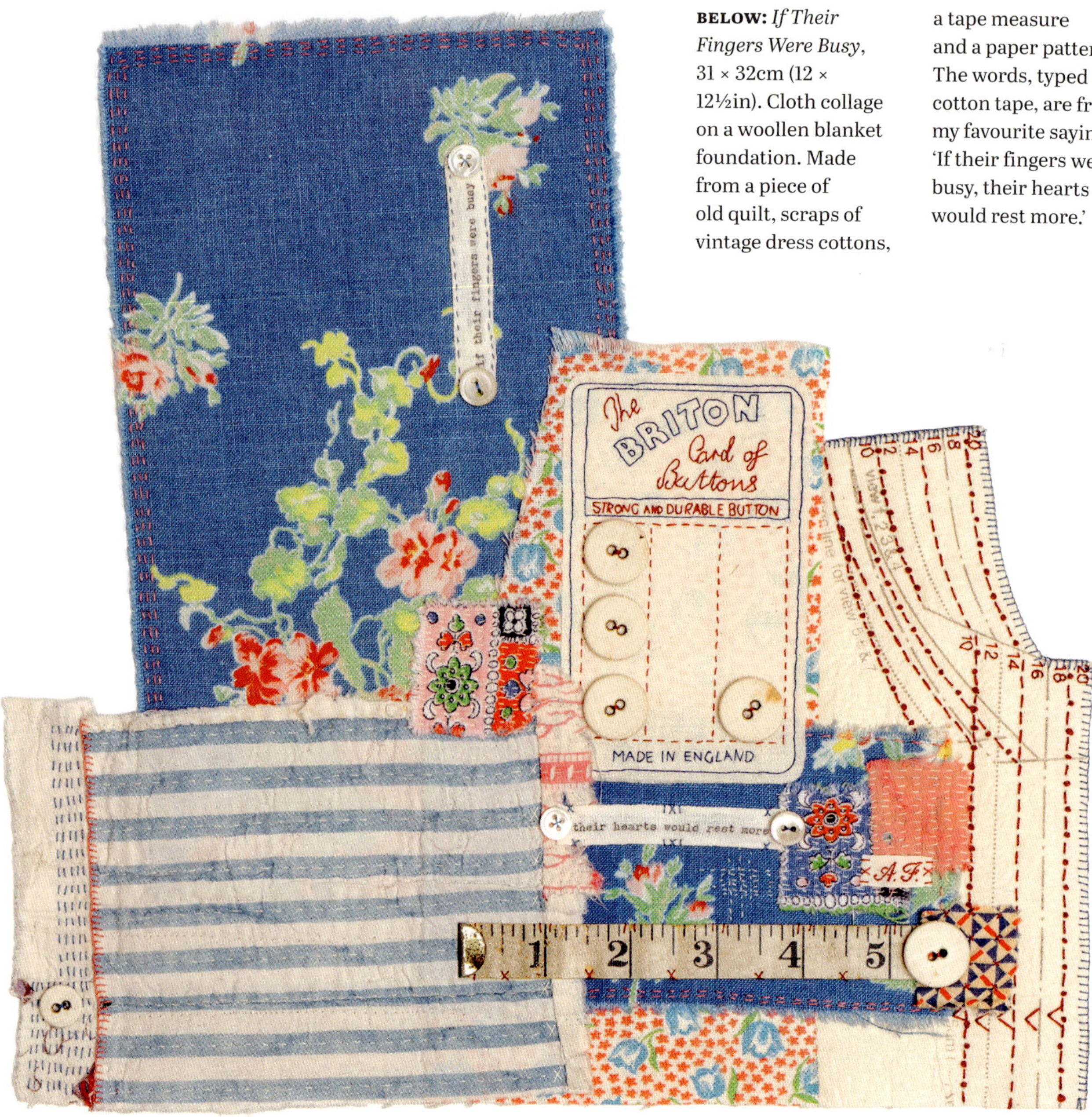

Further reading

Burman, Barbara and Fennetaux, Ariane, *The Pocket*, Yale University Press, 2019
Butler, Anne, *The Batsford Encyclopaedia of Embroidery Stitches*, Batsford , 1979
Ferguson, Ali, *Cloth Stories*, Batsford, 2024
Holmes, Cas, *Embroidering the Everyday*, Batsford, 2021
Kakita, Tomoko, *Furoshiki*, Laurence King Publishing, 2021
Kelly, Anne, *Textile Travels*, Batsford, 2020
McKechnie, Sam, *Gentle Spells & Kind Magic*, Pavilion, 2022
Nicholson, Virginia, *Millions Like Us*, Penguin, 2012
Paine, Sheila, *Amulets*, Thames & Hudson, 2004
Summers, Julie, *Jambusters*, Simon & Schuster, 2013

Further exploration

If you love falling down rabbit holes, here are some topics for your own online research:

- 17th century witch bottles
- Maggie Dickson, Edinburgh
- Scottish fishwives
- Spiritual properties of fabrics
- Symbolism of colour
- Symbolism of numbers
- Symbolism of flowers and herbs
- Symbolism of handkerchiefs

Suppliers and contributing artists

DALSTON MILL FABRICS
For calico, muslin, silk organza and general supplies
www.dalstonmillfabrics.co.uk

PRINFAB
For digital printing on fabric
www.prinfab.com

WEND SHAW
For vintage cloth and paper ephemera
Instagram @ticking_stripes

LISA GILES
For vintage cloth and quilt pieces
Instagram @lovely_hudson_sale

LINDA CLIFT
For vintage cloth, clothing, lace and quilt pieces
Instagram @lespannards

DONNA FLOWER
For vintage cloth and quilt pieces
Instagram @donnaflowervintagefabrics

LIZZIE VAN HASSELT
For vintage textiles and tiny treasures
Instagram @thewasherwoman

CHERRY ABRAMS
For vintage ephemera and books
Instagram @misscherrypievintage

Contributing artists

Darren Ball	Instagram @darrenballtextiles
Lynn Barron	Instagram @seaangelsvintage
Anne Brooke	www.annebrooke.co.uk
Fran Buxton	Instagram @fran_buxton_mixed_media
Cristina Rebeccani Coretti	Instagram @cristina.rebeccani.coretti
Karla Fuller	Instagram @karlafullerartist
Catherine Hill	Instagram @catherine_hill_textile_artist
Victoria Merness	www.littlehouseofvictoria.com
Sam Miller	Instagram @sam_miller_artist

Acknowledgements

My heartfelt thanks to the artists who so generously allowed me to share their work and their stories.

To the fabulous team at Batsford, especially Bella MacConnol, Frida Green and photographer Michael Wicks for their expertise and support.

To my dear friends Carole and Christine whose listening ear and creative input is so very much valued and appreciated.

To my wonderful family for their love and support and my mum who gifted me a childhood of 'making'.

And very special thanks to my husband Paul who simply makes everything possible… and fun!

All photography by Michael Wicks, except for the following:

Lynn Barron, pages 116, 117
Anne Brooke, pages 84, 85
Fran Buxton, pages 68, 69
Cristina Rebeccani Coretti, pages 112, 113
Paul Ferguson, pages 6, 13, 30, 31, 48, 50, 54, 60, 61, 62, 63, 77, 83, 88, 89, 100, 120
Karla Fuller, pages 46, 47
Catherine Hill, pages 86, 87
Victoria Merness, pages 40, 41
Sam Miller, pages 102, 103
Todd-White Photography London, pages 52, 53

Index